GLORIOUS REVOLUTION
1688

K. MERLE CHACKSFIELD

With Best Wishes

K. Merle Chacksfield

Swanage
Dorset.

1987

WINCANTON PRESS
NATIONAL SCHOOL, NORTH STREET
WINCANTON, SOMERSET BA9 9AT

Also by K. Merle Chacksfield

Music and language with Young Children with P. Binns and V. Robins
Plays from the Bible
Sound Ideas, Volumes 1 to 6 with P. Binns
Hør Iydene Musikk og Språkstimulering med små barn
Far away and Over the Hills
Plays for Children
Smuggling Days
Dorset and Somerset Rebellion

For
Rodney Legg
—another escape
into the seventeenth century

Publishing details. First published 1988.
Copyright K. Merle Chacksfield © 1988.

Printing credits.
Typeset by Colin Gay
at MKG Typesetting, Green Dragon Lane,
Bridgwater, Somerset
and printed in the same county by
Wincanton Litho.

Distribution. Trade sales distribution by Dorset Publishing Company
from Knock-na-cre, Milborne Port, Sherborne, Dorset DT9 5HJ,
telephone 0963 32583 or 0963 33643.

International standard book number (ISBN) 0 948699 04 3

Contents

Foreword 5
Preface 5
MAPS: BRIXHAM LANDING & PASSAGE TO LONDON 6
William lands in the West 7
The Dutch Fleet leaves Holland 25
The Prince made welcome 51
The King's last welcome 67
The Vanguard at Sherborne 83
Great excitement in Salisbury 97
Night of Riot and Terror 112
The real troubles now begin 125
Lords and Commons Resolved 135
Insurrection in Scotland 147
DIAGRAM: ROYAL FAMILY TREE 152
Derry Under Siege 153
Base Metal Sovereignty 165
MAP: KINGS CONTEST IRELAND 167
Crossing the Boyne 175
MAP: THE BATTLE OF THE BOYNE 179
Bibliography 187
Acknowledgements 188
Index 189

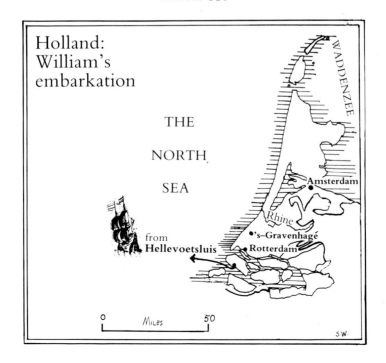

William, Prince of Orange.
Portrait of 1677, after Sir Peter Lely, courtesy the National Portrait Gallery.

Foreword

from

Air Vice-Marshal Sir Bernard A. Chacksfield,

K.B.E., C.B., C.Eng., F.R.Ae.S., R.A.F.(ret.),

Chairman of the Burma Star Association

HISTORY CAN be a dull subject, particularly when, as often, it is reduced to 'bare bones;' but if the skeleton is covered with sinews and flesh, clothed, and enriched with fascinating cameos of events in familiar places, it not only becomes alive and full of interest, but clearly reveals the basis upon which our present way of life is founded. This the author has done with an important episode in the history of our country. I only wish that my history books had been as interesting to read!

Our current thoughts, words and deeds inevitably and inexorably shape the future destiny of our country; indeed, of our world. Similarly the convictions and actions of past patriots have formed the basis for the development of Britain as a great democracy. This is well illustrated here.

Important history does not, however, flow smoothly. Rather, it progresses in a series of steps marked by historic milestones. One such milestone in our history was, of course, Magna Carta. Another was the adoption of the Bill of Rights which followed the Coronation of William and Mary in April 1689 as a result of the *Glorious Revolution* of 1688, the subject of this book.

Merle Chacksfield has clearly gone to great lengths to ferret out important and interesting details of all aspects of this fascinating piece of English history and has given us a well written, readable and enjoyable book. I commend it to you.

Finally, it is good to know that the profits from this work are to be dedicated to the Prince of Wales's Tercentenary Trust.

Bernard A. Chacksfield

Preface

IN WRITING this book I have tried to tell the story largely in the words of those who were there at the time of the Revolution and who left a written record of what they saw and knew, such as the Revd. John Whittle, Dr. Gilbert Burnet, Henry Hyde, the second Earl of Clarendon, and Sir George Savile, the first Marquis of Halifax.

I have also looked over the shoulder of that master of the written word and indefatigable student of history, Thomas Babington Macaulay, and at times I have leaned heavily on his descriptive passages to illustrate the progress of the Prince of Orange.

K. Merle Chacksfield
Swanage, Dorset.

1987.

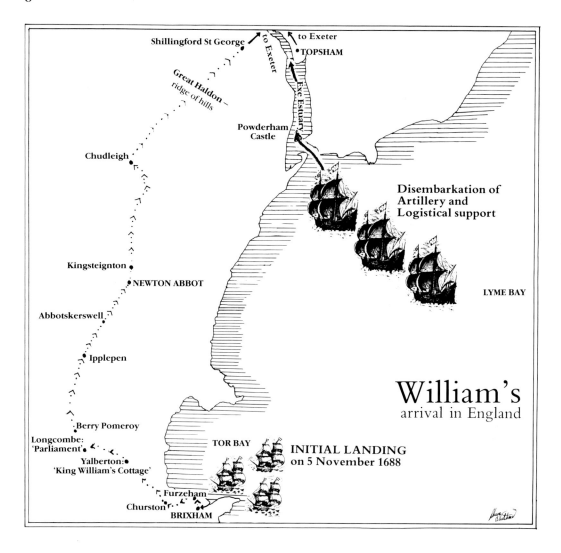

Shillingford St George

to Exeter

to Exeter

•TOPSHAM

Exe Estuary

Great Haldon –
ridge of hills

Powderham
Castle

Chudleigh•

**Disembarkation of
Artillery and
Logistical support**

Kingsteignton•

•NEWTON ABBOT

LYME BAY

Abbotskerswell•

•Ipplepen

William's
arrival in England

•Berry Pomeroy

Longcombe:
'Parliament'•

TOR BAY

INITIAL LANDING
on 5 November 1688

Yalberton:•
'King William's Cottage'

•Furzeham
Churston •
BRIXHAM

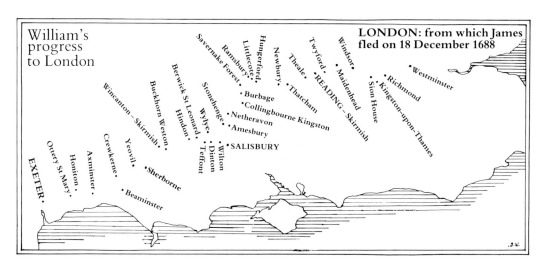

William's
progress
to London

Savernake Forest•

Ramsbury•

Littlecote•

Hungerford•

Newbury•

Twyford•

Windsor•

**LONDON: from which James
fled on 18 December 1688**

Theale•

•READING – Skirmish

Maidenhead•

Thatcham•

•Westminster

•Richmond

Sion House•

Kingston-upon-Thames•

Berwick St Leonard•

Stonehenge•

•Burbage

Wincanton – Skirmish

Buckhorn Weston•

Wylye•

•Collingbourne Kingston

Hindon•

•Netheravon

Crewkerne•

Yeovil•

Teffont•

Dinton•

•Amesbury

Honiton•

Axminster•

Wilton•

•SALISBURY

Ottery St Mary•

•Sherborne

EXETER•

•Beaminster

William Lands in the West

ON NOVEMBER 5, 1688 William Henry, Prince of Orange-Nassau, sailed with his army into Tor Bay, Devonshire, and setting foot on land at Brixham, began the last successful invasion of Britain. This precipitated the "Glorious Revolution," in which William and his wife Mary replaced James II on the British throne. Their accession in 1689 marked a new relationship between the Crown and Parliament which has lasted to this day.

The times were ripe for change. The country was riven between Protestants and Catholics, and there was no wish to return to the days of the absolute monarchy of Charles I. The national mood was for Parliament to be supreme. Many had striven mightily through the Civil War and the Restoration for this, and further, they would not accept religious domination by Rome. As James II leaned increasingly towards Roman Catholicism he stimulated fear and agitation in the minds of most of the people, and made fertile ground for the change in the monarchy that would depose him and enthrone a Protestant king who would make no claim to divine right of kingship.

William, a Protestant, had a legitimate claim to the throne, being by birth and by marriage a member of the Royal Family of Stuart: his mother was a daughter of Charles I and his wife Mary was the daughter of James II. King James II was, therefore, at once his uncle and his father-in-law. In the normal course of events William would have succeeded James, and those in Britain who looked eagerly for this to take place had, reluctantly, to wait.

Mary Beatrice of Modena, however, had become pregnant again, or so it was announced. Mary Beatrice of Modena was the Catholic wife of James II, and if she were to produce an heir to the throne all chance of the succession of William and Mary would vanish. Though the queen had borne several children, all but one had died young, and five years had elapsed since her last pregnancy. The majority of the people believed, as indeed most of them wished, that she would not deliver an heir to the throne. On the other hand, as Macaulay says in his *History of England*, "Nothing seemed more natural and probable than that the Jesuits should have contrived a pious fraud. It was certain that they must consider the accession of the Princess of Orange as one of the greatest calamities which could befall their Church. It was equally certain that they would not be very scrupulous about doing whatever might be necessary to save their Church from a great calamity." It was rumoured abroad that the King's advisers, and even the King himself, had considered schemes for defrauding the Lady Mary, Princess of Orange, of her inheritance, and thus suspicion grew in the minds of the people that royal trickery was planned.

Impudent zealots proclaimed that the baby would be a boy, and backed their opinion by offering odds of twenty to one in guineas. One fanatic announced that the Queen would bear twins, of whom the elder would be King of Great Britain and the younger Pope of Rome. Mary the Queen could not conceal the delight with which she heard this prophecy, and her ladies found that they could not gratify her more than by talking of it.

Mary, Princess of Orange, received news of the Queen's pregnancy with suspicion. In April 1688 she wrote: "I have received an account of the Queen's pregnancy which gives me good cause to suspect that there is some trickery afoot. I do not know what will happen, but as always I will place my trust in God: it is His cause, and He will take care of His Church." It seemed to her that her father meant to deprive her of her inheritance and to destroy the Protestant Church which she fervently supported.

Meanwhile James II was creating the greatest antipathy over one of the most sensitive issues in the political scene of the day, that of religious tolerance. Only a policy of moderation would have ensured national loyalty to the Crown, but the King was not interested in moderation in matters of religion. The law as it stood imposed certain strict disabilities upon Roman Catholics and upon Protestant non-conformists, backed by Test Acts and penal laws. The King antagonised the Church of England as well as Parliament by arbitrarily dispensing, in individual cases, with disabilities imposed by these laws, and replacing Anglican churchmen by Roman Catholics; and finally by making his Declaration of Indulgence. On 18 March, 1687, the King informed the Privy Council that it was his intention to prorogue Parliament until the end of November, "and to grant by his own authority entire liberty of conscience to all his subjects". On 4 April appeared the memorable Declaration of Indulgence, which suspended the penal laws and Test Acts. In this Declaration the King stated that he earnestly wished to see his people members of the Church to which he belonged [namely the Church of Rome]. Since this was not possible, he said that he intended to protect them in the "free exercise of their religion". He promised again that he would protect the Established Church "in the enjoyment of her own legal rights". All penal laws against all classes of non-conformists were suspended, and he authorised both Roman Catholics and Protestant dissenters to worship publicly. His subjects were forbidden to molest any religious assembly. He also "abrogated all those Acts which impose any religious test as a qualification for any civil or military office". The Test Act of 1673 ordered every office-holder under the English Crown to take the sacrament according to the rites of the Church of England, and to declare against the doctrine of transubstantiation. It was aimed mainly at Roman Catholics.

A result of the Queen's reported pregnancy, and the king's abandonment of proper Parliamentary procedure and his promotion of the Roman Catholic faith, might have been foreseen. Men of substance and great influence in England whose greatest wish was to see their country ruled by a Protestant amenable to the will of Parliament were appalled. They immediately began planning to remove James from the throne. Secret messages were sent to William in Holland inviting him to invade England and ascend the throne; for the salvation of their country, as they saw it, lay in the substitution as King of William for James.

Since the failure of Spain to invade England in an attempt to restore the Roman Catholic Church in 1588, the fear of a new attempt to bring this about remained throughout the 17th century. The Gunpowder Plot of 1605, a conspiracy to blow up King James I and his Parliament on 5 November, was instigated by several Roman Catholic gentry, out of patience with the penal laws preventing the practice of their faith. The Popish Plot in 1678 was a false plot of Titus Oates and other perjured witnesses which inferred that all the leading statesmen of England were to be murdered, and that schemes were afoot to murder King Charles II, and it whipped the country into a frenzy of excitement, as a result of which many Roman Catholics were executed.

In 1660, just before his Restoration, Charles had promised in the Declaration of Breda that he would grant "liberty of conscience" to all his subjects in England, Scotland and Ireland. In fact, Charles's parliament did not allow such sweeping tolerance for all sects, and non-conformists were less free to follow their own way of worship than they had been under Cromwell's rule. "I care not who is King so that I can enjoy my religion in my own way," said Joanna Punchard in 1685, when she was haled before the court for not attending service at the Church of England. After 1662, Catholics, and those Protestants who failed to attend its services were fined, and barred from employment in public life.

East Gate, Totnes.
The town was staunchly Protestant.

John Bunyan, the author of *Pilgrim's Progress,* and a non-conformist preacher, was convicted in 1660 for unauthorised preaching. He was released under a Declaration of Indulgence in 1672, but was imprisoned again in 1675 in Bedford jail, where he probably began writing his famous book. Another, Francis Barnfield, held for nine years in Dorchester jail, was re-arrested when he moved to London, and died in Newgate prison. In 1662 Francis Whiddon, a licensed preacher from Totnes in Devon, was removed from this position, but continued his ministry unofficially outside Totnes, although his congregations were fined. Unhappily, the Mayor of Totnes, a Mr. Shapley, discovered that his wife had attended one of the meetings, and he had to pay her fine.

Spain was no longer the international power behind the drive to re-establish the Roman faith in England. The place occupied by Philip II of Spain in the days of Queen Elizabeth had now been taken by King Louis XIV of France. It was he who had been active in arranging the marriage by proxy between James, Duke of York, and Mary Beatrice of Modena, after the death of the Duke's first wife, so ensuring that the Queen, when the Duke succeeded to the English throne, would be a staunch Roman Catholic. He was engaged in persecuting the Protestants in his own country, and as a result a great many fled to England and Holland, where sympathy with their plight strengthened the anti-Catholic feeling in those countries. He even persuaded Charles II to sign a secret treaty on 22 May 1670, in which Charles agreed to "reconcile himself with the Romish Church as soon as the welfare of his kingdom will permit", and to accept "two millions of livres tournoises", and the assistance of Louis "with troops to the number (if required) of 6000 infantry, which are to land wherever Charles shall judge best". The two monarchs agreed "to make war upon the United States of Holland," and promised "to annul any clauses to be found in any preceding treaties made with other states that may happen to be contrary to those of this secret treaty".

Charles must have realised that "the welfare of his kingdom" would never permit the restoration of the Roman Catholic Church in his country, and he undoubtedly entered into the treaty with no small degree of cynicism. Hallam, in his *Constitutional History of England,* remarks regarding the treaty, "This memorable transaction explains and justifies the strenuous opposition made in Parliament to the King and Duke of York, and may be reckoned the first act of a drama which ended in the Revolution." Not such a "secret" treaty after all.

Charles's brother James, Duke of York, was a far more honest and sincere adherent of the Roman Church than ever Charles was, and he was impatient to see that part of the treaty which affected the Roman Catholic religion put into effect immediately. Together with his second wife, Mary Beatrice of Modena, he openly practised the Roman Catholic faith, although by so doing he endangered his prospects of succeeding his brother to the throne. Under the Test Act of 1673 he had to relinquish his position as Lord High Admiral of England. In spite of his brother's professed religion and consequent unpopularity in the country, Charles firmly maintained that James was the legitimate successor to the throne.

Lord Shaftesbury was the head of a political group which strenuously campaigned for the exclusion of James from the succession. They called for him to be replaced by James, Duke of Monmouth, the eldest but supposed illegitimate son of Charles II, or by Mary, Princess of Orange, daughter of the Duke of York by his first wife, and wife of Prince William of Orange. Parliament was urged by some of its most prominent members to put these proposals into effect. They were embodied in the Exclusion Bill, which passed the Commons at its second reading by a majority of seventy-nine. In order to avoid the Bill becoming law, the King dissolved Parliament on 26 May 1679.

Shaftesbury and his associates fomented among the people the strongest fears of a Popish government and its supposed evils. Many people, alarmed that Bibles might become unobtainable, started to make copies of them by hand so that they would not be denied the comfort of their reading. Daniel Defoe, the author of *Robinson Crusoe,* set to work at this himself, and said that he worked like a horse until he had written out the whole Pentateuch, when he grew so tired that he was "willing to risk the rest".

In October 1680, Parliament met again, and the Exclusion Bill went through all its stages in the Commons without difficulty, only to be rejected in the Lords. In March 1681 the King summoned a new Parliament at Oxford, where the University was devoted to the Crown, and the gentry of the neighbourhood were mostly Tories. At the meeting of this Parliament, "the Whig members, who still comprised a majority of the House of Commons, were escorted by great numbers of their armed and mounted tenants and serving men, who exchanged looks of defiance with the royal Guards. The slightest provocation might, under such circumstances, have started a civil war, but neither side dared strike the first blow.

"The King again offered to consent to anything but the Exclusion Bill. The Commons were determined to accept nothing but the Exclusion Bill. In a few days the Parliament was dissolved. The King had triumphed."

Still hostile to Popery, crowds carried banners through the streets of Oxford and London bearing the words "No Popery—No Slavery" but events then quietened down. Shaftesbury escaped to Holland, and died there in 1683. The Rye House Plot of 1683 was a Whig plan conceived by a few desperate and fanatical men, members of the "Green Ribbon Club," to assassinate both the King and the Duke of York in order to secure the accession of the Duke of Monmouth; but it was soon discovered and foiled. It was said that Monmouth himself had no part in the plot, and would have recoiled with horror from the thought of parricide, but the indignation aroused throughout the country extended to include the whole Whig faction. The Earl of Essex was found dead in the Tower of London with his throat slit, and Lord William Russell and Algernon Sidney were executed there. Dr. Gilbert Burnet, a staunch Whig, Chaplain to Charles II and a lecturer at St. Clements, was deprived of his chaplaincy and lectureship for his defence of William, Lord Russell. He retired to the Continent on the accession of James II, and later became a personal friend of William of Orange.

The families of Russell and Sidney, privately vowing vengeance, managed to keep their family estates out of danger. Admiral Edward Russell resigned from the Navy, and with Henry Sidney began secretly to correspond with Prince William of Orange.

The Duke of Monmouth, who was closely associated with and under the influence of prominent Whigs such as Lord Shaftesbury, threw himself on his father's mercy, and the King forgave him, but he thought it prudent to go into voluntary exile, and found refuge in Holland. His arrival there was greeted with full military honours by the English regiments loaned to William of Orange.

Relations between Charles and William became strained, and it became clear that William was not welcome at the English Court, although communication continued between Whitehall and The Hague, and William watched events in England with close attention, being particularly interested in the growing opposition to James, Duke of York. He was also wary of his enemy, the formidable Louis XIV, King of France, not only because he had, with the support of Charles II, invaded Holland in 1672, but also because in 1682 he had annexed the small principality of Orange, near Avignon, of which William was ruler, and appropriated its revenues.

James Duke of York, the legitimate heir to the throne, succeeded Charles II on his death in February 1685. By this time, the Duke of Monmouth and the Earl of Argyll, both in exile in Holland, were deeply involved in plots to remove James II from the throne. England's need for a Protestant King was apparent and in Monmouth, eldest son, if illegitimate, of Charles II, and an avowed Protestant, the people saw their ideal leader. He was particularly popular in the West Country, where the ordinary people had taken him to their hearts during a tour which he made there in 1680.

In April 1685 King James's special envoy at The Hague, Bevil Skelton, arrived to warn the Dutch authorities against the exiles who had taken refuge in their country, and to try to persuade them to banish them, and so prevent them from raising a rebellion in England. William informed James that he knew nothing of these activities. Both the Duke of Monmouth and the Earl of Argyll were active in Holland at the time raising money, men and ships in order to invade England and Scotland respectively, and when these preparations were complete in 1685, both expeditions sailed without either help or hindrance from William. Skelton received orders to request the return to England of the Scottish and English regiments then in Holland, and not only did William comply promptly with this request, but offered to lead them himself against Monmouth. James did not agree to this offer.

Argyll landed in Scotland, and after a brief campaign was defeated and taken, ending his life under the headsman's axe in Edinburgh on 30 June. Monmouth, whose youth and charm, as well as his Protestant religion, so appealed to the West Country folk, landed at Lyme Regis in Dorset on 11 June and raised a rustic army in rebellion against the King. He was defeated at the battle of Sedgemoor, and after fleeing for his life, was finally captured in a Dorset ditch on 8 July and beheaded on Tower Hill on 15 July 1685. Those who suffered the aftermath of Monmouth's rebellion, either from the cruelties of Colonel Percy Kirke and his "lambs" or in the judicial horrors of Judge Jeffreys's Bloody Assizes, are remembered to this day. It was estimated that about seven percent of the rebel army were either killed in battle or executed afterwards. The West Country lost something in the region of four thousand men from its working population. Over a thousand prisoners were either hanged or transported, and not until the General Pardon of March 1688 did hundreds more dare to re-appear. The intolerance and brutality of the regime of James II personified in Judge Jeffreys led eventually to a great upsurge of revulsion among the people.

On his accession to the throne James inherited a peaceful nation, and by the autumn of 1685 his power was at its height. Parliament was manageable, consisting largely of men he had wanted elected, who were loyal to him. He had been voted a generous income for life, which was sufficient to maintain an army of twenty thousand men. His brother's reign had proved that a policy of moderation would encourage national loyalty; but James did not pursue a moderate policy. He began to reveal his intention of returning the country to the Church of Rome. One of his small but significant acts concerned the wording cut into the plinth of Wren's monument commemorating the Great Fire of London of 1666, which stood by the house in Pudding Lane where the fire started. James ordered the obliteration of that part of the inscription which blamed the papists for the catastrophe. [In the reign of William and Mary the inscription was re-cut, more deeply, only to be finally erased in 1831.]

In making appointments, he used his royal prerogative to excess. Roman Catholic officers were appointed to the army and the navy, and tactlessly he even tried to replace with a Catholic officer the commander of the English regiments loaned to Prince

The Monument – James had its anti-Catholic inscription excised. William had it re-cut.
The tower was erected by Wren to mark the place where the Great Fire of London had started in 1666.

The Monument,
London

William in Holland. His ministers were expected to attend mass with him, and there was a Papal Nuncio in London. Reporting the scene at the time, Dr. Burnet wrote,"Affairs in Scotland went on at much the same rate as they did in England." There were a few converts to Rome, but they had little effect. On the other hand, the Irish supported James with enthusiasm. Under the Earl of Tyrconnel, whom James made Lord Lieutenant of Ireland, Irish papists were appointed to army posts as they became vacant, and on the slightest pretext he "broke" English Protestant officers to make the vacancies, and in the end he turned them all out. The King resolved to make Ireland "a nursery for his army in England, and to be sure at least of an army there," but to "go on more slowly in Britain," wrote Burnet.

The people of Britain watched with dismay the persecution of the Protestants across the Channel under the regime of Louis XIV, where children were torn from their parents to be educated in convents. When in October 1685 Louis revoked the Edict of Nantes, a law which had given a degree of protection to the Protestant Huguenots, and unleashed upon the unfortunate people a fury of cruelty and persecution, many Huguenots left their homes in France and made their way to England, where they settled in various areas of London. This influx of a considerable number of skilled and industrious people, incidentally, enriched in no small degree their new country. A wave of sympathy for these refugees swept this country, and James's popularity was further damaged when many people began to fear that he was following along the same road as Louis, and that similar persecution might develop in Britain.

In 1686 a group of gentlemen of the West Country who were greatly concerned about the general situation met at Charborough Park near Wareham in Dorset, the seat of Thomas Erle, Esquire. John Hutchins, in his *History and Antiquities of the County of Dorset,* remarks that "The Erles were a very ancient and knightly family". So secret was this meeting ("One could easily lose one's head in those days", Mr. H. W. Drax, the present owner of Charborough Park, observed wryly) that it was held in an ice-house in the grounds of the great house. The ice-house still exists. It is an underground cavern built into the side of a high bank a little to the north of the main house, with a decorative stone facing and a sunken entrance approached through a short tunnel from the grounds; an ideal spot, in fact, for a secret meeting and the plotting of sedition. We have of course no record of what transpired, but it was of sufficient importance for the occasion to be commemorated when it became safe to do so, and on a marble slab over the entrance to the ice-house is the following inscription:

Under this roof in the year MDCLXXXVI
a set of patriotic Gentlemen
of this neighbourhood
concerted the great plan
of
THE GLORIOUS REVOLUTION
with
THE IMMORTAL KING WILLIAM
to whom we owe our deliverance
from Popery and Slavery
the expulsion of the tyrant race
of STUARTS
the restoration of our Liberties
security of our Properties
and Establishment of National Honor and Wealth

Ice-house at Charborough Park, near Wareham, Dorset.
Secret meeting place in 1686 of conspirators plotting the overthrow of James II. Photograph courtesy the *Dorset Encyclopedic Guide* [Dorset Publishing Company, 1988].

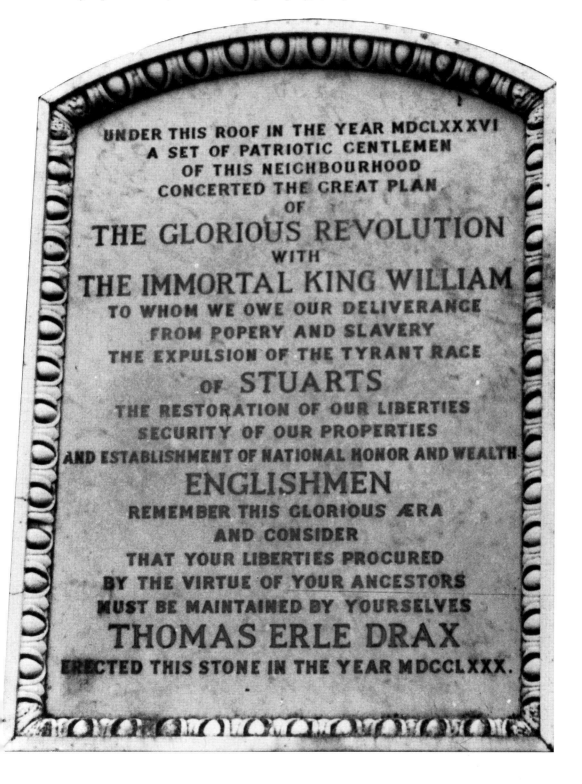

UNDER THIS ROOF IN THE YEAR MDCLXXXVI
A SET OF PATRIOTIC GENTLEMEN
OF THIS NEIGHBOURHOOD
CONCERTED THE GREAT PLAN
OF
THE GLORIOUS REVOLUTION
WITH
THE IMMORTAL KING WILLIAM
TO WHOM WE OWE OUR DELIVERANCE
FROM POPERY AND SLAVERY
THE EXPULSION OF THE TYRANT RACE
OF STUARTS
THE RESTORATION OF OUR LIBERTIES
SECURITY OF OUR PROPERTIES
AND ESTABLISHMENT OF NATIONAL HONOR AND WEALTH
ENGLISHMEN
REMEMBER THIS GLORIOUS ÆRA
AND CONSIDER
THAT YOUR LIBERTIES PROCURED
BY THE VIRTUE OF YOUR ANCESTORS
MUST BE MAINTAINED BY YOURSELVES
THOMAS ERLE DRAX
ERECTED THIS STONE IN THE YEAR MDCCLXXX.

ENGLISHMEN
REMEMBER THIS GLORIOUS ERA
and consider
that your liberties procured
by the virtue of your Ancestors
must be maintained by yourselves
THOMAS ERLE DRAX
erected this stone in the year MDCCLXXX

James went on increasingly to disregard the inclinations of the majority of his people, the existing laws, his oath given to Parliament in his first speech there, and even his coronation oath. The King could, on his own authority, annul a statute made by Parliament, but to use this prerogative in religious matters was, to say the least, a most delicate matter. Even Queen Elizabeth I, a monarch whose powers were far more absolute than those of James, had cleverly avoided trouble and had maintained a happy state of affairs with regard to the Church of England and the people without using her authority in the religious field.

Unlike Elizabeth's times, at the Restoration it was Parliament which had recalled the monarch, and the King's was no longer the final authority in the country. James refused to acknowledge this. Finally, in 1687, his Declaration of Indulgence dispensed with all religious tests. In 1688 he demanded that the Declaration be read twice in all churches in the realm, and so aroused the entire Church of England against him. Seven bishops who protested that his orders were contrary to the law of the land were, with heavy hand, prosecuted and sent to the Tower, passing through crowds of kneeling people as they went. There was a trial, and they were acquitted, and the public rejoiced. On 30 June 1688 James was inspecting his own forces on Hounslow Heath, and it was observed that even they cheered the news of the acquittal after he had departed. Amongst the seven bishops was the Cornishman Trelawney. The version we know of the famous song *And shall Trelawney die?* was written in the nineteenth century by R. S. Hawker, but the refrain had been sung when the bishop was in the Tower, and even earlier, when his grandfather had suffered similarly under Charles I.

The bishops had hardly entered the Tower when it was announced that the Queen had given birth to a son, the unfortunate James Francis Edward Stuart. According to Macaulay, no-one of any note was present at the birth, which was a month premature. Princess Anne, James's daughter, was away in Bath on her father's orders "to take the waters". Sancroft, the highly respected Archbishop of Canterbury, was in the Tower. The Dutch ambassador had not been invited, and of the Privy Councillors present, half were Roman Catholics. The only witness to the delivery was the midwife. The news of the birth was not well received in the country, and the suspicion that an imposture had been practised grew. Rumour spread that a baby had been "smuggled, by means of a warming pan, into the royal bed, and then handed round in triumph, as heir of three kingdoms". After this all royal births were attended by the Home Secretary, a decree that was not put aside until the birth of children to Queen Elizabeth II.

Prince William of Orange, who had previously been urged by Lord Mordaunt in September 1686 to come to England with an army, and had refused, now listened to representations from Admiral Edward Russell, who had gone to The Hague in May, 1686, before the birth of the Prince of Wales. The Prince was advised to bring a strong body of troops to England and "to call the people to arms". Russell informed him of the mood of the English. William recognised the significance of the crisis, and is reported

The seven bishops approaching the Tower of London.
Dutch print, courtesy the BBC Hulton Picture Library.

to have said in Latin to his close friend Van Dykvelt, "Now, or never!" He was more guarded in his reply to Russell, but he said, according to Dr. Burnet, that "if he was invited by some men of the best interest, and the most valued in their nation, who should both in their own name and in the name of others who trusted them, invite him to come and rescue the nation and the religion, he believed he could be ready by the end of September to come over." In other words, he agreed to come.

Mary of Orange and her sister Anne, although finding little evidence to throw doubt on the royal baby's birth, were still able to believe the worst. Mary had little reason to think that her father was fond of her. She had not seen him for a long time, and he had shown her no affection since her marriage to William, nor did he give her any financial help, wealthy though he was, although he gave her sister Anne thirty or forty thousand pounds a year. He had tried to disturb her happiness by having her spied upon in her home, and he made sure that the rumour that her husband was having an affaire with one of her maids of honour, Elizabeth Villiers, was brought to her notice. She felt that James would have no hesitation in joining with the King of France in war against her husband.

Dr. Burnet became one of her trusted advisers. He gives a very good opinion of her in his book. "Her person was majestic," he writes, "and created respect. She had great knowledge, with a true understanding, and a noble expression. There was a sweetness in her deportment that charmed, and an exactness in piety and virtue that made her a pattern to all that saw her." She had read much, both in history and divinity, and the good Doctor informed her in detail about affairs in England since the Restoration of which she knew little. Of greater importance, he was responsible for ensuring that she knew what William's role would be on her accession to the throne of England. She had not realised that he would be only her consort, and had envisaged that they would be joint rulers. Burnet pressed her to talk this over with William, and this she did, "in a very frank manner. She did not think that the husband was ever to be obedient to the wife; she promised him that he should always bear rule, and she asked only that he would obey the command 'Husbands love your wives', as she should do that of 'Wives be obedient to your husbands in all things'." Having cleared up this point, the way was plain for them to go ahead with any plans they wished to make for the future in succeeding to the English throne.

When Dr. Burnet first came to The Hague on the accession of James II, his impression of the Prince of Orange was that he was cold and reserved. "There was a gravity in his whole deportment", he writes. "He spoke little. He put on some appearance of application, but he hated business of all sorts; yet he hated talking and all house games more. This put him on a perpetual course of hunting, to which he gave himself up, beyond any man I ever knew: but I looked on that as always flying from company and business. He had a way that was affable and obliging to the Dutch, but he could not bring himself to comply enough with the temper of the English, his coldness and slowness being very contrary to the genius of the nation." With Mary he became affectionate, and he was relaxed and at his best with his troops. Even as a young man he had the qualities of a great ruler, and was intelligent and hard-working. He spoke and wrote English and German fluently, and had some knowledge of French, Latin, Italian and Spanish. He was of a delicate constitution, and plagued by asthma.

Macaulay describes his appearance: "He had a slender and feeble frame, a lofty and ample forehead, a nose curved like the beak of an eagle, an eye rivalling that of an eagle in brightness and keenness, a thoughtful and somewhat sullen brow, a firm and somewhat peevish mouth, and a cheek pale, thin and deeply furrowed by sickness and care." Thirty-eight at the time of the Revolution, he was courageous and enjoyed the excitement of danger. He gained the respect of the troops he led, and his calm presence and composure gave confidence to all about him.

An invitation to William, written on 30 June 1688, was conveyed to him in the greatest secrecy by Admiral Herbert, who came disguised as an ordinary seaman. The letter outlined the situation current then in England, and reassured William that invasion was feasible. He was warned of difficulties ahead, but "if the Prince of Orange, after due consideration, shall think fit to venture upon the attempt", he was urged that no more time should be lost. The letter was signed in code, using numbers instead of names. The signatories, sometimes known as the "Immortal Seven", were in fact:

(24) Devonshire; (25) Shrewsbury; (27) Danby; (29) Lumley;
(31) Compton, Bishop of London; (33) Sidney; (35) Russell.

Wasting no time, the Prince began his campaign. He obtained the sanction of the States General for his expedition, and instructed Marshal Schomberg, his friend and confidant, to prepare for an autumn invasion of England. He invited Dr. Burnet to go with him as his chaplain, and so ensured that an invaluable record would be made for posterity. On 16 October 1688 the wind turned easterly, and the Prince was ready to go. He took his leave of the States General, thanking them for the kindness which they had shown him on many occasions, and leaving his wife in their care. "He assured them", wrote Burnet, "that she loved their country perfectly and equally with her own:

he hoped that, whatever might happen to him, they would still protect her, and use her as she well deserved; and so he took leave."

Having ensured that the States were safe "on all hands" for this winter, the only risks the Prince felt he had to run on his expedition were "the seas and the weather". He arrived at Helvoet-Sluys on 19 October and went aboard his frigate *Den Briel*. That night the whole fleet sailed. It was a considerable armada. Escorted by fifty or so naval vessels were between five and six hundred transports and auxiliary ships and boats comprising frigates, merchant ships, pinks [flat-bottomed craft from the shallow Dutch inshore waters], flyboats [swift, narrow long boats], fireships and Schieveninger fishing boats, and aboard them was an army of approximately 15,000 men, together with some 3000 horses. About 200 cannon were in the artillery train accompanying them.

A chaplain accompanying the army of the Prince of Orange, the Revd. John Whittle, kept a personal diary of events from the time the expedition set out from Holland to the coronation of William and Mary in London. There are some discrepancies in dates throughout the diary, which are explained by the fact that England in 1688 was still using the Julian Calendar, whereas most of Europe by that time had changed to the more accurate Gregorian Calendar. There was a difference of ten days between the two. The Revd. Whittle vividly describes the beginning of the voyage:

Saturday 29 Oct 1688:

"It was about four a Clock in the Afternoon on Saturday, when the Fleet first weighed their Anchors, and made sail, upon the coming of the Prince of Orange on board. The Evening draw'd on us very fast, the days being short and the nights long; so when the darkness seized us, and night was shutting upon us, every Vessel set up a Light in the Lanthorn: the Men of War set up two, and the Ship wherein the Prince was, had three for a mark of distinction.

"After night, the Wind began to arise high, and the Seas wax'd rough, the Waves began to roar and swell, lifting up their head aloft, and many now began to suspect the Weather, as well they might: for within a while the Winds turn'd and blew a very dreadful Storm, insomuch that all thought we should never see Land more: for there were sundry circumstances which did add to the peril of the Storm, as many skilful Mariners said, The Darkness of the Night, the manner of Carriage, Horses, which will rowl from side to side, if they break their Stays, our Pipes of Water, barrels of Powder and Ball, and the vast number of Ships together, which was worst of all; for while the Schipper intended to escape one on his Starboard, then is he in no small peril of running against the other on his Larboard-side; nay, behind, and before, and all around, there were Ships throwing themselves from side to side, after an exceedingly fearful manner, so that no Steerman knew which way to steer: the Winds blew as if they would have blown the very Elements away before them; the Seas raged and foamed, being all in white froth for anger; the Waves rowled one upon the back of another, as so many great Mountains; the Ships threw themselves, and the people in them, from side to side, and from the fore-part of the Vessel unto the hinder part, as if they would have beaten themselves all to pieces; and if it had not been the good providence of the Almighty, we had most certainly dash'd against each other, and so perished one by the other . . .

"Now the people being thus toss'd and tumbl'd about the Ship, many wax'd exceeding sick, and vomitted continually after a dreadful rate; you could hear the men groan after a pitiful manner; others were sighing, and not a few praying, and committing their souls unto God, for they thought their Bodies must be Meat for the Fish of the Sea. The Sea-men that did belong to each Ship were almost kill'd in working so hard for to preserve their own and our Lives; but now and then they would refresh themselves with a dram of the Brandy-bottle . . .

"Thus did we tumble and rowl about the Seas, and among the unnatural Waves, all this Night . . . Many ships had their Sails blown off; others had their Masts broken with the violence of the Storm, the Waves often-times rowling themselves over the labouring Ships, some had their main-yard broken.

"The Morning-light approaching, we were all very much comforted, especially when we saw that our Vessels were whole and sound, and very little water in her Pump, when it was fathom'd.

"Now we longed for to hear of our great Master, how he did after such a terrible Night, which had befallen us. The Seas continued raging, and the Waves roaring, and exalting their tops as they would touch the Clouds, and we rowled about, and could not tell what to do, or which way to steer after his Highness the Prince of Orange . . . The Prince of Orange, seeing the Winds so stormy, and the Seas so very tempestuous, return'd unto the Holland Coasts, and came into the Haven of Hellevoot-sluys, with a considerable number of Men of War and Merchant-men, Pinks and Fly-boats; and many Men of War more could have come into the Haven, but staid out on purpose to secure the Fleet. When we and other Ships had heard, that the Prince of Orange was safe in Harbour, we gave thanks to God, and were not a little joyful at this good News, and made towards Hellevoot-sluys as fast as we could: Many Vessels in this Storm were driven near the Coasts of England, others towards the North, some into the Texel, and others into Zeeland, and every day they came into the Haven from one place or other."

Of the demeanour of the Prince during the storm, Whittle writes: "His Highness the Prince of Orange was not in the least dismay'd in all the Storm, when most mens hearts were as stones, dead with fear, his Countenance was observed not to alter as other mens did, but, like a true Paul, or servant of Jesus Christ, he encouraged all in the Ship where he was, making them cheerful when their Spirits were dejected."

Orders were immediately given for the repair and revictualling of the fleet, and the smiths and carpenters worked day and night. In less than two weeks, "the whole Fleet being once more in readiness, longed to be under sail".

Towards evening on the last day of October, "the Wind turned about, and came full East, and the Prince of Orange hearing thereof, and feeling the Wind blow so fresh, was fully resolved (by the blessing of God) to set to Sea on the Morrow, not to lose any time, and therefore every Ship took care to have all things in a readiness, insomuch that many were forced to work hard all Night, to get Water and other things convenient on board, for they had heard that his Highness was resolved to tarry for nothing, and therefore he would leave all behind which were not ready.

"So upon Thursday, Novemb. 1 Old Stile, Novemb. 11. New Stile, after the Prince of Orange had dined with all English, Dutch, Scotch and French Lords, Knights and Gentlemen attending his Sacred Person, about three or four of Clock in the Afternoon he went on board a new Vessel of about Twenty eight Guns with the Rotterdam's Admiral, call'd the Brill, as some will have it [other authorities suppose it was called *Den Briel*], and being now in his Cabin, fired, for to give notice unto all the Fleet, to weigh their Anchors and make Sail, which was accordingly done by every Ship, with all possible expedition."

An Exact

D I A R Y

OF THE

Late Expedition

O F

His Illuſtrious Highneſs

T H E

Prince of Orange,

(Now K I N G of *Great Britain*)

From his Palace at the *H A G U E,*

To his Landing at *T O R B A Y;*

And from thence

To his Arrival at *W H I T E-H A L L.*

Giving a particular A C C O U N T

Of all that happened, and every Day's March.

By a Miniſter, Chaplain in the A R M Y.

L O N D O N:
Printed for *Richard Baldwin,* near the *Black Bull* in the
Old-Baily. M D C L X X X I X.

Title-page of Reverend John Whittle's 'Exact Diary'.
This, the most detailed contemporary record of the 'Late Expedition', was published in 1689.

OVERLEAF: the fleet of the Prince of Orange leaving Helvoetsluys for the invasion of England, October 1688.
Daniel Marot's superb print is reproduced by courtesy of the Rijksmuseum, Amsterdam. Marot returned to Holland and is remembered as the architect who designed the great audience chamber in The Hague Palace.

A Sijn Hoogheijt met sijn Hof siende aenkomen de Amsterdamse vloot.
B Den Marschalck van Schombergh met den Grave Carel sijn Soon
ende den Heer dela Caillemotte Soon vande Marquis de Ruvigny

Gesichte vande
hoogheijt den
Tot
den 2

B

D

D. Mort. Fecit

Doorluchtige
van Orangien.
fluys.
1688.

C *Jacht van Syn Hooghejst in het welke waren den Heer van Odyck
ende den Marschalk van Schombergh.*

D *De hoofden van Helleveet-sluijs.*

[32]

Now we could fee the Fire on feveral Towers and places as we fail'd along the Channel towards the Weft, and
many thought that thefe Fires (which were only to direct
all ftrange Ships in the Night) had been Beacons fet up
by the Countrey, according to the Order of the late
King *James*, on purpofe to alarum the Land; when we had
fail'd fome hours after Night, we all ftruck fail, as we
had done before ; the Weather was very good, and the
Wind very favourable, and moft of our Hearts exceedingly reviv'd thereby.

On the Morrow-morning, being the Lord's day, *Novemb.* 4. *Old Stile* , which was the happy Birth-day of
his thrice Illuftrious Highnefs, the Prince of *Orange*; moft
men were of opinion, that we fhould land either in the
Ifle of Wight, Portfmouth, or fome other convenient place,
about which matter they were much miftaken ; for the
Prince of *Orange* did not fail, but obferve the duty of the
day ; fo all were driven of the Waves. Prayers and Sermon being done, he went to Dinner, with fome Nobles attending him, and about Four of Clock in the Afternoon
made fail, all the whole Fleet following the example of
his Ship; now every Schipper endeavour'd for to keep
fight of the three Lanthorns or Admiral of *Rotterdam*'s
Ship, for the fake of his Highnefs therein. The darknefs
fhutting upon us, all our Lights were fet out, as before :
It was no ordinary fight, for to behold the Seas all cover'd with Lights, the Lanthorns appearing at a diftance
like unto fo many Stars in the Water, dancing to and fro,
here and there, according to the motion of the Ship; but
above all, the Cabin of that Veffel wherein the Prince
was, having fo many Wax Lights burning within it, glit-
tered moft glorioufly, and (at a certain diftance) being
well gilt and varnifhed, it feem'd a Paradife for pleafure
and delight.

An extract from Reverend John Whittle's 'Exact Diary'.
It describes the passage of the Prince's fleet down the English Channel.

NEXT SPREAD: the landing of the Prince of Orange at Brixham, Devon.
A Dutch print, courtesy of the Mansell Collection.

The Dutch Fleet leaves Holland

Thursday, 1 November 1688:

Taking advantage of the east winds—the "Protestant winds"— William led his newly organised fleet towards the north of England where he intended to land, to be greeted by his supporters. However, intelligence reached him that James was expecting him to land in Yorkshire, and he could expect to meet resistance there, so he signalled his fleet to turn and run before the gales southwards, into the English Channel.

The same winds which were advantageous to William prevented the English ships under Lord Dartmouth from leaving the Thames to oppose him. Some of these ships which had reached the sea were driven back by the storms, whilst the more advanced of them were pinned down off the Essex coast at Gunfleet, close to Clacton-on-Sea.

Saturday, 3 November:

Running before the gales, with William in the "Brill" [*Den Briel*] leading, the Dutch Armada, under the command of Lieutenant Admiral General Herbert, reached the Straits of Dover at about 10 a.m. Macaulay describes the scene: "More than six hundred vessels, with canvas spread to a favourable wind, followed in his train. The transports were in the centre. The men of war, more than fifty in number, formed an outer rampart . . . His fleet spread to within a league of Dover on the North and of Calais on the South. The men of war on the extreme right and left saluted both fortresses at once . . . The troops appeared under arms on the decks. The flourish of trumpets, the clash of cymbals and the rolling of drums were distinctly heard at once on the English and French shores." Large crowds both in England and France saw the fleet as it passed by.

By sunset, the Armada was off Beachy Head, "then the lights were kindled. The sea was in a blaze for many miles. But the eyes of all the seamen were directed throughout the night to three huge lanterns which flamed on the stern of the Brill". What a sight this must have been! Steering clear of Portsmouth, where James had sent reinforcements, the fleet sailed on through the night.

Sunday, 4 November:

The dawn of the anniversary of William's birthday, and of his marriage, saw the great assembly of ships off the Isle of Wight, and here, divine service was held aboard them all. William had now determined to land at Tor Bay in Devon, and to disembark his army there. At noon Lord Russell brought an English pilot aboard the *Brill*, and his orders were "to sail so that next morning we should be short of Dartmouth: for it was intended that some of the ships should land there, and the rest should sail into Torbay."

Monday, 5 November:

In the mists of the November dawn the pilot missed his sea marks, and the fleet sailed on past Tor Bay and Dartmouth. It was not possible to return in the face of the easterly wind, and in such a dilemma the fleet would be carried on to Plymouth, where a Catholic garrison had been posted under the Governor, Lord Bath, and any attempt at landing would be strongly opposed. When Lord Russell realised what the pilot had done, he told Dr. Burnet to go to his prayers, for all was lost. As soon as he had spoken, the wind veered to the south, and ". . . a soft and happy gale of wind carried in the whole fleet in four hours time into Tor Bay". Here, the mist had dispersed, and in the light of an autumnal noon-day sun the Armada rounded the great promontory of Berry Head and sailed into the sheltered waters of Tor Bay.

The quiet shores were dotted with scattered shelters and huts of the farmworkers and fishermen. Countryfolk came from miles around to see the fleet, a magnificent spectacle, with every vessel displaying its colours. The Prince of Orange ordered his standard to be run up, with a white flag above it to show peaceful intentions to those who wished for peace, and beneath it a red flag to signify war to those who opposed him.

The Devonshire people had a hatred of Popery, and remembered with affection Monmouth and all he stood for, and William's standard, with its motto upholding the Protestant religion and Liberty, moved them to his support.

Whittle describes the scene: "Before we came into the Bay's mouth, as we were near the rocks, the people ran from Place to Place after us, and we being so near as to discern the Habit of the Country People, and they able to see us and hear our voices, a certain Minister in the Fleet, on board the Golden Sun, went up to the top of the uppermost cabin, where the Colours hang out, a place where he could easily behold all the People on the Shore, and where they might most perfectly see and hear him, and pulling a Bible out of his pocket he open'd it, and held it so in his right hand, making many flourishes with it unto the people, whose Eyes were fixed on him and duly observ'd him, thereby signifying to the People the flourishing of the Holy Gospel (by God's Blessing upon the Prince of Orange's Endeavours) and calling out as loud as he was able, and said unto them on the top of the Rock, 'For the Protestant Religion, and Maintaining of the Gospel in the Truth and Purity thereof, are we all by the Goodness and Providence of God come hither, after so many Storms and Tempests. 'Moreover,' said he, 'It is the Prince of Orange that's come, a zealous Defender of that Faith which is truly Ancient, Catholick, and Apostolical, who is the Supreme Governour of this very great and formidable Fleet'."

"Whereupon all the People shouted for Joy, and Huzza's did now echo into the Air, many amongst them throwing up their Hats, and all making Signs with their Hands.

"'Tis, methinks, impossible for any Man to be so blinded as not to discern the Design of God in this Expedition, from the beginning to the end thereof, for a very favourable wind now fill'd our Sails, and brought us into the long-desired Haven, to the Joy of our Hearts and the Comfort of England."

According to contemporary reports, six warships then began patrolling the entrance to the bay, whilst another six guarded the coast. The transports, and the remainder of the fleet then came to anchor in the bay whilst the Prince conferred with his commanders. Very soon there was considerable activity among the transports, and some sixty boats bearing troops made for the shore. The first troops to land were six regiments of English and Scots, bearing a red flag, under General Mackay. The Dragoons, bearing a white flag, followed, led by Count Solms. They were accompanied by "the little Porpus with eighteen guns" to cover their landing.

Then William's own barge, bearing the Prince himself, was seen to be approaching. It was low tide, and the Prince's boat grounded in the shallow water. He, standing up in the boat, said to the waiting crowd on shore, "Mine good people, I am come for your goods. I am come for all your goods"—meaning, in all probability, "for your good". A Mr. Youlden replied, "You'm welcome," to which William answered, "If I am welcome, come and carry me ashore," whereupon a Brixham fisherman by the name of Peter Varwell waded out to the boat and brought the Prince ashore on his shoulders.

Once he was ashore William's personal standard was raised. It bore the arms of Nassau quartered with those of England, and the motto: "Liberate et Religion Je Meintiendray" [I will uphold Liberty and Religion]. Brixham's coat of arms to this day

Know all men

by these Presents that WE the URBAN DISTRICT COUNCIL OF BRIXHAM DO HEREBY WILL AND ORDAIN that no other ARMS than those herein shewn be blazoned the true and lawful arms to be borne by this Urban District as it is constitutionally represented by us the Council thereof

B L A Z O N	per pale or and azure billety of the first, a lion rampant gules and of the first, within a bordure engrailed sables bearing fifteen heraldic fountains
Crest:	on a wreath argent and azure, two dolphins naiant counter naiant counter embowed in saltire, vert
Mantling:	azure doubled argent
Motto:	Je meintiendray - "I Will Maintain"

A R G U M E N T

These Arms shew a dimidiation (halving) of the arms of, on the dexter, the Pomeroy Family and, on the sinister, the House of Orange-Nassau. De la Pomerai's held interests in the Manors of Lupton and Briseham in the twelfth century, and the town's connection with the House of Orange-Nassau is through Stadhouder William, Prince of Orange, who landed at Brixham in 1688 when he came to this country and became King William III. This was the occasion at which William quoted his family motto - long since adopted as the town's motto in its English translation - to say "I Will Maintain the Liberties of England and the Protestant Religion." The landing has been commemorated in the Seal of the Local Government Board, and, later, the Common Seal of the Council and the tradition is here continued. The border is black and powdered with roundels similar to that borne in the arms of the Valletort family, who also had interests in the District's two Manors in the twelfth century. That family came from Cornwall and because of a personal connection the arms bore the same border as the arms of Richard Plantagenet, Earl of Cornwall, Count of Poictou, King of the Romans, Emperor of the Germans, Son of King John and nephew of King Richard I, the Lion Heart. Originally the roundels were besants (gold coins) representing golden peas (poix) in punning allusion to Poictou, but Brixham uses fountains to shew its connection with the sea. Similarly, the straight inner edge of the Valletort-Cornwall border is here engrailed so as to shew a further connection with the Pomeroy family (which used a red engrailed border) and to avoid any apparent implication that Brixham, Devon, is in the County of Cornwall, even though at that time it was within Richard's seignory. Indeed the arms of the Redvers, the first Earls of Devon and from them, the arms of the present County of Devon, and the crest of the City of Exeter, bear the rampant lion of Richard Plantagenet, and Brixham will maintain the tradition, save that our charge is uncrowned.

GIVEN under our Common Seal this twentieth day of March One thousand nine hundred and fifty-six

Chairman *Alfred. E. Bulley*

Clerk *W. A. Saxton*

Brixham's Coat of Arms.

The Charter of Arms of 1956 states: "These Arms show a dimidiation (halving) of the arms of, on the dexter, the Pomeroy Family and, on the sinister, the House of Orange-Nassau. De la Pomerais held interests in the Manors of Lupton and Briseham in the twelfth century, and the town's connection with the House of Orange-Nassau is through Stadhouder William, Prince of Orange, who landed at Brixham in 1688 when he came to this country and became King William III. This was the occasion at which William quoted his family motto – long since adopted as the town's motto in its English translation – to say, 'I will Maintain the Liberties of England and the Protestant Religion.' The landing has been commemorated in the Seal of the local Government Board, and later, the Common Seal of the Council and the tradition is here continued." Courtesy of the Town Clerk and Chief Executive Officer, Borough of Torbay.

includes the words from William's standard, "Je Meintiendray", a lasting memorial to the Prince who came to uphold the religion of the people, and to establish true democracy. The welcoming people regarded his arrival on Guy Fawke's Day as a good omen for their future.

It is not known exactly where the Prince of Orange first set his foot on landing in England. Mrs. M. Godley of Brixham said that her father maintained that Churston Quay was the site, but others say that it was on the north bank of the inlet. The New Quay has on it an obelisk, into the base of which is built a slab of stone from the rock on which the Prince is alleged to have landed, and it is inscribed, "On this stone and near this spot William Prince of Orange first set foot on his landing in England fifth November 1688."

Another, more imposing, monument in the form of a marble statue of William on a suitably inscribed plinth, gazing into Brixham, stands at the waterside on the Strand. The foundation stone was laid on the bicentenary of the landing by the Netherlands Ambassador, His Excellency the Count de Bylandt, and just one year later, on 5 November 1889, the statue was unveiled by Charles Aldenbury Bentinck, J.P., of Bovey Tracey, a direct descendant of Hans William Bentinck, Earl of Portland, a loyal supporter of the Prince of Orange.

William's Brixham statue (opposite) and commemorative stone.
Glimpsed behind, to the left, is a replica of the previous century's shipping; 'castles' were on the way down by William's day.

In 1688 Brixham was a very different place from the busy fishing port and seaside resort which it has become today. Now, the fishing boats land their catches at the New Quay, which was built in 1803, and has been further extended since, and the fish market alongside bustles with commercial activity. The wharves and quayside, and the harbourside street known as the Strand, are thronged with holidaymakers in the summer, crowding the old inns and the many shops. There are unspoilt, narrow streets, and steep steps which climb up to the rows of cottages and houses rising in tiers from the harbour. A map of 1688 shows "The Antient Harbour of Brixham," with an old stone pier, the Eastern Quay, which existed in 1300, at its mouth. The sea came well inland as far as "Combers Bottom" along an inlet which divided the lower part of the town in two. The two parts were linked by a ferry at the point which is now the lower end of Station Hill and Bolton Street.

A local story of the landing relates how a Mr. Youlden formally welcomed William with the words:

> "And it please your Majesty King William
> You'm welcome to Brixham Quay,
> To eat buckhorn and drink Bohea
> Along o' we"

The words "Your Majesty King William" must have seemed a good augury to the Prince as he and Marshal Schomberg stood on the shore of a country where he was not yet crowned. The greetings which William received, and the fact that their landing was unopposed by the people, must have cheered them all greatly. As one of them wrote, ". . . there was no opposition, for the people bid us heartily welcome to England, and gave us all manner of Provisions for our refreshment".

Without wasting any time we are told, William, as arranged beforehand, sent a yellow quince to the Earl of Bath at Plymouth to signify a successful landing in England. Apparently Lord Bath was secretly well-disposed to the Prince.

Again the Revd. Whittle describes the scene: "So the Prince, with Mareschal Schomberg and divers Lords, Knights and Gentlemen, marched up the hill, which all the Fleet could see over the Houses, the Colours flying and flourishing before his Highness, the Trumpets sounding, the Hoitboys played, the Drums beat, and the Lords, Knights, Gentlemen and Guards shouted; and sundry Huzza's did now echo in the Fleet,

WILLIAM
PRINCE OF ORANGE,
AFTERWARDS
WILLIAM III,
KING OF GREAT BRITAIN & IRELAND,
LANDED NEAR THIS SPOT
5TH NOVEMBER 1688,
AND ISSUED HIS FAMOUS DECLARATION
"THE LIBERTIES OF ENGLAND
AND
THE PROTESTANT RELIGION
I WILL MAINTAIN."

ENGELANDS VRIJHEID

DOOR ORANJE HERSTELD

from off the Hill, insomuch that our very Hearts below on the Water, were even ravished for Joy thereof."

Their own horses being not yet landed, William asked the people for some, and two were procured from a neighbouring village, whereupon the Prince and Schomberg mounted and rode off to reconnoitre the area. Meanwhile, Dr. Burnet was landing, and as soon as he had done so he sought out the Prince and congratulated him. "The Prince," he wrote, "took me heartily by the hand, and asked me if I would not now believe in pre-destination. I told him I would never forget that providence of God which had appeared so signally on this occasion. He was more cheerful than ordinary. Yet he returned soon to his usual gravity."

Calling together all the local fishermen, William asked them where they thought the best place for landing the horses would be. He then directed the encamping of his men on Furzeham Common, the area on the hill above the town which he had previously surveyed, and that done, he returned down the hill to the fishermen's houses to find his own lodging for the first night. It is said that he made his headquarters that night at Peter Varwell's cottage in Middle Street. There may be seen in Brixham Museum "Peter Varwell's Chair," a wooden chair reputed to have belonged to the Brixham fisherman who carried the Prince from his barge to Brixham Quay on his arrival. His descendants are alive today.

Inscriptions on William's monument on Brixham's Strand (opposite) and then and now views of Brixham Harbour.
William landed in the inner harbour, on the left-hand side. 'England's freedom restored by Orange' the Dutch inscription translates.

The house in Middle Street, Brixham, where the Prince of Orange is said to have spent his first night ashore in the West Country, on 5 November 1688.
It has since been demolished.

In recognition of his services, William is said to have asked him what he would like as a token of his favour.   His reply was that he hoped that the press gang would never come to Brixham.   According to local tradition, Varwell rode with the Prince to Newton, Exeter and later, to London, where he was rewarded with one hundred pounds, which enabled him to build another house in Brixham.

Meanwhile there was great and continuing activity in the town.   By nightfall, two thousand men had landed, disembarkation having continued all the afternoon, and it went on through the night, speed being essential lest James II's forces should attack during the darkness, although the Royal fleet had only reached Beachy Head at this time.   William's army was settling down on Furzeham Common.

Whittle wrote: "The night was now as the Day for Labour; and this was done lest the Enemy should come before we were in all readiness to receive them.   Officers and Souldiers were continually marching up the Hill after the manner of the Guards, with their Colours flying and Flourishing, Hoitboys playing, drums beating, and all shouting and echoing forth Huzza's.

"As soon as the Prince had view'd well the Ground upon the top of the Hill, and found the most commodious place for all his Army to Encamp, he then gave orders for every thing, and so returned down the hill unto the Fishermen's little Houses: one of which he made his Palace at that time, instead of those at Loo, Honfleurdyke, and the Hague."   The area round Peter Varwell's house was well guarded.

Peter Varwell's chair is in Brixham Museum. The Overgang is the flight of steps up from the seafront.
Peter Varwell was the fisherman who carried Prince William ashore from his barge. The steps were ascended by the Prince's army, on its way to camp on Furzeham Common.

"The Horse Guard and some Foot were round about him at every House, and a strong Guard a little below the House wherein his Highness lay. All the Lords were quartered up and down at these Fishermen's Houses, whereof these poor Men were glad.

"Now the camp began to be filled with Officers and Souldiers; for no Officer must move from his Company or Post. Foot Guards belonging to the Prince of Orange did encamp within an Inclosure of plowed Land, about which there was a natural Fence, good Hedges and little Stone Walls, so that no Horse could touch them."

The Prince had ordered that everything needed by the forces must be paid for, which pleased the local people, but there was little provision for them in Brixham. On the following day, people from the surrounding villages brought in goods for the men, and they even rolled apples down into the town for the soldiers. Others came from Totnes after their morning service, many of whom were non-conformists. They were quite fearless, confident that they would not be harmed by the invaders.

Greetings were brought from Dartmouth by Nicholas Roope, probably the first "man of substance" to visit William in Brixham. He later became Governor of Dartmouth Castle. An invitation to the Prince to stay at Forde House on his arrival at Newton Abbot was extended by the son of Sir William Courtney.

By now, over fifteen thousand men and roughly a thousand officers were encamped in the area, and that night Furzeham Common was alight with the glow of hundreds of camp fires. Whittle goes on to say: "It was a cold, frosty night and the Stars twinkled exceedingly; besides the Ground was very wet after so much Rain and Ill Weather. The Souldiers were to stand to their Arms all Night, at least to be in Readiness if any thing should happen, or the Enemy make an Assault; and therefore sundry Souldiers went to fetch some old Hedges and cut down green Wood therewith, to make some Fire. Now one Regiment beginning, all the rest soon followed their Example. Those that had Provision in their Snap-sacks (as most of the Souldiers had) did broil it at the Fire, and others went into the Villages there-abouts to buy some fresh Provisions for their Officers, being we were newly come from the Sea; but Alas! here was little Provision to be gotten."

As Whittle says, overnight the army stayed on guard, prepared for any attack, but James's forces were still only at Warminster and Salisbury, awaiting further orders. The Prince had taken the precaution of leaving a force of warships in Lyme Bay to afford protection to his fleet at Brixham, and a man of war had been sent to Plymouth to secure that port for William. Lord Bath, in command of the garrison there, had told Lord Russell secretly that he would join the Prince, "yet it was not likely that he would be so forward as to receive us at our first meeting". Messengers had also been sent ahead to Exeter to give the news of William's successful landing.

Tuesday, 6 November:

With the coming of daylight the Prince reviewed his troops on Furzeham Common, and then went with the fishermen who were to show him where his horses might be landed. Fortunately the winds were still gentle, and the sea was like glass, and stayed dead calm all morning. At the chosen beach the horse transports were brought in to within sixty feet of the shore, and in three hours—instead of the several days it was thought might be the case—hundreds of horses swam safely ashore.

"The Navy was like a little City, the masts appearing like so many Spires. The people were like Bees, swarming all over the Bay, and now all the Schievelingers are set to work to carry the Men and Horses unto Shore with speed, for as yet they had done nothing."

Dartmouth Castle – to the right of the harbour entrance.
Nicholas Roope, who visited William at Brixham, later became its governor.

Brixham's outer harbour and Tor Bay, from Furzeham.
William's troops camped here on the common for their first night in England.

Topsham, near Exeter.
William's artillery and heavy baggage
were landed here, five miles up the
sheltered waters of the Exe estuary.

Roughly four thousand horses had to be disembarked. Some of the animals were pushed overboard and guided ashore with a rope, whilst others were brought by ship to the quay, and came ashore fully harnessed. With so many of the beasts milling about, the local people were amazed at the speed with which each soldier found his own horse.

By three o'clock all the forces who were to land were ashore, together with as much baggage as they needed to get them to Exeter.

"Officers and Souldiers crowded the Boats extreamly, many being ready to sink under the Weight: happy was that Man which could get to Land soonest; and such was the eagerness of both Officers and Souldiers, that divers jeoparded their lives for haste; sundry Oars were broken in rowing, because too many laid hands on them; some jumped up to their Knees in Water, and one or two were over Head and Ears."

The artillery and heavy baggage were left aboard to be taken by sea to Topsham, from where they could be more easily transported to Exeter, where William intended to make his first headquarters.

No sooner had the disembarkation been completed than the winds again increased to gale force from the west, which was very providential for William, since the King's Fleet in pursuit of him, now off the Isle of Wight—and some ships were even in sight of the topmasts in Torbay—had to put in to Portsmouth Harbour for safety and shelter. Many said that the winds served the Protestant cause so well that it was reminiscent of the Spanish Armada one hundred years before, when the "Invincible Armada" had been scattered by the wrath of God. "Civil freedom and divine truth were again in jeopardy; and again the obedient elements had fought for the good cause."

William stayed another night in Brixham, where his officers doubtless availed themselves again of the facilities of the local hostelry. "There was a little Alehouse amongst the Fishermen's Houses which was so extreamly throng'd and crowded that a Man could not thrust in his Head, nor get Bread or Ale for Mony. It was a happy time for the Landlord, who strutted about as if indeed he had been a Lord himself, because he was honoured with Lords Company."

Wednesday, 7 November:

The army now began to move out on the march to Exeter. Outriders had been sent ahead to search the houses of known Catholics for horses and weapons. One such house was Torre Abbey, which still stands close to the sea in the centre of the popular seaside resort of Torquay, at the upper end of Tor Bay. It is now the property of the Corporation of Torquay, and has been repaired inside and is used as a picture gallery. It is open to the public. In 1688, Torre Abbey belonged to a Mr. Cary, a well known Catholic His household, on seeing the approach of William's fleet, had at first mistaken the ships for those of the French Navy, as identified by a priest who was staying at the house. When William's officer, a certain Captain M., asked for arms and horses, Lady Cary politely informed him that her husband was in Plymouth. When asked if anyone could speak Dutch, the inhabitants of the house fled, except for Lady Cary and a few retainers. She was put to no further trouble.

"At the upper end of Torbay there is a fair House belonging to one Mr. Carey, a very rigid Papist, who entertained a Priest in his House; This Priest going to recreate himself on the Leads, on the top thereof, it being a most delightsome day, as he was walking there, he happened to cast his Eyes towards the Sea, and espying the Fleet at a distance he presently concludes that 'twas the French Navy (because he saw divers white Flags). . . and being transported with Joy, he hastened to inform his own Disciples of the House, and forthwith they sung Te Deum . . . And because false Reports were spread abroad, that the People of this House had shot several of the Prince of Orange's Souldiers, and thereupon they had burnt down the house; I must inform the candid Reader, that there was nothing at all in it, for our People did not give them one reviling word, nor they us; some lodged there while we were at Torbay."

Torre Abbey, Torquay.
In 1688 it was the home of Mr Cary, a known Catholic. Most of its occupants fled when they were asked if anyone could speak Dutch.

Countryfolk flocked to see William.
He was a celebrity before he left Brixham.

The countryfolk came from far and wide to see William before he left Brixham.   A certain Mr. Samuel Windeatt, a non-conformist, with his young son, rode at speed from Bridgetown over the Somerset border for the honour, but it was noticeable that very few men of substance welcomed him at this stage.   One who did was Sir Edward Seymour, "foremost among the Tory gentlemen of England," who, it is said, invited the Prince to his great house, Berry Pomeroy Castle.   There is no evidence to show that William accepted this invitation, but records show that the saddle which Sir Edward used when he rode to Torbay on this occasion was discovered many years later "in a very good state of preservation" buried in a box at the castle.

Berry Pomeroy Castle lies to the north of the Paignton-Totnes road in woodland near the village of Berry Pomeroy.   It is no longer in the possession of the Seymour family, who lived there for some four hundred years, but has passed into the care of the Department of the Environment.   At the time of writing it is being restored.

Other notable people, no doubt remembering the fate of those who supported the rebellion three years earlier of the hapless Duke of Monmouth, were afraid to show their hand at this early stage of the enterprise.   If William failed in his attempt to depose James II, his followers could expect savage retribution at the hands of the King.

The Prince and his army had, on landing, publicly given thanks for God's protection which had blessed the "Great Enterprise". "The Troops, taught to regard themselves as the favourites of Heaven", were encouraged afresh to carry out their duties, but this feeling of wellbeing began to wear off when their energy was further taxed, and their marching orders included carrying extra baggage. Obviously many were still feeling the after-effects of the sea voyage. "Upon Wednesday about Noon, Order was given to march towards Exeter, and so every Souldier was commanded by their Officers to carry something or other besides his own Arms and Snap-sack; and this made many grumble exceedingly. As we marched here upon good Ground, the Souldiers would stumble and sometimes fall because of a Dissiness in the Heads after they had been so long toss'd at Sea, the very Ground seem'd to rowl up and down for some days, according to the manner of the Waves. Therefore it was the Lord's Goodness that our Foes did not come upon us in this juncture and unfit Condition."

Little is known about any casualties which may have been left behind at Brixham when the troops moved out. Certainly there does not appear to have been any military opposition to the forces, and there is only mention made in St. Mary's burial register on November 21st 1688 of "A fforeigner belonging to the Prenz of Oringe".

The army was ordered to move in three "lines", or divisions, fanning out over the countryside towards Exeter. They left Furzeham Common and took the old Brixham road through Churston and Paignton, then made their way down the country lanes and across the old High Road towards Newton Abbot and Kingsteignton. An officer of one of the divisions marching towards Newton Abbot wrote of his route, "We marched to Painton, a village situated the other side of the bay, where our troops encamped. On the morrow we proceeded to Newton Bushell where we were joined by the cavalry, who

Berry Pomeroy Castle was the seat of Sir Edward Seymour.
He joined William at Brixham.

Churston.
William's army marched through,
en route to Newton Abbot.

OPPOSITE: King William's Cottage at Yalberton.
Lean-to at the rear pictured before renovation.

had taken one day more to disembark." Pouring rain hampered the troops, making their clothes heavy and their baggage waterlogged. Red mud in the lanes made the going difficult, and the Dutchmen found to their cost that English roads were inferior to the excellent roads in Holland.

"This first day we marched some hours after Night, in the Dark and Rain. The lanes hereabout were very narrow and not used to Wagons, Carts or Coaches, and therefore extream rough and stony, which hindered us very much from making any speed: divers of the Dutchmen being unaccustomed to such bad ways and hard marching in the Dirt, wish'd themselves back again in their own Country, and murmur'd because of the Dark and Rain. At length we came to the Cornstubble Inclosures on the side of a Hill, where we encamped that Night: It was a red Clay, and it rain'd very hard the greatest part of the Night, the Winds being high and stormy.

"Nevertheless the poor Souldiers, being much wearied with the Tent-Polls, spare Arms, and other Utensils for War, which they had carried all day and some hours after Night, as well as with the badness of the March, lay down to take their repose; and verily the Water ran over and under some of their Legs the major part of the Night, and their Heads, Backs and Arms sunck deep into the Clay, being so very wet and soft; notwithstanding, they slep all Night very sweetly in their Pee, or Campagne Coats."

Local folk by the wayside continued to welcome them, but "did not know what to say or think, being afraid that we should be served as the D. of Monmouth's handful of men were". Some brave country people did say that they supported William's forces and "pray'd for the Prince of Orange," but they said the Irish would come and "cut them in pieces if it should be known". There were others also who were afraid, remembering Jeffreys and the Bloody Assize and wholesale slaughter of the peasants after the Monmouth Rebellion. One courageous farmer, who left notes of the incident, was a Mr. Webber from Staverton. He and his son William brought a load of apples to the soldiers as they came to a crossroad on the "High Road from Brixham to Exeter," and invited them to take some as they went by.

King William's Cottage at Yalberton.
The ceiling roundel is said to have been set above the spot where the Prince dined.

Whittle reports, "His Highness, with Mareschal Schomberg, Count Solms, Count Nassau, Heer Benting, Heer Zulustein, Earl of Shrewsbury, Earl of Macclesfield, Viscount Mordant, Lord Wiltshire, and divers other Knights and Gentlemen came in the rear of the middle line. The Prince was commonly or always in the middlemost line, which was the meetest place. So he went unto a certain Gentleman's House about two little miles off, where the last line encamp'd the second night, and lodged there, his own Guards being with him."

The "certain Gentleman's House" is still there. It is a thatched cottage, long and low, crouching by the roadside down a country lane in Yalberton, off the new ring road to the west of Paignton, and the words over the entrance porch are KING WILLIAM'S COTTAGE. From the look of the old buildings at the rear, parts of the cottage must have been old in 1688, although obviously there have been alterations and renovations over the years. Inside the front door, which is just off-centre of the building, is a door on the left which leads into a low-ceilinged room. This pleasant chamber looks out over the countryside, and is of interesting proportions. There is plaster cove moulding all round the room, and the date 1777 is incorporated in the coving above one wall. On the ceiling close to the window is a slightly oval roundel said to have been set there by the proud owner of the cottage to commemorate William's visit. The table where he was supposed to have dined stood under the area of ceiling where the roundel was later added. The original floor of closely packed pink pebbles on which the table stood is still in place, and in good condition.

Having rested and refreshed himself at Yalberton, William and his personal guard rode the few miles to a farmhouse near the village of Longcombe. It appears to have

'Parliament' is now the name of this old farmhouse at Longcombe.
The Prince of Orange is reputed to have held his first Council meeting here, though its commemorative stone (right) elevates the event into a Parliament.

been here that Sir Edward Seymour of Berry Pomeroy greeted the Prince, and together with other "Gentlemen of the West," conferred in council and made plans for the future development of the Prince's enterprise. Edward Seymour had, the year before, been ousted from his position as Recorder of Totnes by order of James II so that a Roman Catholic, Sir John Southcote, might be appointed in his place, and no doubt this had soured his loyalty to the King and given him good reason to support William. Moreover, he brought many of the Devonshire gentry with him. At this Council in Longcombe—or "Parliament," as it has come to be called—Sir Edward proposed that those supporters who were present should form an Association, and "come out for the Prince" when he reached Exeter.

Like King William's Cottage at Yalberton, the historical farmhouse at Longcombe still stands. Now divided into three attractive cottages, it is called PARLIAMENT, and marked on the Ordnance Survey map under that name. The building is situated down a country lane leading off the Paignton-Totnes road, and by the front garden wall is a sturdy, upright stone inscribed:

WILLIAM
PRINCE OF
ORANGE
IS SAID TO HAVE
HELD HIS FIRST
PARLIAMENT
HERE
IN NOVEMBER
1688

Meanwhile, the Division which John Whittle accompanied was having a rough time. The army was well disciplined, and the men were ready to pay for all that they needed, but food and fuel were not easily found in this dark countryside, where all was unfamiliar.

"The Souldiers here fetched some old Hedges and Gates to make their Officers and themselves some Fires, else some would have perished in the Cold, being all over a Froth with Sweat in marching. And the old Hedges and Gates not being enough, they fetched away the new Ones.

"The Souldiers had some good Holland's Beef in their Snap-sacks which they brought, and their Officers were very glad to get Part with them, so they broil'd it at the Fire. Some had bought Chickens by the way, but raw, which they broil'd and ate, as a most delicate Dish.

"Sundry Captains offer'd any Mony for a Guide to bring them to a House thereabouts, where they might have some Provision for their Mony, but no Guide could be found, it was exceeding dark, and being all Strangers, and unacquainted with the country, we could not tell where to find one House, for those few that were scattering here and there, were either in some little grove of Trees, and so hid from our Eyes, or else in a bottom amongst the Hills, and so could not be seen.

"We thought this night almost as long as that in the Storm at Sea, and judged it to be Dawn of the Day some hours before it was. The Morning appearing rejoiced our very Hearts, for we thought now we should march presently; and we were sure of this, that worse Quarters we could never meet with, but much better we hoped to find.

"A private Souldier going in the next Croft for to seek a convenient place, he found it be an Inclosure with Turnips; so bringing his Burden away with him, he came to the

Fire, and gave those there some, telling his Comrades of the Place, who soon hastened there and brought enow with them: Some roasted them, and others eat them raw, and made a brave Banquet.

"The Souldiers were busy in discharging their Musquets, after the Wett and Rain, for they durst not trust to that Charge; and about 11 of the clock the Army receiv'd Orders to march. The Place where we encamp'd was trodden to Dirt, and stuck to our Shoes wretchedly."

As a result of the difficulties experienced in trying to accommodate such large numbers of men in one area, orders were given to divide the "lines" into regiments and to move them forward over a wider front. In this way, the number in one area would be much reduced. Conditions were hard enough for the foreign troops, for they could neither speak nor understand English, so no matter how friendly the natives were, it was not easy to communicate with them.

The soldiers were renowned for their huge appetites, and to feed them adequately was a problem for the country folk. Progress was slow along the muddy tracks towards Exeter, but eventually some regiments advanced as far as Newton Abbot. Here, "The Declaration" was read to the people by "a certain Divine".

This Declaration had been "drawn up from several drafts sent from England by Pensioner Fagel". In the final version, Dr. Burnet wrote that "The Prince could not enter into a discussion of the law and government of England; that was to be left to Parliament: the Prince could only set forth the present and public grievances as they were transmitted to him by those upon whose invitation he was going over. This was not without some difficulty overcome, by allowing some few expressions in the first draught, and leaving out some circumstances. So the declaration was printed over again, with some amendments." Although the final document was still lengthy, the gist of it was that the Prince, "being earnestly invited by men of all ranks and in principal by many of the Peers both spiritual and temporal, he resolved to go over into England and to seek for proper and effectual remedies for redressing such growing evils in a Parliament that should be lawfully chosen and should sit in full freedom, according to the ancient custom and constitution of England, with which he would concur in all things that might tend to the peace and happiness of the nation, and in particular that he would preserve the Church and the established religions . . . and that he would suffer such as would live peaceably to enjoy all due freedom in their consciences."

"Signed and sealed on 10th October."

William's Declaration had, in fact, preceded his invasion. "On the 1st November," states Macaulay, "it began to be mentioned in mysterious whispers by the politicians of London, was passed secretly from man to man, and was slipped into the boxes of the post office." One of the agents was arrested and his packages were taken to Whitehall. King James was "greatly troubled" when he read what was in the Declaration. He burned every copy but one of those delivered to him, "and that one he would scarcely trust out of his own hands". Naturally, the paragraph which most upset him was that which referred to "some of the Peers, Spiritual and Temporal," who had invited the Prince of Orange to invade England. On the day after James had first received the package of copies of the Declaration a proclamation appeared "'threatening with the severest punishment all who should circulate, or who should even dare to read, William's manifesto". Meanwhile the Prince had set sail for England, and now his advance regiments were in Newton Abbot.

The Reverend Whittle writes of a "certain Divine" who at the Cross in Newton Abbot read the Declaration to the many people gathered there on their market day. The

Commemorative stone beside St Leonard's Tower in Newton Abbot.
It marks the spot where William's Declaration was read to the populace.

The nearby Wolborough Inn sign depicts the event.
Reverend John Reynel was the reader.

Cross was the area where the three streets which then formed Newton Abbot intersected, and today the spot where the reading took place is marked by a stone standing in front of St. Leonard's Tower, which was once part of an ancient church, in Besigheim Place. The stone is inscribed as follows:

THE FIRST DECLARATION OF WILLIAM III PRINCE OF ORANGE THE GLORIOUS DEFENDER OF THE PROTESTANT RELIGION AND THE LIBERTIES OF ENGLAND WAS READ ON THIS PEDESTAL BY THE REV. JOHN REYNEL RECTOR OF THIS PARISH ON THE 5th NOVEMBER 1688

An interesting inn sign, that of the Wolborough Inn in Newton Abbot, depicts "a Divine" reading the Declaration by St. Leonard's Tower. This inn, which was once two cottages, is now a listed building.

"Now being on their March to Newton Abbot, a certain Divine [Whittle himself?] went before the Army, and finding it was their Market Day, he went unto the Cross, or Town Hall, where, pulling out the Declaration of the Prince of Orange, with undaunted Resolution, he began, with a loud and audible Voice, to read as follows: William Henry by the Grace of God, Prince of Orange, &c. Of the Reasons inducing him to appear in Arms in the Kingdom of England, for preserving of the Protestant Religion, and restoring the Law and Liberties of England, Scotland and Ireland &c. When the people heard the Prince of Orange's name mentioned, they immediately crowded about him in a prodigious manner to hear him, insomuch that some jeoparded their lives. The Declaration being ended, he said, God Bless and preserve the Prince of Orange: to which the People, with one heart and voice, answered Amen, Amen, and forthwith shouted for joy and made the town ring with their echoing Huzza's.

"The Minister, nolens volens, was carried into a Chamber near the Place; the Windows were shut, the Doors lock'd and bolted, to prevent the crowd from rushing in.

"The people of the House, and others, very kindly asked him, Sir, what will you be pleased to eat? Or, What shall we provide for you? Name what you love best, it shall be had. The Minister answered, What you please, give me what you will. So they brought forth such as was ready, and having eaten and drunk well, they desired him to spare them one Declaration. Yes, says he, for I have enow in my Pocket; and pulling them out he gave Three, because they were of distinct Parishes.

"He told the people that he would go and visit their Minister, and cause their bells to ring because the Prince of Orange was come into the Parish, at Sir Will Court[e]ney's, tho' not into the Town. And (says he) this being the first market town, I cannot but think it much the more proper and expedient. Whereupon he went to the Minister's House [the old Parsonage was in Wolborough Street] and enquiring for him, he was courteously invited in and desired to sit down. The Reverend Minister of the Parish coming presently to him, they saluted each other; and after some Communications passed between them, this Divine from the Army, desired the Keys of his Church-doors for to welcome the Prince of Orange to England with a Peal (that being the first Market-town they came to).

"The Minister answered, Sir: for my own part I am ready to serve his Highness any way, but of my own accord cannot give the Keys; but you know you may command them, or anything else in my House, in the Name of the Prince of Orange, and then I will readily grant it. So the Divine said, Sir: I demand your Keys of the Church Door only for an hour, to give his Highness a Peal, and then I will return them safely unto you.

"The Minister presently directed him to the Clerk's house and desired him to come and take a Glass of Wine with him after the Peal was ended (but the Ringers coming together, they rung sundry Peals) and he returned the Keys to the Minister.

"The people of the Town were exceedingly joyful, and began to drink the Prince of Orange's Health. The Country People in the Town were well inclin'd towards us, and here was the first favour we met with worth mentioning. His Highness was most kindly receiv'd at Sir Will Court[e]ney's, the Souldiers generally well treated by the Vulgar."

Forde House, near Newton Abbot, (above) and Powderham Castle, on the Exe estuary (below).
The Prince stayed at Forde House and here he held his first Council of State in England. Powderham Castle was the home of the Earl of Devon.

The Prince made welcome

WITH SOME of his forward regiments in Newton Abbot, William took up the invitation which Sir William Courteney's son had extended to him previously, and for two or three days made his headquarters at Forde House. The Courteneys were an old-established family, and their seat, Forde House, stood on the outskirts of Newton Abbot. The house was completed in 1602 by Sir Richard Reynell, Lord of the Manor of Wolborough, and later it had passed by marriage to the Courteney family. Today the building and surrounding parkland are in the care of the local authority.

Sir William Courteney was a staunch Whig, but he was careful not to imperil his life and fortune by becoming implicated in what would be a crime if James II were to defeat William, so he prudently left Forde House before William arrived in the area. Nevertheless, the Prince was made most welcome and entertained lavishly, being "Magnificently lodged and feasted there". The room in which he slept is to this day known as "The Orange Room".

There is evidence to show that in 1689 the Earl of Shrewsbury wrote to Sir William on behalf of King William offering him a Baronetcy. He declined this favour, probably because he felt that by right he was the Earl of Devon.

In Powderham Castle, the home of the Earl of Devon beside the Exe estuary, there stands today in the dining room the chair in which Prince William sat for his first Council of State at Forde House.

Chair from Forde House, in which William is said to have sat for his first English Council of State.
It is now in Powderham Castle.

A further link with the Prince in that part of Devon may be found in the several members of the Vooght family, living at Ideford, Luton Chudleigh, Bovey Tracey and Harberton. Mrs. Marjorie Vooght, of Little Bovey Farm, Bovey Tracey, relates how two Dutchmen, the brothers Vooght, landed with the Prince of Orange at Brixham, and left his army on the march up through Devon. One was a doctor, who was reputed to have a cure for the "King's Evil" [scrofula], whilst the other is said to have set up as a farmer. The original family house, Marsden Farm at Luton Ideford, exists today, and is still occupied by members of the Vooght family.

Remains of the mediaeval Exeter bridge. Over which the Prince of Orange and his troops marched into the city.

The transport ships had reached Topsham whilst the Prince was at Forde House, and were unloading the heavy supplies and munitions, including two hundred cannon, a weight of armament which contrasts hugely with the four little cannon which were all that the Duke of Monmouth could muster for his ill-starred rebellion, and which were dragged behind him on all his marching from Lyme Regis until he ended his adventure on the marshes at Sedgemoor.

Wednesday, 7 November:

Mr. Hicks, son of the non-conformist Minister who was executed in the aftermath of the Monmouth Rebellion for complicity in the uprising, went ahead of the Prince's army and reached Exeter with the news of the successful landing at Brixham. Having declaimed this in public, he was inundated by those who wished to enlist in the Prince's army. His activities did not meet with the approval of Sir Thomas Jefford, the Mayor of the City of Exeter, who was a loyal supporter of James II. Mr. Hicks was called to the Guildhall for interrogation, and committed to prison because he would not divulge any of William's plans. This treatment provoked a demonstration by the crowd of such anger that the Mayor allowed him to remain in the Guildhall, where he was supplied with "excellent provisions". At the same time, Dr. Burnet and Lord Mordant were riding to Exeter to prepare quarters for the Prince.

Thursday, 8 November:

When Mordant, at the head of four troops of dragoons, and Dr. Burnet came to the west gates of the city they found them locked, on the orders of the Mayor and Aldermen. Lord Mordant ordered the porter, "on pain of death," to open the gates, and when he had done so, he was threatened with the same penalty if he should close them again. Exeter was in a state of agitation. The Bishop, Lamplugh, on hearing of the invasion at Brixham, had fled to London, and the Dean ran away from the Deanery. Dr Burnet took advantage of the Dean's flight and began to prepare the Deanery for the Prince's occupation. News of the plight of Mr. Hicks came to Lord Mordant and Dr. Burnet, and his Lordship went immediately to the Guildhall and demanded his release. On learning that Hicks had been well looked after, Lord Mordant rewarded his guards with two guineas.

The Prince left Forde House at Newton Abbot, and Whittle describes how "The Army moved toward Exeter, some Regiments being at one Town and some in another: And as they were marching over the Heath or Common between Newton Abbot and Exeter, about five miles off the city, sundry Companies of young Men met them, with each a Club in his Hand, and as they approached near, they gave sundry Shouts and Huzza's, saying God Bless the Prince of Orange, and grant him Victory over all his Enemies. We are his true Servants, and come to fight for him as long as we are able. So we all bid them welcome. Here the Army passed by a Popish Lady's House, which was cruel to all her Protestant tenants; she forced them to turn Papists, or Apostates. But had the French King's Army passed thus by a Protestant House, it should soon have been fired, the People put to the Sword, or burnt; But we have not so learn'd Christ, nor been thus taught by His Ministers in our Land . . . for no Man molested this House, nor did any visit it, unless a Captain and some Gentlemen, which would have bought themselves Horses there, having lost their own at Sea, and so constrained to walk on foot till they could supply themselves with more."

About a mile from Chudleigh is Ugbrooke, and possibly this was the "Popish Lady's" House. An old chapel, an integral part of the house, was built in 1671 by Thomas, Baron Clifford, who owned Ugbrooke, and this chapel is possibly the oldest Roman Catholic parish church in the south west. It has been suggested that Baron Clifford's wife, a member of the Martin family of Lindridge, Bishopsteignton, was the "Popish Lady".

The Prince insisted on good behaviour and firm discipline amongst his troops, and the people through whose territory they passed acknowledged that "never better Order could be kept in any Army than in this". In fact, when they were in Exeter, Whittle says, "when we were there, the City was more quiet in the Night and freer from

Ugbrooke, near Chudleigh, the seat of Thomas, Baron Clifford. It was on the line of William's march to Exeter and seems to have aroused anger as the 'Popish Lady's House' – but William ordered it should be left unmolested.

Chudleigh Rocks (right). Reverend John Gawler and other Protestants hid here from James II's forces.

Debauch'd and disorderly persons than 'twas before".

Chudleigh, the ancient wool town, with a charter going back as far as 1309 A.D., lies between Kingsteignton and the eight hundred foot Great Haldon ridge on the route to Exeter. His Highness made his headquarters in Cholwichs, a house in Chudleigh town centre, which was later burnt down. At the time the Poulett family owned it, and Bridget, a granddaughter, and her husband the Revd John Gawler, lived there. King James had no liking for this Protestant clergyman, and when he was warned that he was to be arrested by the King's men, he and other Protestants in the area left their homes and hid in a cave at Black Rock, which is in a beautiful area of countryside known today as Chudleigh Rocks. The King's forces stayed at Cholwichs during the daytime, returning to their barracks at night, and the Protestants were then able to creep home for provisions. Eventually the guards became suspicious, and soldiers were on duty both day and night. Mrs. Gawler then smuggled food in a covered basket to the cave-dwellers at great risk to herself. As soon as William's troops were in the area the King's forces must have withdrawn, for there is no record of any fighting here. The Revd John Gawler was, some years later, Vicar of Sampford Peverell, where the Pouletts had their seat.

When the Prince arrived at Chudleigh he was warmly welcomed by the Gawler family amongst others. Inhabitants from the neighbouring villages crowded in to see him, and a party of "young peasants, brandishing their cudgels, had assembled on the top of Haldon Hill, whence the Army marching from Chudleigh first descried the rich valley of the Exe, and the two massive towers rising from the cloud of smoke which overhung the capital of the West". As the troops marched down the long descent to the city, "the road, and through the Plain to the River, was lined mile after mile with spectators".

So Prince William of Orange arrived amid great rejoicing at Exeter. The Mayor and Magistrates, who represented and were loyal to the King, refused to receive him when he made his entrance in state to the city, but, as Macaulay says, "The pomp of the day, however, could well spare them. Such a sight had never been seen in Devonshire. Many of the citizens went forth half a day's journey to meet the champion of their religion. From the West Gate to the Cathedral Close the pressing and shouting on each side was such as reminded Londoners of the crowds on the Lord Mayor's Day. The houses were gaily decorated. Doors, windows, balconies and roofs were thronged with gazers."

The infantry, who had slogged for mile after mile through the wet, with the red mud of Devon over their ankles at times, were not an impressive sight. As Whittle says,"The Foot Souldiers did not appear well, because they were sorely weatherbeaten, and much dabbled in marching in the Dirt and Rain, and looked very pale and thin after such a hard day's march, which made some people conjecture that they were dull sluggish Men". In spite of this, the Devon people, who were not used to "the splendour of well-ordered camps, were overwhelmed with delight and awe".

The army itself was a never-ending source of wonder to the people, composed as it was of men from many different races. There were towering Dutchmen, flaxen-haired men from northern climes, and blacks from the sugar plantations. The citizens of Exeter were astonished by the Africans with their embroidered turbans and white feathers, and fascinated by a squadron of Swedish horsemen in black armour and fur cloaks. Amazing rumours sped swiftly saying that they had come from a land where the ocean was frozen, and where the night lasted for six months of the year, and that they had killed huge bears for the skins which they wore. Broadsheets describing the spectacle, entitled "A true and exact relation of the Prince of Orange, his Publick

Entrance into Exeter" were published and circulated all over the country. One such, which appears in Joyce Packe's "The Prince it is that's come" reads: "Since the foundation of Monarchy, Imperial Orations or the triumphs of the Caesars, in the Manner, Grandeur, and magnificence of their most sumptuous cavalcades, there was never any that exceeded this of the most Illustrious Hero the Prince of Orange his entrance into Exeter, which was in the manner and form following:

"1. The Right honourable the Earl of Macclesfield with 200 horses, the most part of which were English Gentlemen, Richly mounted on Flanders Steeds, manag'd and us'd to war in Headpieces, Back and Breast, Bright Armour.

"2. 200 Blacks brought from the plantations of the Netherlands in America, Imbroyder'd Caps lined with white Fur and plumes of white Feathers to attend the Horse.

"3. 200 Finlanders or Laplanders in Bear Skins taken from the Wild Beasts they had slain, the common Habbit of that cold Climat, with black Armour and Broad Flaming Swords.

"4. 50 Gentlemen, and as many Pages to attend and support the Princes Banner, bearing this inscription God and the Protestant Religion.

"5. 50 Led Horses all Managed and brought up to the Wars, with 2 Grooms to each Horse.

"6. After these Rid the Prince on a Milk White Palfrey, Armed Cap a Pee. A Plume of White Feathers on his head. All in Bright Armour, and 42 Footmen Running by him.

"7. After his Highness followed likewise on Horseback 200 Gentlemen and pages.

"8. 300 Switzers with Fuzies [Note: these were bewhiskered Swiss Infantry].

"9. 500 Voluntiers each 2 led Horses.

"10. His Captain and Guard Armed Cap a Pee. The rest of the Army in the Rere, his Highness with some Principal Officers entered the Town, where they were not only Received but entertained with Loud Huzzas.

"Ringing of Bells Bonfires and such acclamations of Joy as the convenience of the place, and their abilities cou'd afford.   FINIS."

The Prince in his armour made a great impression on the people. His usually grave features relaxed into a smile when an old woman, "perhaps the mother of some rebel who had perished in the carnage of Sedgemoor, or in the more fearful carnage of the Blood Circuit, broke from the crowd, rushed through the drawn swords and curvetting horses, touched the hand of the deliverer, and cried out that now she was happy."

Accompanying the Prince was the renowned Count Schomberg, "the first soldier in Europe," who had resigned as Marshal of France for the sake of his Protestant religion. It is interesting to note that these two men had been on opposing sides at the Battle of Maastricht in 1673, but were now united in a common cause. The people marvelled at the size and strength of the invading soldiers. Some, said the broadsheets, were over six feet in height, and "they wielded such huge pikes, swords and muskets as had never before been seen in England. Nor did the wonder of the population diminish when the artillery arrived. Twenty-one heavy pieces of brass cannon were with difficulty tugged along by sixteen cart horses to each." One structure which caused much comment was a smithy on wheels. It had all the tools and equipment necessary for the repair of the arms and vehicles accompanying the army.

This spectacular cavalcade moved majestically over the old Exeter bridge, now a well-preserved relic close to the modern bridge over the River Exe. What astonished the populace was a temporary bridge of boats which was laid with great speed over the river to facilitate the crossing of the waggons, and which was then with equal speed dismantled and moved on.

The army was eventually stationed on the north and east sides of Exeter, with forward lines advancing towards Tiverton, Cullompton and Honiton, and some were encamped on Clyst Heath. Rigid discipline was maintained, and the troops were ordered to behave in a civil manner towards the populace. Those citizens who had suffered the coarse and cruel conduct of Colonel Kirke and his "Lambs" during and after the Monmouth Rebellion were "amazed to see soldiers who never swore at a landlady, or took an egg without paying for it". As a result, the army received ample provisions which were not expensive. So strict was the control that two soldiers were hanged for chicken-stealing.

The ordinary people of Exeter had warmly welcomed the Prince of Orange, but now much depended on the attitude of the Church, and the action that the Bishop and chapter of Exeter might take. They were the first who had to show where their allegiance lay. The Prince had given Dr. Burnet full authority to protect the clergy and their homes, but they "stood off, though they were sent for and very gently spoken to by the Prince". The Canons, leaderless without their Bishop and Dean, could not decide how to receive the Prince, and when Dr. Burnet ordered a service of thanksgiving in the Cathedral for William's safe arrival they were not present in their stalls, but some choristers, and some of the clergy were in attendance. The Prince, with due ceremony, took his place on the Bishop's throne, "a stately throne rich with the carving of the fifteenth century," and Dr. Burnet stood below him. The scene is described by John Whittle:

"After the Prince was come unto the Deanery, and had refresh'd himself, with all his Lords and Gentlemen, then was he pleased to go and render his hearty Thanks to Almighty God in the Cathedral Church for his safe Arrival, and the whole Fleet. The People thronged the Streets to see him as he went, and crouded the Quire where he was to come very much. Now there were sundry Men with Holbards who cleared the way, besides Sentinels: So being conducted to the Bishop's Seat, he sat down, with about six of his Life-Guard-Men on his Right hand, and many more before him and about him in the Quire. As he came all along the body of the Church the Organ played very sweetly, tho' 'twas not the right Organist himself, he being gone aside on purpose, as I was inform'd there. And being sat, the Quire began and sung Te Deum for the safe arrival of the Prince of Orange and his Army in England (as also for his whole Fleet).

"After the Collects were ended, the Reverend Dr. Burnet began to read the Declaration of his Highness . . . at the very beginning of which Declaration the Ministers of the Church there present, rushed immediately out of their Seats and bustled through all the Croud, going out of the Church; the People remained, and were very attentive to the Doctor's reading, and the Declaration being ended, he said, God save the Prince of Orange, unto which the major part of the Multitude answered, Amen. So his Highness returned to the Deanery, the People echoing forth Huzza's as he went along."

Several copies of the Declaration had been printed on the printing press which William had brought with him. He thought of everything! In the Declaration the Prince indicated that he had not come in order to dethrone James, but to force him to ask Parliament to put the country's affairs in order.

Sunday, 11 November:

On the first Sunday after William had entered Exeter, service was held again in the Cathedral, and the Prince was present. The Cathedral clergy disapproved of Dr.

Burnet preaching the sermon from their pulpit.   Whittle records the scene:

"The first Sunday after the Prince was come unto Exeter, being Novemb. 11, the Reverend Dr. Burnet preached before him in the Morning, the Quire and Body thereof being extreamly throng'd with people which came to see his Highness, some placing themselves in Seats by eight in the Morning.   When his Highness came he was pleased for to sit in the Bishop's Seat in the Body of the Church as he had done in the Quire before.   Sundry Sentinels stood just behind him, two just before him, and many more in the Church Isle; the Doctor's Text was Psalm 107:43.   Whoso is wise and will observe those things, even they shall understand the loving Kindness of the Lord.

"The Doctor very accurately shewed the loving Kindness of the Lord unto the Prince of Orange, and his Fleet; how he caused the Winds to turn at Tor-Bay, where the whole Fleet was to tack about to come into the Bay; and then shewed the upright Design of the Prince to promote the Glory of God, and good of his Church in England, Scotland and Ireland; having ended his Sermon, he read the Prayer for the Expedition, and so concluded with the Blessing, &c."

Monday, 12 November:

William began to lose patience.   So far, no one of real standing had come to support him, and he wondered what had happened to those who had invited him to come to England.   An explanation for their absence could have been that his friends in the North had expected him to land there and so allow them to join him.   He had made no such arrangements in the West Country, and his supporters there had not expected to find themselves in the forefront of the initial invasion, and in such an important and perilous situation, but their tardiness was of no comfort to William, who had hoped to

Exeter Cathedral.
A service gave thanks for William's arrival.

find his supporters awaiting him at Exeter.

The position looked advantageous for King James, who found this lack of support for William encouraging. The Prince had been in England now for seven days without any demonstration of support from men of influence and position. Things were quiet in the North and East of the country, and none of James's Ministers appeared to have deserted him. His army, superior in numbers to William's forces, was gathering at Salisbury.

The people of the West Country could be forgiven for their caution. Barely three years had passed since the Monmouth Rebellion, which had taken such toll of the lives of the families of so many of them, so that many were still in mourning for their loss. At the same time, it was understandable that "William, who, trusting to promises from England, had put to hazard not only his own fame and fortunes, but also the prosperity and independence of his native land, should feel deeply mortified." He felt so humiliated that he even considered returning to Holland with his troops. A turning point came when Captain Burrington, who lived in the neighbourhood at Crediton and commanded a section of the local militia, arrived to offer his services to the Prince's cause, and soon after, more and more of the gentry from all over Devon, Somerset and Dorset came to him. Sir Walter Yonge of Escot House, which stands between two and three miles from Ottery St. Mary, set off for Exeter as soon as he heard that William's headquarters were at the Deanery there. Sir Walter and other local gentry arranged together to provide accommodation for the Dutch troops in their area, and soon Ottery and Honiton were swarming with soldiers, whilst the local people were happy to welcome them and provide them with food.

The ice was now broken, and other men of substance followed Sir Walter's lead, although some of William's potential supporters were still awaiting the outcome of battle with the King's forces before committing themselves, and neither James nor William seemed particularly anxious to engage their forces. One unit of the Royal forces was, however, advancing to the West, and would give William's cause a boost.

Wednesday, 14 November:

Lord Cornbury, a Colonel of the Royal Dragoons stationed at Salisbury, conceived the notion of deserting with three regiments, and transferring this valuable force to William's army at Honiton. He led them through Blandford and Dorchester, where they rested for an hour or two, and then proceeded towards Axminster.

Suspicious of their Colonel's actions, some of his officers demanded an explanation, and he told them that he had received orders to carry out a night attack on William's troops encamped at Honiton. After considerable pressure from the officers to produce these orders Cornbury realised that he would not be able to carry out his scheme, and had to see the majority of his force turn about and return to Salisbury with the loyal officers. A portion, however, "who had been detached from the main body", and who had no suspicion of the designs of their commander, continued under him to Honiton. Here they found themselves in the midst of a large force which was fully prepared to receive them. Resistance was useless, and their leader pressed them to take service under William. A gratuity of a month's pay was offered to them, and most accepted. There were finally about two hundred men and as many horses with Cornbury. The desertion of these troops to William was very good propaganda for the Protestant cause, and a bad omen for James.

Thursday, 15 November:

News of Cornbury's defection reached the King after the arrival at Court from Exeter of Bishop Lamplugh. According to Macaulay, James had been in high good humour, but on receiving the information he was exceedingly downcast, for it was a severe and unexpected shock to him. Cornbury's father, Lord Clarendon, was ashamed.

"Oh God", he said, "that a son of mine should be a rebel!" Macaulay comments, "A fortnight later he made up his mind to be a rebel himself."

Friday, 16 November:

It seemed that William was not unduly discouraged now by the slowness of his supporters in England to join him. He seemed to be in good spirits when he wrote from Exeter to his friend the Prince of Waldeck in Holland:

"The state of things here is in accordance with representations made to me before my departure from Holland, so that I can hope, with God's blessing, to succeed in this great undertaking. The beginning is favourable. It is unfortunate that we have been obliged by the wind to land here in the west, where we are so much out of the way of correspondence with Holland that we are quite out of the world, knowing nothing but what happens in the neighbourhood. I hope in two days to be able to advance, and then we shall know in a short time whether we shall be forced to fight to decide the business. Some reports say the the King and his army will not dare to go far from London, from which we are fifty leagues away and consequently a long march".

Saturday, 17 November:

On November 17th Sir Edward Seymour arrived in Exeter. Sir Edward, who had just inherited a baronetcy, and was one of the most influential Tories in England, came in with several other gentlemen of quality and estate from the West Country. At the time, William was away in Ottery St. Mary reviewing his troops, and inspecting Lord Cornbury's Dragoons, a useful addition to his forces.

As the news of Cornbury's defection spread, many more of the landed gentry came to join him, including Edward Russell, son of the Earl of Bedford and brother to the Earl of Shrewsbury, of the "Immortal Seven". He was accompanied by Sir William Portman of Bryanston, Dorset.

Sir William Portman's residence was on the site now occupied by Bryanston, the well known public school on the banks of the Stour just outside Blandford, but his actual house no longer exists, and the school occupies the building designed for the Portman family by Norman Shaw, and completed in 1897. Sir William, like so many of his contemporaries, made a complete about-face in deserting James and supporting William, a move even more surprising in his case when it is considered that it was he who was in command of the Sussex Militia when they apprehended the fugitive Duke of Monmouth and delivered him into the hands of the King. William was obviously recognised by men like Sir William to be a true leader, and to be far more likely to succeed in ousting James than ever Monmouth was.

Amongst others who now joined William was General Thomas Erle of Charborough Park near Wareham, who, as Mr. Erle, had been appointed Deputy Lieutenant of Dorset in May 1685. As Major Erle he rallied a band of Dorset men to Prince William's banner after the landing at Brixham, undoubtedly as the outcome of the cloak-and-dagger meeting in the ice-house in Charborough Park in 1686. Sir Francis Warre of Hestercombe came too, representing Somerset.

In welcoming his tardy supporters the Prince is credited with observing, "We expected that you that dwelt so near the place of our landing would have found us sooner."

Two days later, the Earl of Bath, with the 13th Foot, had seized the fort at Plymouth for the Prince, and arrested all the Roman Catholic officers there, "so now all behind him was safe". The first Peer of the Realm, James Bertie, Earl of Abingdon, presented himself at William's headquarters. Lord Colchester, the eldest son of the Earl of

**Sir William Portman
of Bryanston, Dorset.**
The trusted Jacobite who arrested the
Duke of Monmouth now gave allegiance
to Prince William of Orange.

Bryanston: Sir William's residence.
In a sketch by Thomas Robins. This house
was pulled down to make way for a James
Wyatt house in 1788 and replaced in turn
by its present Norman Shaw public
school building a century later. These
illustrations are courtesy of the Hon. Mrs
Marjorie Portman's *Bryanston: Picture
of a Family* [Dorset Publishing
Company, 1987].

Rivers, appeared with between sixty and seventy horse, and the "bold and turbulent" Lord Thomas Wharton accompanied him.

The Prince felt that it was time that these new adherents of his bound themselves more formally to his cause. Dr. Burnet records how Seymour, having had audience of Prince William, said, "When I came to him he asked me why we had not an association signed by all that came to us, since, till we had that done, we were as a rope of sand; men might leave us when they pleased, and we had them under no tie; whereas if they signed an association, they would reckon themselves bound to stick to us. I answered, it was because we had not a man of his authority and credit to offer and support such an advice."

"I went from him to the Prince," says Burnet, "who approved of the motion; as did also the Earl of Shrewsbury, and all that were with us. So I was ordered to draw it."

It was, in a few words, an engagement to stick together in pursuing the ends of the Prince's declaration; and that if any attempt should be made on his person, it should be revenged on all by whom, or from whom, any such attempt should be made. This was agreed by all those that came in to him. The Prince put Devonshire and Exeter under the government of Seymour, who was recorder at Exeter.

In the splendid oak-panelled hall in his headquarters, the Deanery, William held court. Macaulay describes the daily scene: "More than sixty men of rank and fortune were lodged at Exeter; and the daily display of rich liveries, and of coaches drawn by six horses, in the Cathedral Close, gave to that quiet precinct something of the splendour and gaiety of Whitehall."

The Prince thought that the time was right to give a reception for the "whole body of noblemen and gentlemen who had assembled at Exeter". Although he did not know them all yet, he said he had a list of their names, and knew how highly esteemed they were in the country.

"Therefore," he said, "gentlemen, friends and fellow Protestants, we bid you and all your followers most heartily welcome to our court and camp."

The Deanery, Exeter.
Headquarters for the Prince of Orange during his stay in the city.

The Mayor and Aldermen of the City visited the Prince. The Mayor appears to have been forgiven for his earlier refusal to submit to William's demands at the City gates, for when he was about to leave Exeter, the Prince said that the Mayor "is worthy to be trusted, for being faithful to his trust".

Substantial numbers of the common people volunteered for duty in William's army. So many were there that he could have formed many regiments of infantry had he needed to do so.

"The People of the City," says Whittle, "began now to be more and more inclin'd towards our Army, and all fear almost of the other Army was banish'd out of their Thoughts, so that they would discourse more freely now than at the first. The Drums beat for Volunteers, and every Regiment of English or Scotch which wanted any Men, was now compleated. The Regiment of Sir John Guyes, and Sir Robert Peyton, fill'd up very fast; for Men came into the City daily from all parts to list themselves, insomuch that many Captains pick'd and chose their Souldiers. Very great crowding was here at the Deanery (it being the Prince of Orange's Court) by all sorts of People: Many coming 20 miles on purpose to see him, and all the People of the adjacent Places were waiting there daily, insomuch that the Sentinels could hardly keep them out. The Guard was before the entrance into the Deanery, and sundry Sentinels, two at each door."

Information reached the Prince that "our Friends were up in the North of England," including Lord Delamere, the Earls of Devonshire, Stamford and Danby, Sir Scroop How, Sir William Russell "with divers others". A report of Lord Delamere's successful rising in Cheshire states that he had promised his tenants in return for their support that "their leases would be extended to them", and he urged every man who had a good horse to join him, or at least to provide a substitute. He was able to "declare for William" with 200 horse. His neighbours, others of the "Immortal Seven," were also active.

The Earl of Devonshire had laid plans to take Nottingham, and no problems were expected there. Danby's task was less easy. He had to seize York, which was already garrisoned by a small force of loyal King's men commanded by Sir John Reasby. Macaulay describes the action:

"Danby acted with rare dexterity. A meeting of the Gentry and Freeholders of Yorkshire had been summoned for the 22nd of November to address the King on the state of affairs. All the Deputy Lieutenants of the three Ridings, several noblemen, and a multitude of opulent esquires and substantial yeomen had been attracted to the provincial capital. Four troops of militia had been drawn out under arms to preserve the public peace. The Common Hall was crowded with freeholders, and the discussion had begun, when a cry was suddenly raised that the Papists were up, and were slaying the Protestants. The Papists of York were much more likely to be employed in seeking for hiding places than in attacking enemies who outnumbered them in proportion of a hundred to one. But at that time no story of Popish atrocity could be so wild and marvellous as not to find ready belief. The meeting separated in dismay. The whole City was in confusion. At this moment, Danby, at the head of about a hundred horsemen, rode up to the militia and raised a cry, "No Popery! A free Parliament! The Protestant Religion!" The militia echoed the shout. The garrison was instantly surprised and disarmed. The governor was placed under arrest. The gates were closed. Sentinels were posted everywhere. The populace was suffered to pull down a Roman Catholic chapel, but no other harm appears to have been done. On the following morning the Guildhall was crowded with the first gentlemen of the shire, and with the principal magistrates of the city. The Lord Mayor was placed in the chair. Denby proposed a Declaration setting forth the reasons which had induced the friends of the Constitution and of the Protestant Religion to rise in arms. The Declaration was eagerly adopted, and it received in a few hours the signatures of six peers, of five baronets, of six knights, and of many gentlemen of high consideration."

Meanwhile the Earl of Devonshire took up arms, left Chatsworth, which he was then in the process of building, and went on to Derby. There he informed the City Council why he was acting in such a manner. Moving on to Nottingham he set up the headquarters of the uprising, and delivered a proclamation.

"The name of rebellion, it was said, was a bugbear which could frighten no reasonable man. Was it rebellion to defend those laws and that religion which every king of England bound himself by oath to maintain? How that oath had lately been observed was a question on which, it was to be hoped, a free Parliament would soon pronounce. In the meantime the insurgents declared that they held it not to be a rebellion, but legitimate self-defence, to resist a tyrant who knew no law but his own will."

Four powerful and wealthy Earls, Manchester, Stamford, Rutland and Chesterfield, met in Nottingham and were joined there by Lord Cholmondely and Lord Grey de Ruthyn, and Newcastle on Tyne declared for the Prince.

All this was very encouraging news for William, and he felt emboldened to consider leaving Exeter for the next phase of the campaign. Accordingly, he made arrangements to move, and more troops were sent out in advance.

Sunday, 18 November:
Before he set out to meet James the Prince attended Divine Service in Exeter. The Rev. John Whittle was exercising his priestly calling at the same time, though not without some trouble from the Churchwardens. He writes:

"I preached in St. Carion's Church in Exeter, November 18th. My Text being Isaiah 8: 12, 13, 14. Neither fear ye their fear, nor be afraid. Sanctify the Lord of Hosts himself, and let him be your fear, and let him be your dread. And he shall be for a Sanctuary.

"Now the Church Wardens of this Parish, altho' there was no Minister to preach, were unwilling to give the Keys (because they were no true Friends of our good Cause) insomuch that I was forc'd to threaten them for their great rudeness. The Clerk of the Parish going along with me the Day before for the Key, one of the Church Wardens very rudely broke his Head in sundry places, for which intolerable Action I immediately had him brought before the Honourable Colonel Cutts for this bold Fact, who upon a due submission and acknowledgement of his Faults, dismissed him with a sharp Reprehension. For Modesty-sake I conceal his Name, hoping that he's reformed with the Times."

Lieutenant-General John Churchill, one of the King's most able and trusted commanders, who had three years earlier played a prominent part in the defeat of Monmouth was, together with his wife Sarah, a close friend of James's daughter Anne. On Churchill's instigation, Princess Anne had written to her brother-in-law Prince William telling him that his father-in-law the King had left London for Salisbury accompanied by her husband Prince George of Denmark and John Churchill, and she added that Prince George would probably soon be joining him.

Whilst William was making such encouraging progress through the West Country, Salisbury became the centre of extraordinary and momentous activity. Sir Richard Colt Hoare in his *History of Modern Wiltshire* [1843] describes the events there:

"On the intelligence that the Prince had disembarked in Torbay, James proceeded with the utmost activity to collect his disposable force, and a train of artillery. These were ordered to concentrate themselves in the neighbourhood of Salisbury, as the key of the West. Accordingly, on the 8th of November, the city was filled with soldiery, and the surrounding villages occupied by various divisions of the royal army. On Sunday the 18th, three regiments of cavalry, the flower of the army, entered Salisbury. These were, the regiment of the Duke of Berwick, commanded by Lieutenant-Colonel Sir Francis Compton; that of the Duke of St. Albans, by Lieutenant-Colonel Langton; and that of Sir John Fenwick, by Lieutenant-Colonel Sutherland.

"No sooner had these regiments arrived, than the principal officers of each held a meeting to consider of the part it became them to take in the actual situation of the country.

"The loss of the national liberties, and the subversion of the Protestant religion, they were aware, must necessarily follow the success of the King. Their only alternative, therefore, was to espouse the cause, or, at least, not to withstand the progress of the Prince. But surrounded as they were with a numerous body of men, whose dispositions were as yet untried, it was dangerous to indicate their intentions by any overt act. Accordingly, on mounting guard for the night, the Quarter-masters and Adjutants were directed to wait the arrival of the post, by which it was alleged, a marching order might be expected. The post arrived about midnight, and Langton, who was prepared with an expedient for concealing his purpose, opened the bag, in the presence of the other officers. Under a feigned order, the three regiments were directed to be in readiness to proceed westward; and the signal being given, at an early hour in the morning, they took the road to Exeter, with the expectation of being the first to be led against the outposts of the Prince."

Monday, 19 November:

James, in dejected mood following the news of the uprisings and defections from his cause in the north and west, arrived at Salisbury to join his army.

Right Reverend Dr Gilbert Burnet.
The personal Chaplain to the Prince of Orange, who has been quoted here. In 1689 William appointed him Bishop of Salisbury. Courtesy of the Cathedral School, Salisbury, and the Paul Mellon Centre for Studies in British Art.

Old Bishop's Palace, The Close, Salisbury.
This was the headquarters in the city for James II and then Prince William of Orange. This view shows the original thirteenth century part. The Palace now houses the Cathedral School.

The King's last welcome

HIS SPIRITS must have lifted when he was greeted with such acclaim by the people of Salisbury. The London Gazette reported:

"Salisbury, Nov. 19. This evening, about 4 o'clock, the Duke of Berwick, the Earl of Feversham, Sir John Fenwick, and several other officers, on horseback, met his Majesty, about a mile from hence; and attended him to the gates of the City, where his Majesty was met by the Mayor and Aldermen, in their gowns, who waited upon his Majesty to the Bishop's Palace, which is appointed for his lodgings, the people in very great multitudes following his Majesty's coach, from his entrance into the City gate, to the doors of the palace, with huzzas and demonstrations of joy and satisfaction, the bells ringing all the while."

This was, perhaps, the last time that the King was fully recognised and acknowledged as the Sovereign.

The old Bishop's Palace, which was appointed for the King's lodging, was originally a medieval building, and has been occupied since 1947 by the Salisbury Cathedral School. It houses paintings of Dr. Burnet, who became Bishop of Salisbury in 1689, under William and Mary, and of Bishop Seth Ward, the Bishop when James came to the City as described above. A senile old man, Seth Ward was away from the palace when James arrived and made it his headquarters.

Very soon after the King's arrival, friction inevitably developed between the clergy representing the established church and the retinue of popish priests who accompanied James. Richard Colt Hoare describes a scene which occurred at the palace in the chapel there which had been reserved for the royal use:

"Pursuing that course of hypocrisy [the King's sudden changes of policy to curry favour with his people] which his proud mind had now been compelled to assume, James was attended while here by Mr. Knightly Chetwood, under the title of his Protestant Chaplain. This clergyman, finding the chapel of the Episcopal Palace, which had been reserved for the use of the King, pre-occupied by Popish priests, publicly announced his intention to withdraw from the royal service. Such a step, in the actual situation of affairs, might have been attended with the most serious consequences. After some hesitation, therefore, the Papists were ordered to give way; and the service, according to the ritual of the Church of England, was performed to crowded congregations. The feelings of the soldiery on this subject were evinced by their attendance on the Protestant worship, and their acclamations, as the preacher passed through the streets. On every hand he was welcomed by the troops with marks of encouragement, and uncouth but hearty declarations, that they would risk their lives for the Church of England."

These demonstrations must have seemed ominous to the troubled monarch.

In the meantime, further news of the progress of the King and his army had reached William. Whittle's information was:

"The late King James we heard now was advanced as far towards us as Salisbury, with a very brave Army of about thirty-five thousand Men, and a prodigious great Train of Artillery, which made the poor Country People tremble. Moreover we heard, that he was fully resolved to encamp his Army about Sarum, in the Plain, where he intended to fight us. Some of our Men, being of the Van-guard, were advanced as far as Wincaunton to provide Carriage, at which place there was a small Skirmish or Action between 26 of our Souldiers, and about 150 of the late King's Party; which you shall have a particular account of by and by. We soon received information of this Skirmish at Exeter."

James was anxious to draw William's forces into battle, for if there was bloodshed, then his opponent's popularity would be damaged. William was well aware of this, and so planned his movements as to avoid direct confrontation between the armies until such time as he thought it would be to his advantage. Skirmishing between the advanced units of the two armies was bound to occur sooner or later, but when it happened, William wanted to be sure that it would not alienate the sympathy of the majority of the people. It happened that the King's forward units were chiefly Irish, and in any conflict against Irishmen William's men would have the support of most Englishmen. The first of these encounters occurred at Wincanton in Somerset, and John Whittle received "an account thereof from the Minister (Mr. Bulgin) and from Mr. Webb a Cornet of Horse belonging to the late King James, who was shot there, between his Back-bones and Reins, [loins, or kidneys] and lay desperately ill when we marched by.

"A Lieutenant having his Post at this Town, with about four and twenty Souldiers belonging to the Regiment of the Honourable Major General Mackay, hearing that a party of Horse belonging to the late King James were posting thither, he was so magnanimous as to resolve to fight them; and in order thereto, posted his men as securely as he could, in a small Inclosure, at the East end of the Town, on the left side; there was a good hedg between them and the Road, which was to defend them against the Horse, and through which they were to fire upon the Enemy; but there was a little Gate at one Corner, and a weak dead Hedg. In this Field he posted most of his Men; and on the other side of the way. Just opposite to this place, he posted about six Souldiers in a little Garden, who had a thick old Hedg to cover them from the Horse, and through which they were to fire. The Officer himself, with four or five Men, keeping the Road. The Enemies Horse being now advanced within Musquet-shot, the Souldiers would have fired upon them; but the Lieutenant, whose name was Cambel, not knowing what they might be; whether Friends or Foes, would not permit them, and the more, because a Regiment of Horse belonging to my Lord Cornbury, was come in and joined our Forces, and so advancing each towards other, our Officer first gave them the Word, saying, Stand, Stand, For who are ye? To which the Enemies Officer, at the Head of the Party of Horse, answered, I am for King James, who art thou for? To which our Officer replied, I am for the Prince of Orange.

"God damn me, says the Enemies Officer, I will Prince thee. Whereupon our Officer said, Fire; and went boldly up to this Popish Officer and shot him in at his Mouth and through his Brains, so he drop'd down dead; our Souldiers firing upon them through the Hedges on each side, maul'd them desperately, and killed several of them. They carried off their Dead presently, being ten to one (for the Enemies Party was about one hundred and fifty, and our party but five and twenty.) They rode to find out a Place to break in upon our Men; so some Horse broke in at the upper end of the Croft, some at the lower Corner, and others got in at the little Gate, which, as is said, was open'd by a Townsman that stood near the Place, so that our Men charged as fast as they could to fire upon them, but were now surrounded with the Enemy; our Souldiers were divers of them kill'd. They defended themselves as well as 'twas possible, for such a handful against so many; and one or two of them being shot in five or six places, were offer'd Quarter by the Enemy for their great Courage, but they would not accept of it from the Hands of Papists, and therefore chose rather to die.

"Now the little Company in the Garden fired divers times, and the Officer, with his

Wincanton, Somerset, from the River Cale.
James's troops ambushed William's army. Courtesy the Ashmolean Museum.

Men, kept their Ground awhile, and then got into the Garden to their own Party. The Towns-people were much alarmed by this Action, and came thronging into the Streets; and kind Providence having so ordain'd it, for the Saving of our Men (else, no doubt, they would all have been cut off, being so mightily overpowred) that a certain Miller came riding in at the other end of the Town, and hearing of this Skirmish, presently reported, that he had overtaken a strong Party of Horse belonging to the Prince of Orange, and that he believed they were now entring the Town; This was brought to the Enemies Ears very quickly, and moreover he call'd to them, and said, Away, for your Lives, save your selves, the Enemies are at hand. Now these Souldiers of the late King James, seeing the People of the Town so thick in the Streets, running here and there, judged that it might be so, and hereupon they retreated with all speed, galloping away in a confused manner; however, they left more behind kill'd on their side, than they had kill'd of our Men, for 'twas the Judgement of all here that this handful of Souldiers (appertaining to his Highness the Prince of Orange) kill'd more of their Enemies than they themselves were in number.

"There were about fifteen tumbled in one Grave together, and about eight or nine of our men, the rest being of the Enemies Party. Our Officers did most of them visit this Mr. Webb, Cornet of Horse, to hear the manner of this small Action."

There is no help from the Wincanton parish records about this episode. There are gaps in the burial entries around 1688, and no contemporary record of the Prince or his forces passing through the town is to be found. There is a perfunctory note in the Bruton parish register which reports the landing of William at Torbay; "November 5th, The Prince of Orange arrived on this land att Torbay in ye County of Devon in ye year of our Lord 1688", and it does add that "on ye 20th of ye same instant (Nov.) was a skirmish at Wincanton."

In a book *The March of William of Orange through Somerset,* by Emmanuel Green [1892] which was compiled from the London Gazette and early news sheets, a reference to Wincanton may be found. This version of events closely follows Whittle's diary:

"It being reported that some of the prince's party had advanced into Somerset as far as Bruton, thither went Col. Sarsfield from Salisbury with some royal troopers. The colonel, however, missed his intention, as, on his arrival at Bruton, the others had marched to Wincanton, whither he followed on November 20. Lieutenant Campbell at Wincanton, in command of about twenty-five men, hearing of Sarsfield's approach, resolved to fight him. First he posted the majority of his men in a small enclosure at the east end of the town on the left side, a good hedge being between them and the road by which their enemy must come.

"Just opposite this spot, in a little garden also covered by a thick hedge, he placed six men, and then, with four or five others, he took the road, determined to be cautious and not to fire too hastily, as there was the possibility that Sarsfield's men would desert and join him. Presently Sarsfield and his men were seen approaching. Waiting until they were quite near, Campbell then challenged with: "Stand! stand! for whom are ye?" To this the other replied, "I am for King James: who art thou for?" Campbell answered, "For the Prince of Orange". "God damn me!" returned the other, "I'll Prince thee".

Hearing this, Campbell ordered his men to fire, and, himself going up to this "popish officer", shot him in at the mouth and through the brains; so he dropped down dead. Firing now commenced on both sides; but the royalists, a hundred and fifty strong—the Gazette says a hundred and twenty, seventy horse and fifty dragoons—got into the field, some through a dead hedge, some at the lower corner, others by a little gate said to have been opened by a countryman who was looking on; and so they quickly surrounded their opponents, who could do nothing more than fire as fast as possible.

"Defending themselves thus stubbornly, they were joined by their companions from the other side of the road, but at last were overpowered by numbers. The wounded, some of them shot in five or six places, being offered quarter for their bravery "would not accept it from the hands of papists", but chose rather to die. Every man would have been killed had not a miller riding into the town proclaimed to the townspeople, who in alarm and terror had thronged into the streets, that a strong party of Orange horsemen was just entering on the other side. The miller further called out to the king's men, "Away! Away for your lives! save yourselves! the enemies are at hand!" On hearing this and seeing the great confusion in the streets, the troopers judged it was true and galloped away.

"The result of all this was that, on the Orange side, Lieutenant Campbell and eight or nine others were killed, and six prisoners were taken, of whom, however, three got away. Of the King's side four were reported killed and two wounded. If the two wounded died, the general account may be considered correct, as in the end fifteen dead were tumbled into one grave. This narrative was taken from Mr. Bulgin the minister; and from Cornet Webb of the king's force as he lay wounded, shot through the back and reins.

"Besides this, the only episode in Somerset was the arrival of a party of Orangemen at Bridgwater, where they secured some twenty horses from the market people."

George Sweetman, in his *History of Wincanton* [1903] says that he had great difficulty in locating the site of the Wincanton skirmish. He writes: "The last account says distinctly the east end of the town, and in that direction Campbell might well have expected the enemy to have come from Salisbury. There, too, was a garden, and the high hedges where shelter could have been taken. In that case, what is now Colyton Terrace would be the spot; but Sarsfield's party coming from Bruton would have had to come through the town to meet the Prince's soldiers, unless they had come by way of Hunter's Lodge from Bruton. Legend gives us no help, inasmuch as Lawrence Hill, Whitehall, The Croft in Common Lane, are mentioned in this connection, and the field in front of Cutt's Close is said to have been the burial place of the dead soldiers. On the whole, I incline to the belief that it was at the east end of the town, and that the King's forces retreated to Salisbury. The parish register gives us no assistance. Mr. Bulgin was the curate from 1664-1726, but if there was any register kept at that time, there is none existing at present from March 1687-1693."

Another account is given in an article written by Frederick Dixon in Temple Bar Magazine, May 1891. This differs as to the scene of the action. "If this account is correct", says Sweetman of Dixon's article, "Lawrence Hill is the spot where the fight took place." Dixon wrote:

"Early in November, William was keeping court at Exeter. The headquarters of the King were at Salisbury. It was evident that the rival outposts may at any moment come in contact. About the middle of the month, Mackay, who commanded the Prince's advanced guard, being in want of transport, sent out a detachment under a lieutenant named Campbell to endeavour to procure it. Sarsfield and his Irish were known to be in the vicinity. Campbell felt his way cautiously. He passed through the sleepy village [!] of Sherborne, with its noble Gothic minster and battered Norman keep, and coming to Wincanton found what he wanted, and turned to go. Scarcely, however, had he cleared the houses when Sarsfield was upon him. The Irish numbered one hundred and twenty sabres. Campbell's force was only fifty strong, but he was a Scotch Presbyterian, who would as soon thought of uncovering to the "host" as of surrendering to a papist. He blocked the road with a handful of his men, massed the remainder in an adjoining enclosure, and prepared to sell his life as dearly as possible. Sarsfield sent his men straight at the enemy. "Stand!" shouted Campbell as they approached, "For whom are you?" "For King James," was the reply. "I am for the Prince of Orange", returned Campbell. "We'll Prince you," roared the other, with a laugh and a curse, and gave the word to charge. Three times before the enemy could close, Campbell's men poured in their fire; one of the Royal officers was killed, a second had his jaw smashed, many of the troopers' saddles were emptied, but the odds were too heavy. The dragoons burst through the hedgerow. In another moment its defenders would have been cut down where they stood, had not a passing miller, who shared to the full the popular antipathy to James and his Irish soldiers, hurried up with the lying information that the Prince's troops were entering Wincanton in force. Sarsfield had no intention of being caught between two fires, so he called off his men and galloped away, leaving Campbell to continue his retreat unopposed."

Sweetman adds the dry comment: "The singular part of the business is that both leaders went on their way after they were killed."

A recent speculation on where the skirmish might have taken place appears in the 1987 issue of Wincanton's Directory, where Rodney Legg writes:

"In the seventeenth century the last buildings in the High Street would have been much closer to the Market Place than they are now; the eastern extremity of the town was the former George Tavern, on the east side of the present Carrington Way corner. The battle must have taken place a short distance up from there, on the left-hand side— problably between Flingers Lane and Ireson lane, which would have had a field between them. Somewhere there is the mass grave into which the dead—numbering about fifteen—were 'tumbled' together."

This skirmish at Wincanton was one of only two engagements which occurred between King James the Second's men and those of William of Orange in a campaign in which little blood was shed. The other, even smaller, action happened at Reading, where a considerable body of King's men was routed when the Prince's troops advanced. The two main forces were very close to each other at this stage, but no great clash developed, for James was unable to depend on the loyalty of his men. As Rodney Legg writes of the Wincanton incident, "any skirmish was a rarity as James's English army was riven with conspirators and fence-sitters, and the king's capacity for leading from the front, from Salisbury was diminished by a violent nose-bleed.

"Delay facilitated Treason, as the *Dictionary of National Biography* puts it, towards the end of November 1688."

Rumour was rife. Yeovil was alarmed by a story which Sir Hugh Speke claimed to have spread to the effect that the Irish, who were looked upon as no better than savages at that time, were advancing westwards. Emmanuel Green quotes a letter from Yeovil dated 19 December 1688 which was published in the London Mercury, and records "that about three in the morning the whole town was alarmed by a report that some thousands of Irish were marching westward, having burned Portsmouth, Lymington and Basingstoke. This report revived the remembrance that during the civil war some Irish had landed on the Somerset coast, and committed many atrocities. The country round as far as Taunton rose at once in arms. All sorts of weapons were seized. Some had swords, some muskets, some clubs, several thousands both horse and foot being thus ready. The report, however, proved to be a false alarm, to the no small joy of everybody."

Dr. Burnet may be allowed the last word on the Wincanton incident, even if he does refer to it as an engagement "at Winkington in Dorsetshire". "Here," he writes, "an advanced party of the Prince's met one of the King's that was thrice their number, yet they drove them before them into a much greater body, where they were overpowered with numbers. Some were killed on both sides, but there were more prisoners taken of the Prince's men. Yet though the loss was of his side, the courage that his men showed in so great an unequality as to number made us reckon that we gained more than we lost on that occasion."

The news of the successful outcome of the skirmish at Wincanton was bad for James, but cheering for William, who decided to proceed with his march from Exeter. Whittle continues: "Order was given for the Army to march in three Lines. Now many Oxen being brought into this town to draw the Artillery, and many Horses being come to carry the Ammunition, and all things necessary for War appertaining to our whole Army; We then were soon on the March."

Wednesday, 21 November:
The Prince left Exeter and advanced with his army. He left a small garrison in the city together with his heavy artillery under Colonel Gibson, who was in charge of the armed forces in the city. Edward Seymour had already been appointed Governor of Exeter, and as such was in overall charge. Whittle says:

"The first Line marched out of the City as far as St. Mary Ottrie, and were Quartered in and near that Place: The next day the second Line march'd forth of Exeter to the same place, and the first Line advanced to Axminster: The third day the last Line march'd, as before, to St. Mary Ottrie, the first Line advancing some to Beminster, and some to Crookhorn, the second to Axminster and the adjacent Towns and the Regiments march'd some one Road and some another; as the first Line advanced, so the whole Army moved, which was always according to the Motion of our great Master; for when he remained anywhere, then did the whole Army abide in the same Quarters. The City of Exeter was now freed of all its Souldiers, only the

By the King.
A DECLARATION.

JAMES · R.

S We cannot Confider this Invafion of Our Kingdoms by the Prince of Orange Without Horror, for fo Unchriftian and Unnatural an Undertaking in a Perfon fo nearly Related to Us; So it is a Matter of the greateft Trouble and Concern to Us, to reflect upon the many Mifchiefs and Calamities which an Army of Foreigners and Rebels muft unavoidably bring upon Our People. It is but too evident by a late Declaration Publifhed by him, That notwithftanding the many fpecious and plaufible Pretences it carries, his Defigns in the bottom do tend to nothing lefs than an Abfolute Ufurping of Our Crown and Royal Authority, as may fully appear by his affuming to himfelf in the faid Declaration the Regal Stile, Requiring the Peers of the Realm, both Spiritual and Temporal, and all other Perfons of all Degrees, to obey and affift him in the Execution of his Defigns; A Prerogative Infeparable from the Imperial Crown of this Realm. And for a more Undeniable Proof of his Immoderate Ambition, and which nothing can fatisfie but the Immediate Poffeffion of the Crown it felf, he calls in Queftion the Legitimacy of the Prince of Wales Our Son, and Heir Apparent, though by the Providence of God there were prefent at his Birth fo many Witneffes of Unqueftionable Credit, as if it feem'd to have been the particular Care of Heaven, on purpofe to difappoint fo Wicked and Unparallell'd an Attempt.

And in Order to the effecting of his Ambitious Defigns, he feems defirous in the Clofe of his Declaration, to fubmit all to the Determination of a Free Parliament, hoping thereby to Ingratiate himfelf with Our People, though nothing is more Evident, than that a Parliament cannot be Free, fo long as there is an Army of Foreigners in the Heart of Our Kingdoms; So that in truth he himfelf is the fole Obftructor of fuch a Free Parliament: We being fully Refolved, as We have already Declared, fo foon as by the Bleffing of God, Our Kingdoms fhall be delivered from this Invafion, to call a Parliament, which can no longer be liable to the leaft Objection of not being freely Chofen, fince We have actually Reftored all the Burroughs and Corporations of this Our Kingdom, to their Ancient Rights and Priviledges, and in which We fhall be ready not only to Receive and Redrefs all the Juft Complaints and Grievances of Our Good Subjects, but alfo to Repeat and Confirm the Affurances We have already given to them, in Our feveral Declarations of Our Refolution, by Gods Bleffing, to Maintain them in their Religion, their Liberties and Properties, and all other their Juft Rights and Priviledges whatfoever. Upon thefe Confiderations, and the Obligations of their Duty and Natural Allegiance, We can no ways doubt, but that all Our Faithful and Loving Subjects, will readily and heartily concur and joyn with Us, in the Entire Suppreffion and Repelling of thofe Our Enemies and Rebellious Subjects, who have fo Injurioufly and Difloyally Invaded and Difturbed the Peace and Tranquillity of thefe Our Kingdoms.

Given at Our Court at *Whitehall* the 6th day of *November*, 1688. In the Fourth Year of Our Reign.

GOD SAVE THE KING.

London, Printed by *Charles Bill*, *Henry Hills*, and *Thomas Newcomb*, Printers to the Kings moft Excellent Majefty. 1688.

'By the King, a Declaration.'
Concilliatory promises, including a pledge to "protect the Church of England", were offered by James on 6 November 1688 – the day after William landed. He withdrew demands that Roman Catholics should be eligible to sit in the House of Commons. Courtesy Somerset Record Office; Simon Heneage deposit of the Walker Heneage bequest reference DD/WHb 306.

Regiment of Sir John Guyes (which was now raised) was order'd to keep this City. I suppose our Army was now in Circumference between 20 and 30 Miles."

Accompanied by many influential gentlemen of the West Country, the Prince made for Axminster by way of Ottery St. Mary. Again it was raining, and the roads were stiff with mud, but by then the Dutch soldiers must have become used to these conditions. Quarters were scarce in Ottery. Every house was crammed with soldiers, and there were hundreds of troops around the town, and as far as Honiton. The good people of Ottery must have been anxious when William advanced through their little town, for again their memories were seared by the punishments which their people had endured under Judge Jeffreys at the Exeter Assize after Monmouth's defeat a mere three years earlier. Nevertheless, William and his troops were civilly received, and he is reputed to have dined at Ottery, or more probably at the newly built house at Escot belonging to Sir Walter Yonge, who would perhaps have entertained him. Situated in serene parkland a few miles to the north of Ottery on the far side of what is now the A30 main road to the West, the present mansion was built on the site after the original building was burnt down. After the accession of William, Sir Walter Yonge became Member of Parliament for Honiton, and was renowned as a man of considerable influence.

William left Ottery and rode on unimpeded to Axminster, where he stayed for some days.

King James, meanwhile, was in Salisbury, and Burnet says of him at this time, "The King wanted support, for his spirits sunk extremely. His blood was in such fermentation that he was bleeding at the nose, which returned upon him every day. He sent many spies over to us. They all took his money and came and joined themselves to the Prince, none of them returning to him. So that he had no intelligence brought him of what the Prince was doing but what common reports furnished, which magnified our numbers, and made him think we were coming near him, while we were still in Exeter."

It was out of character for James to be so dejected, for previously he had stood boldly against the people and Parliament. His opponents had been treated with disdain, and he had outraged and insulted those who would have supported him in this hour of need, and imprisoned and even robbed of their belongings priests and prelates who had preached the upholding of the "anointed delegate of God". Realising his dilemma when the news of William's impending invasion reached him, James set about conciliating his subjects. Macaulay writes: "The Tyrant was overcome by fear. He ceased to repeat that concessions had always ruined princes, and sullenly owned that he must stoop to court the Tories once more." But they did not rise to his aid. He solemnly proclaimed that he would "Protect the Church of England," and would "maintain the Act of Uniformity". He would "no longer insist that Roman Catholics should be admitted into the House of Commons; and he trusted that his people would justly appreciate such a proof of his disposition to meet their wishes." He announced that he would reinstate "all magistrates and Deputy Lieutenants who had been dismissed for refusing to support his policy". He received the Bishops who were in London at the time and listened to their advice. The Primate suggested that "if His Majesty would reconsider the points in dispute between the Churches of Rome and England, perhaps, by the divine blessing, on the arguments which the Bishops wished to lay before him, he might be convinced that it was his duty to return to the religion of his father and of his grandfather . . ."

Daily, reversals in the King's policies were reported, and James clearly thought that all the concessions which he had made so speedily would just as rapidly bring him back into favour with his subjects, but the general feeling was one of distrust. The King was pressed to allow free Parliamentary elections, so that William would no longer have any

The Declaration of the Nobility, Gentry, and Commonalty at the Rendezvous at *Nottingham*, Nov. 22. 1688.

WE the Nobility, Gentry, and Commonalty of these Northern Counties assembled together at *Nottingham*, for the defence of the Laws, Religion, and Properties, according to those free-born Liberties and Priviledges, descended to us from our Ancestors, as the undoubted Birth-right of the Subjects of this Kingdom of *England*, (not doubting but the Infringers and Invaders of our Rights will represent us to the rest of the Nation in the most malicious dress they can put upon us) do here unanimously think it our Duty to declare to the rest of our Protestant Fellow-Subjects the Grounds of our present Undertaking.

We are by innumerable Grievances made sensible, that the very Fundamentals of our Religion, Liberties, and Properties are about to be rooted out by our late Jesuitical Privy-Council, as hath been of late too apparent, 1. By the King's dispensing with all the Establisht Laws at his pleasure. 2. By displacing all Officers out of all Offices of Trust and Advantage, and placing others in their room that are known Papists, deservedly made incapable by the Establisht Laws of our Land. 3. By destroying the Charters of most Corporations in the Land. 4. By discouraging all persons that are not Papists, preferring such as turn to Popery 5. By displacing all honest and conscientious Judges, unless they would, contrary to their Consciences, declare that to be Law which was meerly arbitrary. 6. By branding all men with the name of Rebels that but offered to justifie the Laws in a legal Course against the arbitrary proceedings of the King, or any of his corrupt Ministers. 7. By burthening the Nation with an Army, to maintain the violation of the Rights of the Subjects. 8. By discountenancing the Establisht Reform'd Religion. 9. By forbidding the Subjects the benefit of petitioning, and construing them Libellers; so rendring the Laws a Nose of Wax, to serve their arbitrary Ends. And many more such like, too long here to enumerate.

We being thus made sadly sensible of the Arbitrary, and Tyrannical Government that is by the Influence of Jesuitical Councels coming upon us, do unanimously declare, That not being willing to deliver our posterity over to such a condition of Popery and Slavery, as the aforesaid Oppressions inevitably threaten; we will to the utmost of our power oppose the same, by joining with the Prince of *Orange* (whom we hope God Almighty hath sent to rescue us from the Oppressions aforesaid) will use our utmost Endeavours for the recovery of our almost ruin'd Laws, Liberties, and Religion; and herein we hope all good Protestant Subjects will with their Lives and Fortunes be assistant to us, and not be bugbear'd with the opprobrious terms of Rebels, by which they would fright us, to become perfect Slaves to their tyrannical Insolencies and Usurpations; for we assure our selves, that no rational and unbyassed person will judge it Rebellion to defend our Laws and Religion, which all our Princes have Sworn at their Coronations; which Oath, how well it hath been observed of late, we desire a Free Parliament may have the Consideration of.

We own it Rebellion to resist a King that governs by Law; but he was always accounted a Tyrant that made his Will the Law; and to resist such an one, we justly esteem no Rebellion, but a necessary Defence; and in this Consideration we doubt not of all honest mens assistance, and humbly hope for, and implore the great God's protection, that turneth the hearts of his people as pleaseth him best; it having been observed, That people can never be of one mind without his inspiration, which hath in all Ages confirmed that observation, *Vox Populi est Vox Dei.*

The present restoring of Charters, and reversing the oppressing and unjust Judgment given on *Magdalen* Colledge Fellows, is plain, are but to still the people, like Plums to Children, by deceiving them for a while; but if they shall by this Stratagem be fooled, till this present storm that threatens the Papists, be past, assoon as they shall be resetled, the former Oppression will be put on with greater vigour; but we hope in vain is the Net spread in the sight of the Birds: For (1.) The Papists old Rule is, *That Faith is not to be kept with Hereticks*, as they term Protestants, tho' the Popish Religion is the greatest Heresie. And (2.) Queen *Mary*'s so ill observing her promises to the *Suffolk*-men that helpt her to her Throne. And above all, (3.) the Popes dispensing with the breach of Oaths, Treaties, or Promises, at his pleasure, when it makes for the service of Holy Church, as they term it. These, we say, are such convincing Reasons to hinder us from giving Credit to the aforesaid *Mock-Shews* of Redress, that we think our selves bound in Conscience to rest on no Security that shall not be approved by a freely Elected Parliament, to whom, under God, we refer our Cause.

'**Declaration of the Nobility, Gentry and Commonalty at Nottingham.**'
Grievances against James's "oppresive rule" published on 22 November 1688. Courtesy Somerset Record Office; Simon Heneage deposit of the Walker Heneage bequest reference DD/WHb 3070.

excuse for remaining in the country, but he refused to accept a petition of the Lords for a Parliament. "They came," says Macaulay, "with Sancroft at their head, to present a petition, praying that a free and legal Parliament might be called, and that a negotiation might be opened with the Prince of Orange . . . He received their address ungraciously. He assured them indeed that he passionately desired the meeting of a free Parliament; and he promised them on the faith of a King that he would call one as soon as the Prince of Orange should have left the island. 'But how,' said he, 'can a parliament be free when an enemy is in the kingdom, and can return near a hundred votes?' To the prelates he spoke with peculiar acrimony. 'I could not,' he said, 'prevail on you the other day to declare against this invasion: but you are ready enough to declare against me. Then you would not meddle with politics. You have no scruple about meddling now. You have excited this rebellious temper among your flocks; and now you foment it. You would be better employed in teaching them how to obey than in teaching me how to govern."

Macaulay records that he was much incensed against his nephew Grafton, whose signature stood next to Sancroft, and said to the young man with great asperity, "You know nothing about religion; you care nothing about it; and yet, forsooth, you must pretend to have a conscience".

"It is true, sir", answered Grafton, with impudent frankness, "that I have very little conscience, but I belong to a party which has a great deal."

Burnet gives a similar account of this incident, and describes the Duke of Grafton as a gallant but rough man who had been some time at sea. "The King", he says, "took note of somewhat in his behaviour that looked factious."

After the petitioners had gone the King observed bitterly that he had "done too much already in the hope of satisfying an undutiful and ungrateful people". He further added that he would yield nothing more, repeating again and again, "Not an atom." He made it clear that he would not treat with the invaders, nor would he receive any: the first messenger bringing a flag of truce would be disregarded and "the second should be hanged".

With these feelings of embittered rage James had left London for Salisbury, leaving in charge a "Council of five Lords to represent him". Two of these were papists, a third was the infamous Judge Jeffreys, and the other were Preston and Godolphin, "to whom no serious objection could be made". He had taken the precaution of sending the infant Prince of Wales to the strongly garrisoned port of Portsmouth, and since the Royal fleet under Lord Dartmouth was close at hand, the prince could if necessary easily be taken to France. James, with an army heavily reinforced by Irish regiments which far outnumbered William's forces, established himself in Salisbury, taking up his headquarters at the Bishop's Palace.

Even before he reached Salisbury the news which he had received was disheartening, and now that he was there it became even worse. He knew that William now commanded the city of Exeter and the West Country, and the Duke of Beaufort informed him that Bristol, which had remained loyal during the Monmouth rebellion, could not be relied upon now. Lord Cornbury had already deserted to the Prince of Orange, and James suspected that others would follow. He felt that numerous officers stationed at Salisbury might be disloyal. His fleet had avoided any action against that of William, and was merely watching events from the anchorage at Portsmouth. All this, together with the problems with his health, weighed heavily upon him, and there was little wonder that his normal resistance and inflexibility of purpose were gradually deserting him.

After the skirmish at Wincanton, Lieut. General Churchill, the Duke of Grafton and others, together with Colonels Kirke and Trelawney planned to desert James and join William. Kirke and Trelawney rode to Warminster where their regiments were now stationed. Churchill had previously suggested to the King that he, the King, should visit these troops there, and James agreed to do so.

Wherever he turned his eyes he discovered open enemies, the defection of some of his friends, and others who were confused, hesitant and doubtful. His army was unreliable, and on the night of November 22 he learnt that the Prince of Orange was fast approaching, that London was in a state of commotion, and that in the North disaffection was spreading on every side. Evidence of this last is shown by the "Declaration of the Nobility, Gentry, and Commonalty at the Rendezvous at Nottingham, Nov. 22 1688." This notable document plainly sets out the grievances which lead to the authors "unanimously to declare, That not being willing to deliver our posterity over to such a condition of Popery and Slavery, as the aforesaid Oppressions inevitably threaten; we will to the utmost of our power oppose the same, by joining with the Prince of Orange (whom we hope God Almighty hath sent to rescue us from the Oppressions aforesaid.)". The nine "Oppressions aforesaid" listed include:

"The King's dispensing with all the Established Laws at his pleasure. Displacing of all Officers out of all Offices of Trust and Advantage, and placing others in their room that are known Papists."

"Burthening the Nation with an Army, to maintain the violation of the Rights of the Subjects," and

"Discountenancing the Establisht Reform'd Religion."

They "own it a Rebellion to resist a King that governs by law; but he was always accounted a Tyrant that made his Will the Law; and to resist such an one, we justly esteem no rebellion, but a necessary Defence".

They round off their case with a threefold denunciation of the Papists, and conclude "that we think ourselves bound in conscience to rest on no Security that shall not be approved by a freely Elected Parliament, to whom, under God, we refer our Cause".

The King was suffering great stress under the many reports of defection, trouble and disaster that were reaching him, and he went to the chapel in the Bishop's Palace where his lodging was before leaving for Warminster to review his troops there. As he came from the chapel to enter his coach, which was waiting by the entrance to the Palace, he was seized by a serious nose-bleed, and no means could be found to staunch the flow of blood. He was taken to a room for attention—the same room, incidentally, which is the sick-bay of the Salisbury Cathedral School which today occupies the old Palace of the Bishop. His coach was dismissed and his journey to Warminster cancelled.

The onset of this nose-bleed was regarded by the King's attendants, and even by the King himself, as a sinister omen. James was dogged by incidents which were looked on as ill omens in a superstitious age. At his coronation the crown did not fit his head; it slipped down too far, and covered the upper part of his face. The canopy which was carried over him broke, and his son by Mrs. Sedley died that same day. A similar impression was produced in Salisbury market place after the King had addressed the populace there, declaring that he would defend the Protestant religion to the last drop of his blood. He was then about to enter the Council House when an ornamental crown which had been placed over the door of the building suddenly fell.

The King was compelled to seek medical treatment, and several days passed before the haemorrhage ceased.

There is a note in John Aubrey's *Miscellanies* relating to the cure of nosebleeding which Richard Colt Hoare quotes: "To stop bleeding. Cut an ash of one, two and three

Ante-Chapel of the old Bishop's Palace at Salisbury.
Interior and exterior views of the chapel that was reserved for James's use during his time here. It is now the chapel for Salisbury Cathedral School.

years' growth, at the very hour and minute of the Sun's coming into Taurus. A chip of this will stop it. If it is a shoot, it must be cut down to the ground. Mr. Gill says the stick must not be bound or holden, but dipped or wetted in the blood. When King James the Second was at Salisbury, in 1688, his nose bled near two days, and, after many essays in vain, was stopped by this sympathetic ash, which Mr. William Nash, a chirurgeon at Salisbury, applied."

Although little blood was shed on the battlefield, it certainly played a significant part for James in this so-called bloodless revolution. Whilst he was recovering, rumours reached him that John Churchill, whose loyalty he trusted, and the Duke of Grafton were about to defect. In Macaulay's words, "It was hinted to the King that some who were near his person were not his friends, and that it would be a wise precaution to send Churchill and Grafton under guard to Portsmouth. James rejected this counsel. A propensity to suspicion was not among his vices . . . Nevertheless the reports which he had received of the state of his army disturbed him greatly. He was no longer impatient for battle. He even began to think of retreating."

Saturday, 24 November:

James, "finding his army begin to moulder away", conferred with his principal officers. The Earl of Feversham, who commanded the army, advised him to retreat: Churchill urged attack, but James, distrusting the mood of his forces, ordered a general retreat. At this point John Churchill, sensing, perhaps, that the King had perceived his intending disloyalty, fled before dawn, and Grafton went with him to join the Prince of Orange. He left a letter of explanation to the King. "It was written with that decorum which he never failed to preserve in the midst of guilt and dishonour. He acknowledged that he owed everything to the royal favour. Interest, he said, and gratitude impelled him in the same direction. Under no such government could he hope to be so great and prosperous; but all such considerations must yield to a paramount duty. He was a Protestant; and he could not conscientiously draw a sword against the Protestant cause. As to the rest he would ever be ready to hazard life and fortune in defence of the sacred person and of the lawful rights of his gracious master."

On the next day the whole camp was in a state of chaos. James was informed that Kirke at Warminster had refused to obey orders from Salisbury, and it was obvious that he also was in league with William. James realised that if he had gone to Warminster he could have been captured and taken as a prisoner to William's headquarters. He now regarded what had seemed to him a serious illness to have been the intervention of a "guardian saint".

The news that Marshal Schomberg was approaching with the advanced guard of the Dutch army prompted James to prepare for retreat, and he made plans accordingly. Before departing he published a proclamation promising a free pardon to all his subjects who had joined the Prince of Orange provided they returned to their duty within twenty days.

Sunday, 25 November:

Orders were given to retreat, and a withdrawal towards Reading began, the King reaching Andover that day. Clarendon's Diary for the day records: "An express brought word [to London] that the Duke of Grafton, Lord Churchill and Col. Berkeley were gone over to the Prince of Orange; that the King lay at Andover, and would be at Whitehall tomorrow. In the evening I went to Court; great crowds in the galleries, and consternation in all men's looks."

The retreat, and the sight of the King fleeing, depressed his troops considerably. Whittle's information is that "The Citizens, hearing the Army of the Prince of Orange was advanced within a few Miles of their City; some Persons coming in at one end of the Town, said they saw him not far off: which Report being notified about so Alarmed the Late King James and his Army, that in the middle of his bleeding, he commanded his coach to be made ready, and drive away towards Windsor with all possible speed, which was accordingly done. The Foot Souldiers were ready to desert the late King, and many did, some left their Baggage and Snapsacks behind them; And the Horse likewise being in such a hurry to get away, that they were ready to spoil their Comrades; and the whole Army was in such a confused manner, and marched so disorderly and in such haste, that the Country seeing them, judged they had been routed in Battel."

In Andover that evening James was accompanied by Prince George, his daughter Anne's husband, and the Duke of Ormond, two men who had been in the conspiracy with Churchill. Macaulay observes: "The impenetrable stupidity of Prince George served his turn on this occasion better than cunning would have done. It was his habit, when any news was told him, to exclaim in French, 'Est-il possible?'—'Is it possible?' " This catchword was now of great use to him. 'Est-il possible?' he cried when he had been made to understand that Churchill and Grafton were missing. And when the ill tidings came from Warminster, he again ejaculated, 'Est-il possible?' Prince George and Ormond were invited to sup with the King at Andover. The meal must have been a sad one. The King was overwhelmed by his misfortune."

Prince George, of whom Charles II had said, "I have tried Prince George sober, and I have tried him drunk; and drunk or sober, there is nothing in him", could hardly have been a cheerful guest at the King's table, and neither would Ormond, who was habitually very reserved and uncommunicative, be much of a light relief for James. When the meal was over both Prince George and Ormond, together with Queensbury's eldest son, the Earl of Brumlanrig, a Lieutenant Colonel of Dundee's Regiment—"a band more detested than even Kirke's Lambs"—mounted their horses and rode off to join the invading forces. When James heard of this latest defection he said of Prince George, "What, is 'Est-il possible' gone too? After all, a good trooper would have been a greater loss!"

The King was in no mood of levity, however, but in a rage of vindictive anger against the defectors, and in particular against John Churchill, who had so completely betrayed the trust and confidence which James had placed in him, which had led the King to raise him up from lowly beginnings to a position of power and honour in the land. In rage then, and also in bitter despair, the King returned to London. Dr. Burnet reports:

"And the body of the nation did everywhere discover their inclinations for the Prince so evidently that the King saw he had nothing to trust to but his army. And the ill dispositon among them was so apparent, that he reckoned he could not depend on them. So that he lost heart and head at once. But that which gave him the last and most confounding stroke was that the Lord Churchill and the Duke of Grafton left him, and came and joined the Prince at Axminster, twenty miles on that side of Exeter. After this he could not know on whom he could depend."

Before leaving Andover, the King wrote letters to London explaining his reasons for returning to the capital. He also ordered that Lady Churchill and Lady Berkeley, who were in attendance on Princess Anne at Whitehall, be detained. News soon came to the Princess of the defection of Churchill and Grafton, and of the King's intention to return to London, and she was filled with anxiety and dread. Sarah Churchill was her adored friend and close companion, and Anne was well aware of what the consequences of John Churchill's action would be as far as his wife was concerned. Sarah would be taken, and subjected to the closest of examinations by relentless inquisitors. Anne had no

John Churchill, who was later created Duke of Marlborough.
He was James's most competent professional soldier, but he would no longer fight for his King. Portrait after Sir Godfrey Kneller, when Churchill had won Blenheim and become his nation's hero, courtesy the National Portrait Gallery.

fears for her own safety, but she knew only too well of the women her father had sent to the block or the stake in the past for offences of far less gravity than those which might be found against her dear friend. She was determined to save her from the King, and to flee herself. "I will jump out of the window," she cried, "rather than be found here by my father!"

Lady Churchill was more practical than the Princess, and she immediately began making plans for their escape that night in concert with the Bishop of London, Compton, the ex-tutor of the Princess, who was at the time "lodged very secretly in Suffolk Street," and so on the night of November 25 the princess Anne, accompanied by Sarah, Lady Churchill, left her quarters at the Cockpit in Whitehall. Dr. Burnet describes the flight:

"The Princess went sooner to bed than ordinary. And about midnight she went down a back-stairs from her closet, attended only by the Lady Churchill, in such haste that they carried nothing with them. They were waited for by the Bishop of London, who carried them to the Earl of Dorset's, whose lady furnished them with everything. And so they went northward, as far as Northampton, where the Earl [Devonshire] attended on them with all respect, and quickly brought a body of horse to serve for a guard to the Princess. And in a little while a small army was formed about her, who chose to be commanded by the Bishop of London; of which he too easily accepted."

A further account of the flight is found in the Clarendon Correspondence. The Earl of Clarendon says that he heard the rumour next morning, and the report was that someone had carried the Princess Anne away, but nobody knew whither. The Duchess of Marlborough [then Lady Churchill] managed the escape for her; and the narrative she has given coincides closely with that given by Burnet. After stating the preliminary arrangements she made with the bishop of London, she adds, "The Princess went to bed at the usual time, to prevent suspicion. I came to her soon after, and, by the back stairs which went down from her closet, her Royal Highness, Lady Fitzharding, and I, with one servant, walked to the coach, where we found the Bishop and the Earl of Dorset. They conducted us that night to the Bishop's house in the City, and the next day to my Lord Dorset's at Copt Hall. From thence we went to the Earl of Northampton's, and from thence to Nottingham, where the country gathered round the Princess; nor did she think herself safe till she saw that she was surrounded by the Prince of Orange's friends."

Monday, 26 November:

On the morning after the flight there was consternation at Whitehall when the Princess Anne was not to be found in her room. Her ladies in waiting scurried up and down the palace, wringing their hands and screaming. Lord Craven, in command of the Foot Guards, questioned the sentries, and meanwhile the Chancellor was sealing up the Churchill papers. In all this commotion the Princess's old nurse ran into the royal apartments crying that her dear mistress had been murdered by the papists; rumour spread to Westminster Hall that she had been taken and held captive. Later, it began to be realised that the Princess had escaped of her own free will, and then all kinds of excuses were invented to account for her flight—she had been insulted; threatened; beaten by her cruel stepmother (and the Queen was in danger from the people for a time, so that many Roman Catholics and some Protestant Tories went to the Palace to protect her). In the middle of this confusion a courier brought the news of Prince George's defection to William, and close on his heels came King James himself on his return to London. The King was told of his daughter's disappearance, and after all his suffering and setbacks this was the final blow for James. He burst into tears, saying, "God help me! My own children have forsaken me."

The Vanguard at Sherborne

DURING THESE dramatic events William, Prince of Orange, was calmly receiving more support. Lieutenant General Churchill and the Duke of Grafton, Colonel of the First Regiment of Foot Guards, joined him with four hundred horse from two regiments, and the arrival of these two men of great influence must have given William very considerable encouragement.

William's army had by now cleared Exeter, and Whittle writes: "Our van guard was advanced as far as Sherborn, who coming into the Town at one end and a party of Horse (belonging to the late King James) coming in at the other, but hearing of our Men, retreated back towards Sarum. Our first Line being advanced from Axminster to Crookhorn [Crewkerne] and Beaminster; the second to Axminster and Lyme; and the third Line according to the others stage before them. Then the Prince of Orange rode to Crookhorn with all his Nobles in Attendance.

"The Country People were exceeding desirous to see the prince, and ran in great numbers from one Town to another, when they heard for certain which way he came. Here at Crookhorn his Highness remained the Lord's Day, Novemb. 25, And the Gentlemen of the West came and joyn'd him now almost at every Stage."

A regiment of royal infantry, and the officers of a dragoon regiment also joined the Prince at this time.

Between Crewkerne and Bridport, a mile south of the country town of Beaminster, stands the fine 16th century manor house of Parnham, a most attractive mansion built of the warm, mellow local stone, and with a "William and Mary" staircase. In the 17th

Parnham, in west Dorset, was the seat of the Strode family.
They were unfriendly to the Prince of Orange – it is thought they were the people who, Whittle alleges, gave poisoned meat and beer to some of William's men.

century it was in the hands of the Strode family, who had during the Civil War sheltered King Charles I, and who, in 1688, were no friends of Prince William. Whittle relates:

"Near unto Beminster there lived a Gentleman, whos Name I shall forbear, but a very rigid Papist, and one whom I cannot quite forget, because of his unkindness and curs'd Intention towards the Army: Hearing that some Regiments would pass that way, he resolved to give some their last Meat and Drink (as his own Neighbours at Beminster informed us when we were there) therefore he caused a Beef or two to be kill'd, and poison'd the Flesh, making it into Pyes; and poison'd also a Hogshead or two of Beer, and as much of Sider, for the hungry Souldiers (as he call'd them) against they came that way. Some of his Neighbours hearing of this cursed Design, spread it purposely about the Country, to prevent any of the Prince of Orange's Men from being destroyed; insomuch that every Regiment was timely warn'd hereof: But as in all great Armies, there will be some Straglers, so there was some in ours, tho' not many; and these not hearing of this Bait, accidentally passed that way; and as they approached near the House, they concluded 'twas their best course to call and drink [there] because it shew'd well to the Eye, and People all along were very kind to the Souldiers, and would make them drink, and in many Places eat; Hereupon these Straglers went to the house and asked for some Beer; and the people there made them eat and drink freely, saying Their Master had provided for them. After they had eat and drank, they hastned towards their Regiments, lest the Enemies Party should happen to meet them; Being come a little more than a quarter of a mile from the house, they grew suddenly so weak and faint, that they were not able to go any farther; so they lay down under a Tree, not suspecting what was the matter. As they were in this desperate condition, by meer Providence there came a Surgeon-Major that way, who espying some Souldiers

The Citadel, Plymouth Hoe.
The Earl of Bath, who commanded the garrison here, declared for the Prince of Orange.

(supposed they were some of the Prince of Orange's Men) he went to speak with them; and seeing them look so fearfully (their Eyes being prodigiously swell'd) he ask'd presently, What was the matter with them? or, What did ail them? they told him, they knew not, only they had eat and drank at the Gentlemn's House behind (pointing to the House); The Surgeon, having heard of their evil Preparations, prepared immediately an Antidote, and gave directions what they must do; whereupon they presently began to vomit, and after some time they waxed a little better, and made shift to get to the Waggons which carried sick Souldiers, and were under the Surgeon-Major's hands for some time. At the very next Town, called Yetminster, one Souldier died in the Night, and none could tell what was the matter with him, being very well when he went to bed, which Souldier I buried there according to our Liturgy. The others that were poisoned, were strangely altered, their Eyes being swell'd after an odd manner".

William and his army had by now taken up new positions at Beaminster and Crewkerne. Dr. Burnet continues: "At Crookhorn [Crewkerne] Dr. Finch, son of the earl of Winchelsea, and Warden of All Souls College in Oxford, was sent to the Prince from some of the heads of colleges, assuring him that they would declare for him, and inviting him to come thither, telling him that their plate should be at his service, if he needed it. This was a sudden turn from those principles that they had carried so high a few years before. The Prince had designed to have secured Bristol and Gloucester, and so to have gone to Oxford, the whole West being then in his hands, if there had been any appearance of a stand to be made against him by the king and his army; for, the King being so much superior to him in horse, it was not advisable to march through the great plains of Dorsetshire and Wiltshire. But the King's precipitate return to London put an end to this precaution. The Earl of Bath had prevailed with the garrison of Plymouth, and they declared for the Prince. So now all behind him was safe. When he came to Sherburn, all Dorsetshire came in a body and joined him."

Monday, 26 November:
Whittle confirms that: "On Monday morning the whole Army March'd; The first Line advanced from Sherborn to Wincanton, the second to Sherborn, and the third to Yetminster. The Prince of Orange with all his Nobles and Gentlemen came to Sherborn and lodged at the Castle."

Thursday, 29 November:
"His Highness the Prince of Denmark, with the Duke of Ormond, came and joined the Prince of Orange at Sherborn-Castle, about four of the Clock in the Afternoon; The Report of which made the Hearts of all the Country People to rejoice, as well as our Army, and many Persons of Quality flock'd to the Prince to join him."

Churchill, Grafton and Berkeley, together with Kirke and Trelawney, had made their way to William's forces at Crewkerne, and they were taken before the Prince at the house of the Earl of Bristol at Sherborne. When they came there they were surprised to see Lieutenant Byng, who had ridden from Portsmouth with a secret message for the Prince from some officers of the Fleet under the command of Lord Dartmouth. Byng [who later became Lord Torrington] had slipped away unbeknown to Lord Dartmouth to bring a message of support for the Prince from many ships' captains and officers. Prince George of Denmark and the Duke of Ormond had also joined William at Sherborne. The meeting of William with his latest supporters, as described in a contemporary collection of papers, had a very biblical flavour: "The last news we had was, that the Prince was at the Earl of Bristol's, which is by Sherborne, where we are informed that Prince George, the Duke of Grafton, the Lord Churchill, and Colonel Trelawney met him, and that the Prince saluted them in the words of David to the men

Sherborne Castle, Dorset.
'The Lodge' built by Sir Walter Raleigh became temporary headquarters for the Prince of Orange, at the invitation of John Digby, third Earl of Bristol. Photograph courtesy the *Dorset Encyclopedic Guide* [Dorset Publishing Company, 1988].

of Benjamin, I Chron. xii. 17. 'If ye be come peaceably unto me to help me, mine heart shall be knit unto you; but if ye be come to betray me to mine enemies, seeing there is no wrong in my hands, the God of our fathers look thereon and rebuke it.' But they replied in the words of Amasai in the 18th verse:'Thine are we, David, and on thy side, thou son of Jesse, Peace be unto thee, and peace unto thy helpers; for thy God helpeth thee'."

Sherborne Castle, or "The Lodge," as it was called previously, the middle part of which was built by Sir Walter Raleigh in 1594, was at this time occupied by the third Earl of Bristol, John Digby, who received William here. In his *History of Dorset* the eighteenth century historian, John Hutchins wrote: "It is said that his [William's] proclamation emanated from a printing press set up in the drawing room, where a broken hearth stone bore to the fact until very recently."

Dr. Burnet mentions another declaration, a false one, which had been published in the name of the Prince: "A bold man ventured to draw and publish another declaration in the Prince's name. It was penned with great spirit, and it had as great an effect. It set forth the desperate designs of the papists, and the extreme danger the nation was in by their means, and required all persons immediately to fall on such papists as were in any employments, and to turn them out, and to secure all strong places, and to do everything else that was in their power in order to execute the laws, and to bring all things again into their proper channels. This set all men to work: for no doubt was made that it was truly the Prince's declaration. But he knew nothing of it. And it was never known who was the author of so bold a thing. No person ever claimed the merit of it: for though it had an amazing effect, yet, it seems, he that contrived it apprehended that the Prince would not be well pleased with the author of such an imposture in his name. The King was under such a consternation, that he neither knew what to resolve on, nor whom to trust. This pretended declaration put the City in such a flame that it was carried to the lord mayor, and he was required to execute it. The apprentices got together, and were falling upon all mass-houses, and committing many irregular things. Yet their fury was so well governed, and so little resisted, that no other mischief was done; no blood was shed."

Although Dr. Burnet did not know who had written this false document, according to Emmanuel Green the egregious Sir Hugh Speke, author of the earlier rumour about the wild Irish advancing upon Yeovil, admitted later that he had been responsible for it. "From Sherborne", says Green, "was issued a celebrated document known as the Prince's Third Declaration. The Prince's first declaration was dated October 10, to which an additional one was added, dated October 24. In the first was sketched the conduct of the evil counsellors about the King; the various complaints of the country; and the dismal effect of the assumption of arbitrary power. And it adds, to crown all, there were the great and violent presumptions regarding the birth of a son. During the Queen's pretended bigness, and in the manner in which the birth was managed, there were so many just and visible grounds of suspicion that not only himself, but all good subjects vehemently suspected that the pretended child was not born of the Queen. And since our dearest consort and our selfs have so great an interest in this matter, and a right to the succession, we cannot excuse ourselves from espousing the interests of the English people, and contributing to maintain the Protestant religion, the laws and liberties of the three kingdoms."

The third declaration, having every appearance of being genuine, was dated Sherborne Castle, 28 November. Its effect was immediate and widespread, as its wording so exactly caught the feeling and wishes of that time. It declared the Prince's fervent zeal for the Protestant religion, his resolution to rescue the country from slavery and popery, and that he was resolved to call a free Parliament forthwith. It further promised that no injury should be done to anyone; not even to a papist except when found in arms; then he should be treated as a robber and bandit, and "intirely delivered up to the discretion of the souldiers".

This momentous document was afterwards found to be unauthorised, and for a long time its authorship remained unacknowledged. Sir Hugh Speke eventually claimed it as his: "I wrote it first, and when it was perfected to my liking, I then sealed it up in a sheet of paper and left it with a person in London that I could trust, and charged him to keep the paper till he heard from me out of the west by letter after I was got to the Prince of Orange, and then to dispose of it as I should direct . . . Having informed himself of the exact route and plan of marching from Exeter, Sir Hugh wrote to London accordingly, ordering the insertion of the words 'Given under our hand at Sherborne,' and that the manuscript should be put under a certain bookseller's door, the said bookseller receiving an order to print.

"Be the authorship where it may, this document practically in its effect secured all for the prince."

Twenty-seven years later, the irrepressible Speke avowed the forgery and demanded a reward for so eminent a service rendered to the Protestant religion!

Finally leaving Sherborne and Dorset behind, the invaders made their way through Buckhorn Weston and Wincanton, where there was an isolated act of resistance, and continued in an almost leisurely fashion towards Oxford and London. Whittle continues: "Now the Prince of Orange, with Prince George of Denmark, the Duke of Ormond, and very many Knights and Gentlemen came from Sherborn Castle unto Wincanton and quartered there. This was the place where the first skirmish passed between the two Armies."

'The Dogs' in South Street, Wincanton.
The Prince stayed here whilst his army moved through the town, which had shortly before been the scene of the first armed clash since his landing.

Some interesting information about the Prince and his forces in the Wincanton area was given in a letter published in "The Gentleman's Magazine" for December, 1813. George Sweetman says it was written by Thomas Richards, who died at Roundhill Farm in 1815. Accompanying the letter was a wood-cut representing the brass plate referred to in the letter, which reads:

"Mr. Urban,—As any circumstances connected with the Orange family is, at this time, peculiarly interesting, I send you a brass plate with a figure coarsely engraved, which is evidently designed for William, Prince of Orange, afterwards King William III. The inscription, 'Syr Konink Licke Hoog Heyt', etc., from the information of a Dutch officer, ought to be 'Syn Koninglyke Hoog Heyt', etc., and signifies 'His Royal Highness', &c. The plate, with another with several whole figures [now lost] was dug up in rooting an ancient tree near the churchyard at Charlton Musgrave, near Wincanton, in the county of Somerset, and was probably a badge worn by one of the adherents of King William during his progress from Torbay through the western counties. From the place and manner in which it was found, one might indeed by led to conclude that it belonged to a fugitive from the battle of Sedgemoor, after the Duke of Monmouth's defeat; but I do not recollect that the avowed partisans of William appeared publicly in Monmouth's enterprise.—T.R.."

In Wincanton there is a charming old manor house now known as "The Dogs", built in 1557 by the Churchey family, who were merchants. George Sweetman makes a persuasive case for the Prince having spent some time at this house, and having slept in the "Orange Room" there. He writes: "It has been said that some of the partisans of King William were here in 1688, but that William himself came here is a matter of doubt, and that the "Orange Room" at "The Dogs" derived its name from the colour of its decoration. Let us examine the evidence. In Mr. E. Green's book we read—"At Crookhorn, he remained Sunday, November 25th. Here, besides many gentlemen of the West, a regiment of Royal infantry and the officers of a dragoon regiment joined him. The first line now marched to Wincanton, the second following to Sherborne, whither went also the Prince, and lodged at the Castle, being thus advanced directly upon the King's troops.

"From Sherborne the Prince, with now Prince George of Denmark, and many others who had left the King, marched to Wincanton. When leaving here, a royal trumpeter arrived, asking a pass for messengers to treat. So the Prince, Sir Wm. Portman being with him, advanced by Mere to Salisbury."

Another account is given in *The Harleian Miscellany* Vol. I page 453: Extract of a letter sent by one of the followers of the Prince of Orange, the writer signing himself N.N., to a person of distinction in London. Dated Wincanton, 1st December, 1688. "I shall return again to the prince. When his Highness left Exeter, Wednesday, Nov. 21st, he marched with his own guards, attended by a great many of the gentry, both of Somerset and Dorset [Devon?], to St. Mary Ottery, where he dined, after which he marched to Crookhorn, where he tarried only one night. From thence to Sherborne, where his Highness was splendidly entertained by Lord D. From thence to Wincanton, where he lodged at the house of Mr. Churchill [Churchey?], and is credibly reported designs for Oxford."

The foregoing account appears to have been copied from a pamphlet, now rare, dated from Wincanton, 1st December, 1688, entitled *The expedition of his Highness the Prince of Orange for England. Being an account of the most remarkable passages thereof; from the day of his setting sail from Holland to the first day of this instant December, 1688. In a letter to a person of quality.*

"On Wednesday, November 24th, he marched with his own guards, attended by a great many of the gentry, both of Somersetshire and Devon, to St. Mary Ottery, where he dined; after which he marched to Axminster, where he continued four days. From thence to Sherborne, where his Highness was splendidly entertained by Lord D. [Digby]. From thence he went to Wincanton, where he lodged at the house of one Mr. Churchill, a merchant, and it is credibly reported designs for Oxford.

"Your most obedient servant,—N.N. Wincanton, 1st December, 1688."

These accounts vary somewhat, as the story of any event told by two or more persons would, but it is clear enough that the Prince, with George of Denmark and Sir Wm. Portman, marched here to Wincanton, and that he lodged at the house of Mr. Churchey, a merchant.

In 1688, Richard Churchey, a merchant, lived at "The Dogs", a house which he had recently built. For more than a century before his birth his ancestors were established here as merchants. He was Lord of the Manor, and the owner of about 500 acres of land, with many houses on them.

Sweetman sums up the evidence, and concludes: "Standing by itself, the legend that the Prince slept in the Orange Room, which derived its name from this circumstance, would not count for much; but taken with the other facts, this is as well established as we can expect any event to be which happened over two centuries ago."

And now, three centuries later, the house, a charming old building, is owned by Dr. Samir Mattar, who obviously cherishes it greatly. The whole house exudes a sense of history and of warmth. Low ceilings, fine old double doors, and the oak timbered, panelled staircase evoke pictures of the elaborately dressed Royal party filling the house with their presence. The Orange Room on the first floor, now carefully restored, shows panels of paintings executed by French prisoners during the Napoleonic war. It is a room of comfort, sensitively furnished, with "Orange" touches subtly presented. "The Dogs", in the hands of its present owner, is a store of history.

Incidents from Wincanton's past linger in the folk memory of the people of the town. One is of a wounded officer who was taken into a cottage not far from "The Dogs". Dr. Mattar says that it is believed that William stayed on to see how he fared, and it is said that the ghost of the wounded man still haunts the cottage.

Whilst William was still in Wincanton, his army was already on the move towards Salisbury. Whittle says: "As the Lines advanced towards Sarum All along the West we dispers'd the Declarations; and where we hapn'd to quarter on Sunday, we read it there in the Church, as at Beminster, Collingburn Kingston and several other places."

By the time the Prince was ready to proceed, James had already left Salisbury in haste and returned to London. His appearance was such that Whittle in his Diary records, referring to the King: "and coming thus hastily to Windsor, the Towns-People that saw him judged he had been overthrown in Battel: so coming from Windsor to London, he turn'd out Sir Edw. Hales, who was Governor of the Tower, for he had threatened to Bomb this famous Ancient City, and put Mr. Skelton his late Ambassador in France, Governor, who was but a Prisoner there but a few days before."

After the discovery of his daughter's desertion, and the state of affairs in London, it became apparent to the King how desperate his own situation had become, and he began playing for time in which to plan his escape to France together with his wife and son. He called together his leading ministers, and it was decided that he should invite all the Lords Spiritual and Temporal in London at that time to "solemnly ask their advice" at a meeting the next day.

Tuesday, 27 November:

In the dining hall of the palace there met nine prelates and between thirty and forty Protestant noblemen. Though not Peers of England, Middleton and Preston, the two Secretaries of State, were also there. The King, showing the ravages of mental and physical stress, presided over the assembly. He opened the proceedings by referring to the petition for the convocation of a free Parliament which had been given to him before he left for Salisbury. He stated that as things were at that time he hadn't thought it right to agree to the request, but whilst he had been away from London great changes had taken place, and he had also noticed that his people "seemed anxious that the Houses should meet". Therefore he sought their advice on the matter.

Silence greeted his opening remarks. Then Oxford, "whose pedigree, unrivalled in antiquity and splendour," says Macaulay, "gave him a kind of primacy in the meeting," said that those Lords who had signed the petition ought to explain their views. Rochester then spoke up, and in defending the petition, said that he "still saw no hope for the throne or the country but in a Parliament," although in the present circumstances he thought that even that would not be an effective remedy, but he had no other course to offer. He added that it might be advisable to open negotiations with the Prince of Orange. Jeffreys and Godolphin both agreed with Rochester. Macaulay goes on:

"Then Clarendon rose, and to the astonishment of all who remembered his loud professions of loyalty, and the agony of shame and sorrow into which he had been

Opposite: His Majesty King James II.
Painted in 1684-85 by Godfrey Kneller. By the end of November in 1688 the King was agonising in London as the country slipped from his grasp. Courtesy of the National Portrait Gallery.

thrown only a few days before by the news of his son's defection, broke forth into a vehement invective against tyranny and popery."

Lord Clarendon himself has recorded the occasion in his Diary, where he says: "I spake with great freedom, laying open the most of the late miscarriages; and particularly the raising a regiment of Roman Catholics at this very time, under the command of the Earl of Stafford, to be a guard for the King's person; into which all the French tradesmen in town of that religion were received, and none were to be admitted but Papists. I pressed this so earnestly, that the King called out, and said it was not true; there were no directions for admitting none but Papists: but I went on, saying I had been so informed, &c. My motion was for the calling of a Parliament, and that commissioners might be presently appointed to go to the Prince of Orange in order to a treaty, to make the meeting of a Parliament practicable.

"Lord Halifax spoke very flatteringly; that he would not join in the petition, because he believed it would displease the King; and he should always be very tender of doing that: besides, he thought the meeting of a Parliament at this time very impracticable, though, he must own, he would never at any time advise against the calling of a Parliament: that the sending of commissioners to the Prince of Orange might do well, if the King would make some concessions by way of preliminaries, and would make all things more easy; that the doing of some things at one time might be interpreted to be prudent, which at another time might be thought too complying. This Lord is a strange man: if we would have petitioned at this time, and in his way, all had been well; the displeasing the King was not then thought of. Lord Nottingham endeavoured to cut a feather, and spake much in Lord Halifax's sense. Both these Lords laid all miscarriages open; though in smoother words than I had done. Several concessions were proposed by way of preliminaries; as a pardon to all who were any way engaged with the Prince of Orange, or with the Lords in the North; that the King should immediately put the Roman Catholics out of all employments, military and civil, &c. In conclusion, after a serious and warm debate, the King spake to this effect:- 'My Lords, I have heard you all: you have spoken with great freedom; and I do not take it ill of any of you. I may tell you I will call a Parliament; but for the other things you have proposed, they are of great importance; and you will not wonder that I take one night's time to consider of them.'

"It is to be observed, none of the Popish Lords were present at this meeting; which, I have been told, was prevented by my Lord Godolphin. The Lords Middleton and Preston, the two Secretaries, were present, and sat on each side of the King's chair at a little distance backwards. The King in the debate spake much of the defection of his army; yet seemed to think there were many who would be steady to him. He said he looked upon his bleeding at the nose to be a great providence; for, if it had not returned upon him on the day he intended to view some of his troops at Warminster, he had great reason to believe that Lord Churchill then designed to give him up to the Prince of Orange. The King further said that it would appear that the Prince of Orange came for the crown, whatever he pretended; but that he would not see himself deposed; that he had read the story of King Richard II." [Richard II was compelled to abdicate in 1399 in favour of Henry of Hereford, who had returned to England to reform the government and claim his inheritance].

Taunting the King, Lord Clarendon is reported to have said, "Sir, it is a maxim in our law that the King can do no wrong, but his Ministers may, and be called to an account for it, too. Now in the present juncture of affairs, what would you have us do to appease the nation, since the people have been so provoked by the Papists; as things stand now, what would you have us do for your Majesty's security? When your Majesty was at Salisbury, you might have had some remedy, but the people do now say that the King is run away with his army—we are left defenceless and must therefore side with the prevailing party."

James appeared to be very conciliatory after considering the outcome of the meeting with his advisers.

Wednesday, 28 November:

The King let it be known that a new Parliament was to be called for 13 January 1689, and informed Halifax that he had appointed three commissioners to discuss terms with the Prince of Orange, namely Halifax himself together with Nottingham and Godolphin. James told them that he was prepared to make great sacrifices for the sake of peace, to which Halifax replied, "Your Majesty must not expect that those who have the power in their hands will consent to any terms which would leave the laws at the mercy of the prerogative." Having made himself clear, he accepted the commission which the King wanted him to undertake.

James offered concessions which he had obstinately refused a few hours before. He repeated his offer of a free pardon to all those who had rebelled against him and even declared them eligible to become members of the forthcoming Parliament. They were not even required to lay down their arms. As Whittle recorded, Sir Edward Hales, a Papist, and one of the most unpopular men in the realm as the harsh gaoler of the Bishops, was dismissed from his post as Lieutenant of the Tower and replaced by his late prisoner, Bevil Skelton who, "though he held no high place in the esteem of his countrymen, was at least not disqualified by law for public trust".

Clarendon, in his diary of November 28th writes: "I was at Westminster Hall. The Lord Chancellor had orders to issue out writs for a Parliament to meet on the 15th of January next: this gives infinite satisfaction. Sir Henry Capell dined with me. I told him if the writs were out, I had thought of going to Sarum, to see if I could secure my son's being chosen for that county; and I would then go to the Prince of Orange. He desired to go with me; I promised he should know as soon as I had taken my resolution."

On Friday, 30 November, Lord Clarendon told Lord Halifax and Sir Henry Capell that now that the writs were issued for a Parliament, and a proclamation was due allowing "all men to go to the countries"; he decided to go to Sarum to the Prince of Orange the next day. Sir Henry asked to pick him up at Brentford. Clarendon's Diary continues:

Saturday, 1 December:

"About eight in the morning I set out from Jermin-street. The Lords Drogheda and Blessington went in the coach with me: Sir Arthur Coles, Sir Thomas Fotherly, Mr. Pitt [a younger son of Mr. George Pitt], and Mr. Thomas Jordan, of Witney, went on horseback, besides my own servants. We took up Sir Henry Capell at Brentford: at Staines we found the train of artillery coming from Sarum. At the bridge there was a guard; who only asked who we were, and let us pass. We dined at Bagshott, and in the evening came to Hartfordbridge, where we lay: we found here some of the King's carriages, which stayed for want of horses to bring them home."

Sunday, 2 December:

"We set out from Hartfordbridge as soon as it was light: Mr. Pitt stayed behind, pretending his horse was lame. We dined at Sutton, and got to Stockbridge by the time it was dark; where we lay. The ways were very bad. About midnight Mr. Kitson, brother to the woman of the inn at Hartfordbridge, (Who had been an ensign in Ireland in my time) came post into the house where we were. He came up into my chambers, and told me, about two hours after we were gone from Hartfordbridge, Mr. Pitt took post for London; which he thought strange; and not knowing what might happen, he thought fit to come and give us notice of it. Sir Henry Capell was extremely alarmed, and apprehended we might be taken and carried back; and therefore earnestly desired we might hasten to Sarum. I ordered the horses to be made ready with all speed.

Monday, 3 December:

"About three in the morning we took coach, and got to Sarum about seven. We alighted at the George inn, where we found the Dutch Ambassador: he came hither last night. He told us the Prince of Orange was at Hindon; . . . whereupon we went thither . . . We got thither about four o'clock: here I met my son. As soon as we alighted, we waited on the Prince: we found him in the room where he dined. He received us very obligingly, and after asking us some common questions of our journey, he took me into his bed-chamber; where he talked about half an hour with me. He said he was very glad to see me; that my son's coming over to him was a seasonable service, and he would always remember it."

Dr. Burnet, in his history of the times, describes the appointing of the King's commissioners to the Prince of Orange in these terms:

"The King now sent for all the lords in town, that were known to be firm protestants. And, upon speaking to some of them in private, they advised him to call a general meeting of all the privy councillors and peers, to ask their advice what was fit to be done. All agreed in one opinion that it was fit to send commissioners to the prince to treat with him. This went much against the King's inclinations, yet the dejection he was in, and the desperate state of his affairs, forced him to consent to it. So the marquis of Halifax, the earl of Nottingham, and the lord Godolphin, were ordered to go to the prince, and to ask him what it was that he demanded. The earl of Clarendon reflected the most, on the king's former conduct, of any in that assembly, not without some indecent and insolent words, which were generally condemned. He expected, as was said, to be one of the commissioners, and upon his not being named he came and met the prince near Salisbury. Yet he suggested so many peevish and peculiar things when he came, that some suspected all this was but collusion, and that he was sent to raise a faction among those that were about the prince. The lords sent to the prince to know where they should wait on him, and he named Hungerford."

It was when the Prince was leaving Wincanton that "a royal trumpeter arrived asking a pass for messengers to treat", so the Prince, together with his retinue, accompanied by Sir William Portman, set out for Hungerford by way of Mere and Salisbury.

Whilst he was advancing, news arrived in London of risings in other parts of the country. Lumley had taken Newcastle, where the inhabitants had welcomed him joyously. The King's statue had been hurled into the Tyne. Further south, at Hull, 3 December was long remembered as Towntaking Day. On that day the garrison commander there, Lord Langdale, a Roman Catholic, was arrested, and citizens and soldiers alike declared for the Protestant religion and a free Parliament.

"The Eastern counties were up," wrote Macaulay. "The Duke of Norfolk, attended by three hundred gentlemen armed and mounted, appeared in the stately market place of Norwich. The Mayor and Aldermen met him there, and engaged to stand by him against Popery and arbitrary power."

Amongst other activists were Lord Herbert of Cherbury and Sir Edward Harley, who took up arms in Worcestershire. The Earl of Shrewsbury, unhindered, entered the opened gates of Bristol, the second city of the realm.

Wilton House, the seat of Thomas Herbert, eighth Earl of Pembroke.
William visited the mansion, which John Webb had rebuilt in 1648, and was joined there by the Prince of Denmark. Photograph from the Earl of Pembroke's collection.

Macaulay goes on: "The people of Gloucester rose and delivered Lord Lovelace from confinement. An irregular army soon gathered round him. ["rusty ruffians" as Clarendon called them. Shades of the Monmouth rebellion!] Some of his horsemen had only halters for bridles. Many of his infantry had only clubs for weapons. But this force, such as it was, marched unopposed through counties once devoted to the House of Stuart, and at length entered Oxford in triumph. The magistrates came in state to welcome the insurgents. The University itself, exasperated by recent injuries, was little disposed to pass censure on rebellion." The Heads of Colleges had already sent Dr. Finch to Crewkerne to assure the Prince of their support.

The rhythm of the tune "Lillibulero" was beaten on the drums to cheers as Lord Lovelace, the Whig leader, rode through this stronghold of Toryism, followed by a long procession of horse and foot. Orange ribbons decked the High Street, for already the orange ribbon had become the symbol of civil and religious freedom to the Protestants, as it is today in the troubles in Northern Ireland.

By now, the leisurely advance of William through the West Country had become more of a grand tour as he and his forces steadily approached Salisbury in fine, wintry weather. Clarendon had been joined by the Earl of Oxford and others who had previously denied any connection with the Prince. In his private conversation with William in the Prince's bedchamber, Clarendon records: "He then asked me several questions—How the King came to leave Sarum so suddenly? What was done at the meeting of the Lords on Tuesday last? When the commissioners would be with him? And what their business was? I found by his discourse that the Dutch Ambassador had given him pretty perfect accounts of most things. I told him that the business of the commissioners, as far as I understood, was to agree upon ways to make the meeting of the Parliament safe and easy; that they intended to set out as soon as they had their passes. He asked me what was the general opinion, and what I thought of things. I said, that if his Highness pursued his declaration, we might quickly hope to see a happy settlement. He replied, 'My declaration shall be punctually observed'. He said he had but little acquaintance with Lord Nottingham; but that he did a little wonder, the Lords Halifax and Godolphin came to him in this errand. I then asked him when he went from this place? He said he would go tomorrow to Sarum, and stay one day there."

Tuesday, 4 December:

The Prince took the opportunity of visiting the area round about, and having breakfasted at Berwick St. Leonard, he travelled through Wylye to take in Wilton on the way into Salisbury.

Wilton, a friendly old Wiltshire market town, is an ancient Royal Borough, and claims to be the original capital of Wessex. It stands at the junction of the rivers Wylye and Nadder, about 3 miles west of Salisbury. Wilton House, the seat of the Earl of Pembroke, is famous for its connections with such Elizabethans as Shakespeare and Sidney. It houses a remarkable collection of portraits by Van Dyke, amongst which are paintings of Charles I, who loved Wilton, and Prince Rupert of the Rhine. Prince William went in to see the house and gardens, and he was joined there by the Prince of Denmark.

Clarendon rode ahead of the royal party, and at the bridge at "Salisbury town's end," he found the "Mayor and his bretheren in their formalities". He told them that the Prince of Orange would not be coming in that way, and that they had better make their way to the town hall [Council House] and that he would send a message to them when he arrived. So they did as he advised.

Throughout his journey from Berwick to Salisbury the people flocked to see Prince William, and prayed to God to bless him. As he rode past, he raised his hat and said; "Thank you, good people; I am come to secure the Protestant religion, and to free you from Popery." Whittle gives a graphic account of the entry of the Prince into the city of Salisbury at about 3 o'clock in the afternoon:

"Now the Army being advanced near Sarum, and the first Line being in the City, the second at Wilton and the Towns adjacent, and the Rear Line at Tevent and Dinton; one Line about two or three miles off the City, and the other about seven or eight. The Prince of Orange, with his Highness the Prince of Denmark, his Grace the Duke of Ormond, Mareschal Schomberg, Count Solms, Count Nassau, Heer Zulustein, Heer Benting, Heer Overkirk, the Earl of Shrewsbury, Lord Viscount Mordant, the Earl of Macclesfield, Lord Wiltshire, Lord Cornbury, Lord Colchester, and sundry other Lords, Sir Will. Portman, Sir Rowland Gwynn, Col. Sidney, and many other Knights and Gentlemen, rode into the famous City of Salisbury.

"The manner of their Entrance into this City, was far more glorious than that of Exeter; for here the Mayor and Aldermen met his Highness the Prince of Orange in all their Formalties. First of all marched the Regiment of Foot Guards belonging to Count Solms, with their Colours flying, Drums beating, Hoitboys playing; the People thronging in the Street, and making great Acclamations. Next, some Troops of Horse, with their Kettle-Drums beating, Colours flourishing, Trumpets sounding, the Officers shewing their Courtesy to the People: Then came his Highness the Prince of Orange, with the Prince of Denmark on his right Hand, and the Duke of Ormond on his Left. Never were Windows more crowded with Faces of both Sexes than here; never were Bells ringing more melodiously than now at Sarum; never were People shouting and echoing forth Huzza's in the Air more than now. The Bishop's Palace there being the best and most meet place, both the Princes rode thither, altho afterwards his Highness Prince George went to the quarters assign'd him."

Great excitement in Salisbury

THERE WERE countless spectators, and their excitement was inexhaustible. Crowds from all parts of the surrounding countryside poured into the city to see the Prince, whom they looked on as their country's saviour and the protector of their religion and their laws. So the people greeted the Prince, perhaps with rather more enthusiasm than they had given to James a few days earlier.

In the Fabric Accounts for 1688-89 for Salisbury Cathedral, the following entries are interesting, as they show the Dean and Chapter going with the prevailing wind of change:

No. 19. Ringing when King James came to ye town . . . . £1.4s.
Dec. 4. Ringing when the Prince of Orang came to town £1.
ffeb. 16. Ringing when Kg Willi & Queen Mary were proclaimed . . . . 14s.
18. Ringing on the same occasion . . . . £1.4s.

In a footnote, Colt Hoare shows costs for two other churches in the town: The Churchwardens' Accounts of St. Thomas for the year 1688-9.

Paid for ringing when the King came to town . . . . 10s.
Paid for ringing the thanksgiving day, for the Prince of Orange . . . . £1.2s.
Paid Brown for a form of Prayer for the King and Queen . . . . 1s. 6d.
Paid for ringing when the King was proclaimed . . . . 10s.
Churchwardens' Accounts B.

The accounts of St. Edmunds contain similar items.

Salisbury is a city, a municipal borough, and the county town of Wiltshire. The glorious Cathedral, a perfect example of Early English architecture, was built almost entirely in the 13th Century. Its spire, at 404 ft., is the highest in England and the building is noted for its perfect proportions.

William's great strength was that he was prudent and cautious in his progress towards the English throne. He had always waited to be invited by the people before he made any important move, and he carefully considered the situation before accepting any invitation to treat with those in power. So far, the Prince's venture had been most successful, and had exceeded the highest expectations of those surrounding him, but inevitably there were factions and jealousies among those who had come to support him, and they were divided into two parties. There were the Whigs, many of whom had spent years in exile, out of favour with the King. They would hear of no compromise with regard to the future of James II. They had initially prophesied that he would not be a good King, and now that their worst fears had been realised, they were not willing to leave him on the throne. On the other hand, many Tories were enthusiastic followers of the Prince, and some of these wished to see some form of reconciliation with the King which would not lower the Royal dignity. These men were not traitors, but had taken up arms because they felt that this was the best way of rendering service to the throne—namely to rescue his Majesty, by a little coercion, from the hands of wicked counsellors. Only William's wisdom kept the rival factions from open animosity. Macaulay sums up the situation:

"Surrounded by eager disputants, officious advisers, abject flatterers, vigilant spies, malicious talebearers, he remained serene and inscrutable. He preserved silence while silence was possible. When he was forced to speak, the earnest and peremptory tone in which he uttered his well weighed opinions soon silenced everybody else. Whatever some of his too zealous adherents might say, he uttered not a word indicating any design

The Old Council House, Market Square, Salisbury.
James and, later, William, were received by civic dignitaries. The building burnt down in 1780 and the present Guildhall is on its site.

on the English crown. He was well aware that one false step could bring insurmountable problems.

"Those who ventured to interrogate him learned nothing, and yet could not accuse him of shuffling. He quietly referred them to his Declaration, and assured them that his views has undergone no change since that instrument had been drawn up. So skilfully did he manage his followers that their discord seems rather to have strengthened than to have weakened his hands."

But when William was not in control, their dissension broke up friendly meetings, and even spread so far as to ignore the sanctity of the house of God. An episode which disgusted every good Tory happened in Salisbury Cathedral. Burnet, whose numerous good qualities did not include self-restraint or delicacy, made an exhibition of himself. When the officiating minister read the collect for the King, Burnet "rose from his knees, sat down in his stall, and made an ugly noise with his mouth". When Clarendon asked him later why he had behaved like that, he said that he could not join in the collect for the King.

Some days had passed since the royal Commissioners had been appointed, and the delay in ordering them to proceed seems strange in the light of the prevailing urgency, but it appears that neither James nor William was in a hurry to begin negotiations. James needed time to make his personal plans and preparations, and William's position daily became stronger. Ultimately the Prince informed the Commissioners that he would meet them at Hungerford.

Thursday, 6 December:

After resting one night at Salisbury, the Prince resumed his march and took the route to Oxford, following after the disordered regiments of the royal army. Lord Clarendon records that William left Salisbury at about eleven o'clock in the morning, and that he hoped to lodge that night at Collingbourne. The army, which had already left the Salisbury area, was enjoying the conditions underfoot. The springy turf of

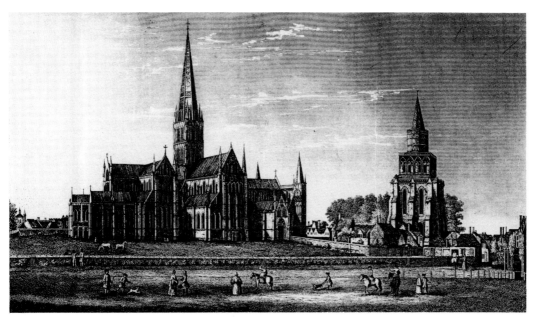

Salisbury Cathedral and the separate Bell Tower.
Its bells rang for James, and similarly for William.

Salisbury Plain seemed "luxuriously smooth to men who had been toiling through the miry ruts of Devonshire and Somersetshire highways". Their route took them close to Stonehenge, and the regiments stopped to look at the "mysterious ruin, celebrated all over the Continent as the greatest wonder of our Island".

Whittle describes the scene as they left Salisbury: "After some stay here, the Prince of Orange went to Am[s]bury, attended with the Duke of Ormond, and many of the English Nobility and Gentry, besides Dutch, Scotch, and French. The first Line was advanced towards the most renowned City of London, a considerable way, the Roads here being good for marching: and as the Regiments marched over the Plains, they made pleasant Figures, sometimes marching in Battalia, and sometimes in a Line: The Weather now was very favourable, and the way very good. And being to march near one of the Wonders of the World, called Stonehenge, most Regiments made an halt to view this strange Sight; none that saw it could render any satisfactory Account concerning it: Certain Officers ask'd the Minister of Am[s]bury what was his Opinion, because they presumed 'twas within the Bounds of his Parish; who told them, that he supposed it to be a Trophy, or Monument erected in token of some notable Victory which was obtain'd there: I must confess, this is the general Opinion of the greatest Antiquaries of our Nation.

"The Custom of erecting a Trophy, or Monument, in token of Victory is of great Antiquity, and first began among the Greeks, who used in that place where the Enemies were vanquish'd to cut down the Boughs of great Trees, and in the Stocks, or Bodies of them, to hang up Armour, or other Spoils, taken from the Enemy. Others argued strongly that these prodigious Stones were brought out of Ireland by Merlin's Magical Art, and so curiously fram'd and put together. To corroborate this Opinion, they assured us, that a piece broken off from these Stones, and put into the Wall of any Well, or cast into the Water, shall, for certain, kill and destroy all the venomous Creatures therein.

'One of the Wonders of the World, called Stonehenge.'
Reverend John Whittle's words: William's men were its visitors of the day. This 1810 print, by French
traveller L. Simond, is from Rodney Legg's *Stonehenge Antiquaries* [Dorset Publishing Company, 1986].

"To proceed, the Army moved daily according to the Motion of his Highness, who
rode from Am[s]bury unto a certain Gentleman's House near Collingburn
[Collingbourne Kingston]. The late King James being almost past all hopes, sent the
Marquess of Hallifax, Earl of Nottingham, and the Lord Godolphin as Commissioners,
to treat with the Prince of Orange, immediately; and a Trumpeter was sent down to
know his Highness's pleasure, Whether he would admit them as such? And his
Highness was pleased to grant them leave. The place appointed them was Hungerford.
His Highness with all his Nobles, went to Littlecott, December 8."

Friday, 7 December:

Having visited Hampsted Marshall, known as a "Miniature Heidelburg",on the way
to visit a stately mansion belonging to the Earl of Craven, the Prince reached
Hungerford just before dark.

Hungerford is a market town in Berkshire on the River Kennet. Four miles away is
the well known landmark Inkpen Beacon, one of the two peaks of the highest chalk
downs in the country, and also nearby is Littlecote, recognised as one of the finest
manor houses in England. William, escorted by a strong body of troops, took up his
lodgings at the Bear Inn in the town centre. The little town was soon full of nobles and
high ranking officers. "The northern Lords brought with them hundreds of irregular
cavalry, whose accoutrements and horsemanship moved the mirth of men accustomed to
the splendid aspect and exact movements of regular armies," wrote Macaulay.

The Commissioners, having left the capital, made their first stop at Windsor, where
they stayed the night, and then they moved on to Reading. Here, they found their
messenger dead drunk, and there was some delay whilst another, more trustworthy,
man was found to ride to the Prince of Orange. This caused a delay at Hungerford.
Halifax records that he and his fellow Commissioners received their passes on the
5 December; on the next day they went on to Andover, and on 7 December they took up
their quarters, which the Prince had arranged for them, at Ramsbury. He informed
them that he would expect them at 9 o'clock on the following morning at Hungerford.

Saturday, 8 December:

"The Commissioners, the Marquis of Halifax, Earl of Nottingham, and Lord Godolphin came to the Prince. The Foot Guards were drawn up, and drums beat as they passed. The Prince called several English Nobles to him, then Monsieur Bentinck, Lord Chamberlain, led the Commissioners to the Prince. They had desired to speak with him in private, but he refused, without the Lords present."

Clarendon goes on to say that the Prince received them in his bed-chamber, and "as soon as the Commissioners had delivered their errand by word of mouth, and their credentials, they withdrew into a room appointed for them. Mr Bentinck attended them. The Prince then read the King's letter to the company. It was in French; upon which he said (and I thought it came with some tenderness from him) this was the first letter he had ever had from the King in French; that he always used to write to him in English, and in his own hand. I took the liberty to say, 'Sir, your Highness being here as a foreign Prince, and this being a formal credential, (which are in Latin or French) it ought to be in the Secretary's hand'."

The Prince then asked the Commissioners to put into writing all that they had said to him, and he sent the Earl of Oxford, Clarendon and Marshal Schomberg to join them. William then sent for Dr. Burnet, as Clarendon had told him that Halifax desired to see him. Although Halifax and Burnet were completely different characters, "Burnet was utterly destitute of delicacy and tact, Halifax's taste was fastidious, and his sense of the ludicrous morbidly quick," nevertheless they had been friends for a long time, and were "drawn to each other by a mutual attraction." They liked each other's conversation, and each appreciated the other's abilities, interchanged opinions freely, and interchanged also good offices in perilous times. This time, however, Halifax wanted to talk to Burnet because the Commissioners were anxious to obtain some inside information on the Prince's plans. Burnet was notoriously garrulous and indiscrete, and Halifax could easily have manipulated him. William well knew this, and could not refrain from exclaiming to Clarendon on hearing of Halifax's request, "If they get together there will be fine tattling." The request was denied.

The garrulous Doctor himself made records: "When they [the Commissioners] came thither [to Hungerford] and had delivered their message, the Prince called all the peers and others of chief note about him, and advised with them what answers should be made. A day was taken to consider of an answer. The Marquis of Halifax sent for me. But the Prince said, though he would suspect nothing from our meeting, others might. So I did not speak with him in private, but in the hearing of others. Yet he took occasion to ask me, so as nobody observed it, 'If we had a mind to have the King in our hands?' I said, 'By no means; for we would not hurt his person.' He asked next, 'What if he had a mind to go away?' I said, 'Nothing was so much to be wished for.' This I told the Prince. And he approved of both my answers. The Prince ordered the Earls of Oxford, Shrewsbury, and Clarendon, to treat with the lords the King had sent. And they delivered the Prince's answer to them on Sunday the eighth of December.

"He desired a parliament might be presently called, that no men should continue in any employment who were not qualified by law, and had not taken the tests; that the Tower of London might be put in the keeping of the City; that the fleet, and all the strong places of the kingdom, might be put in the hands of protestants; that a proportion of the revenue might be set off for the pay of the prince's army; and that during the sitting of the parliament, the armies of both sides might not come within twenty miles of London; but, that the Prince might come on to London, and have the same number of his guards about him that the King kept about his person. The lords seemed to be very well satisfied with this answer. They sent it up by an express, and went back next day to London."

The paper in which the Commissioners set out what they had told the Prince is contained in the *Notes of Halifax,* from a sheet printed by Joshua Churchill for William Churchill, 1688, and authorised by the Prince of Orange, as follows:

"Hungerford Decemb: 8 1688.

"Sir,—The King commandeth us to acquaint you, that he observeth all the Differences and Causes of Complaint alledged by your Highness, seems to be referr'd to a Free Parliament.

"His Majesty as he hath already declared, was resolved before this to call one, but thought that in this present state of affairs, it was advisable to defer it till things were more composed.

"Yet seeing that his People still continue to desire it he hath put forth his Proclamation in order to it, and hath Issued forth his Writs for the Calling of it.

"And to prevent any cause of interruption in it, he will consent to everything that can be reasonably required for the Security of all those that shall come to it.

"His Majesty hath therefore sent us to attend your Highness for the adjusting of all Matters that shall be agreed to be necessary to the freedom of Elections, and the Security of Sitting, and is ready immediately to enter into a Treaty in order to it.

"His Majesty proposeth, that in the mean time, the respective Armies may be restrained, within such Limits, and at such a distance from London, as may prevent the Apprehensions that the Parliament may be in any kind disturbed, being desirous that the Meeting of it may be no longer delayed than it must be by the usual and neccesary forms. (Signed Hallifax, Nottingham, Godolphin.)"

There is also a letter describing the day's proceedings written by the Commissioners to the Earl of Middleton, Secretary of State, from "Ramesbury House, 8. Dre. 88."

"My Lord,—We were last night appointed to wait of the Prince at 10 a clock this morning at Hungerford; when we came thither, We found the Prince with severall Lords about him, and having delivered him his Ma'ties Letter, We asked him, if we should say to him what we had in command, there; or if he would hear Us elsewhere? hee replyed, there; And then I the M. of Hallifax, delivered him what we had aggreed should be said; a Copy whereof goeth herewith inclosed. The Prince said he did not doubt but We had seen his Declaration and he had little more to say, than what was therein expressed, touching the Grounds and reasons, of his Coming into England, which was to maintain the Protestant Religion, and to preserve the Lawes, and liberties of the people; But that those Lords who had joined with him, being concerned in the matter, he would send some of them to speak with us further about it.

"Being retired into another Room, there came to Us presently after, the M'al de Schomberg, and ye Earles of Oxford and Clarendon, who from ye Prince, desired Us to putt into Writing what had been said, and to signe it, that the Lords might consider it; which We did and delivered it to them; who Carried it back to the Prince; and in a little while after M'or. Benting came to Us, and told us from the Prince, he would give Us an Answer to morrow; and We intend accordingly to go and receive it at Littlecott, whither ye Prince is removed this night, by reason of the straitnesse and inconveniencie of his Quarters at Hungerford. We observed that there was particular care taken, that none of the English should speake to Us, the reason for it being given Us, that it was to avoyd giving any Cause of Jealousy to any of ye Lords who might be disposed to it; and it was hinted to Us, that many of the Lords are very suspicious, least an Accomodation should be made which might not provide so largely for their Security as they expected.

"M'or Benting came from ye Prince and invited us to dinner, and nothing passed but indifferent things; After dinner We had promiscuous discourse with severall of the English who came into the Room where the Prince had dined, and by that means and by putting together severall things that were says to Us there, we cannot but form some kind of Conjecture, tho We are not able to determine anything positively, till we receive an Answer to what We delivered.

"That which We apprehend At present is, yt there is no kind of Disposition to stopp the march of their Army; the Generall opinion of the Lords and other English being so much against it, that there is little grounds to hope, that the Prince will go about to Over-rule it.

"Some of the particulars which We can gather by common discourse, they may probably insist upon, are these: That all Papists be removed out of all offices and Trusts, Military as well as Civill, for while any of that party have armes in their hands, they cannot think their sitting in Parliament sufficiently secured, That they cannot accept of any Pardons, for that they will thereby own themselves to be Criminalls; But expect to have some Declaration that what they have done, in defence of the Lawes, needs no Pardon.

"It is also sayd by some, that tho' they could be secure in coming to Parliament, yet if the King should bee perswaded to Dissolve it, before their Grievances bee redressed, and their Libertyes secured, it would be a certaine delay, and very much hazzard their dessein for the Good of the Publick, wch by the methods they are now in, they think, they shall quickly obtaine;

"These things We desire your Ldp to lay before his Ma'tie as Our Conjectures onely; which wee thought our duty to send by Expresse, that We might give his Maiestie all the Light we can as soon as may be.

We remaine, My Lord,

Your Lordps Most faithfull humble Servants

Halifax.   Nottingham.   Godolphin.

"We must not Omitt to tell yor Ldps that ye Association wch was begun in Devonshire is signed by all Noblemen and Gent whatsoever that come in to ye Prince as he marcheth."

This despatch must have seemed ominous to James when he received it at Whitehall the next day.

At the Bear Inn William had said that he wanted the answer to the King's communication to be representative of the Lords and Gentlemen who had been with him at the meeting as well as from himself, so he said that he would withdraw and leave them to discuss it amongst themselves. After dinner he went to Littlecote Hall, about two miles from Hungerford, and decided to leave the Bear Inn and stay there instead, as the inn was "very unquiet". Since they would need the afternoon to prepare their reply, he asked his Lords to bring it to him in the evening. There was much wrangling before a rough draft was prepared and taken to the Prince, and further heated argument before he calmly overruled his aggressive followers and announced that he would have the answer "fairly transcribed" and handed to the Commissioners at a meeting at Littlecote the following morning.

Littlecote, near Hungerford.
Here the Prince of Orange received King James's commissioners.

William's bedroom at Littlecote.
The room where William of Orange slept; a print of him as King William III hangs beside the four-poster.
The large tapestry over the fireplace is one of 16 made for him in Brussels.
Photographs courtesy Country Life.

Sunday, 9 December:

According to the Halifax papers, the terms which were offered to James were as follows:

"We with the Advise of the Lords and Gentlemen assembled with Us have in answer made these following Proposals.

"I. That all Papists, and such Persons as are not qualified at Law, be Disarmed, Disbanded and Removed from all Employments Civil and Military.

"II. That all Proclamations which reflect upon us, or have come to us, or declared for us, be recalled, and that if any persons for having so assisted us have been committed, that they be forthwith set at liberty.

"III. That for the Security and Safety of the City of London, the Custody and Government of the Tower be immediately put into the hands of the said City.

"IV. That if His Majesty should think fit to be in London during the Sitting of the Parliament, that we may be there also with an equal number of our Guards, or if His Majesty shall be pleased to be in any place from London, at whatever distance he thinks fit, that we may be at a place of the same distance. And that the respective Armies do remove from London 40 miles. And that no further forces be brought into the Kingdom.

"V. That for the Security of the City of London, and their Trade, Tilbury Fort be put in the hands of the said City.

"VI. That to prevent the Landing of French or other Forreign Troops, Portsmouth may be put into such hands, as by Your Majesty and Us shall be agreed on.

"VII. That some sufficient part of the publick Revenue be assigned us, for the Support and Maintenance of our Forces, till the meeting of a Free Parliament.

Given at Littlecote, the ninth of December, 1688.   Prince of Orange".

These were firm but reasonable requirements, and showed that James could keep the throne, but with diminished authority.

Monday, 10 December:

The Commissioners returned the following reply:

"Upon consideration of the Princes answer, delivered by the Earles of Oxford and Shrewsbury and Monsr Bentinck, We offer to his Hss that there are some particulars therein contain'd, to which We had power to have aggreed; But there are others of such a nature that are above our Commission to determine, wch makes it necessary that they should be presented to the King; And altho' the most expeditious way of knowing his mind might be to receive it by Expresse, Yet we conceive it may be more effectuall for Us to lay them before Him ourselves. In the mean time we propose that ye Prince will not permitt any of his Troopes to advance nearer to London, than the distance of 30 sic miles mentioned in one of the articles of his Hss's paper, till after Thursday night, wch by our Computation is the soonest that an Answer can be returned. Littlecott ye 10th of Decr 1688.   Halifax   Nottingham   Godolphin "

Halifax concludes with: "The Commissioners despatched their intelligence by express to Whitehall, and took their own departure to town."

At this time, whilst William was at Hungerford, a sharp encounter took place between two hundred and fifty of the Prince's troops and six hundred Irish, who were stationed at Reading. William's well-disciplined forces, although greatly outnumbered, created havoc among the Irish, whom they had come upon within the town itself. They charged furiously, and the Irish retreated in disorder through the street and into the market place. Here they attempted to make a stand, but with the invaders attacking them from the front, and the inhabitants shooting at them from the windows of their houses, the Irish soldiers broke and fled, leaving behind their colours and fifty dead. Of William's force, five men only fell. The event did not upset the nobles who had joined the Prince, because the Dutch had not defeated the English, "but had assisted an English town to free itself from the insupportable dominion of the Irish".

Whittle, with greater modesty, puts the number of Irish slain at "about 20". He says; "As part of our Regiments of Horse were coming to Reading, the Irish Souldiers gave out great swelling Words, and lofty Speeches, how they would hack them to pieces there, and how they would defend the seven Bridges; This was on the Lord's Day. (And as we were informed there, by divers Persons of Credit, they designed to massacre the People at their Worship, had they not been prevented) which obliged the Inhabitants to send to the advanc'd part of the Prince's Army, then a few miles distant, who readily came to their Assistance, being conducted a by-way into the Town, and fought so courageously, that in a few minutes they put the Irish to flight, took some, and kill'd about 20 upon the place, with the loss only of the Officer that led them, and the Guide that conducted them into the Town."

Whilst the advanced forces were engaged at Reading, Whittle reports a false alarm in one of the villages near Hungerford. "The first Line," he writes, "was now advanced to Newberry [Newbury], the second to Hungerford, and the Rear Line to Collingburn Kingstone, and the adjacent Villages; who on Saturday Night December 8th, received an Alarm (tho it proved a false One) sundry Tradesmen riding home from Hungerford Market, late in the Evening, were seen by some of our Scouts, who presently apprehended them to be a Party of the Enemy's Horse (being 'twas both late and dark) who thereupon speedily made report unto some of the Officers commanding in Chief; insomuch that the Souldiers were knock'd up in their Quarters to come presently to their Arms: The Country People were thereupon in a great fear, not knowing what to do; and this Alarm came from one Regiment to another; for Colonel Fagell's Regiment sent to advertise the Regiment of Colonel Sidney, That they might be ready to receive the Enemy. Now they thought this Alarm the rather to be true, because they had heard, that the late King James's Souldiers were resolv'd to make an Attempt upon those Men with the Artillery and Magazine, That, if possible, they might destroy our great Guns and Ammunition. The Souldiers being thus hurried out of their Beds, ran here and there to seek the Enemy: thus were they marching to and fro the whole Night in the Rain. The Morrow Morning (being the Lord's Day) divers Officers went to search the Woods near to the place where those Tradesmen were first seen, lest they should lie in Ambush till the Regiments were march'd away, and then attack the Artillery and Magazine-Forces: But none could be found, or heard of thereabout; only they were now inform'd of these Tradesmen, and so they return'd to their Regiments."

As for King James, it now became obvious to the Commissioners, whom he had deliberately insulted by failing to await their return from Hungerford, and to the rest of the world, that he had merely pretended to make concessions only as a sop to the Lords and to the nation in order to conceal his true intentions. In a letter to the French Ambassador on December 1, he showed that he did not propose to conduct any negotiations with the Prince of Orange: "This negotiation is a mere feint. I must send commissioners to me nephew that I may gain time to ship off my wife and the Prince of Wales. You know the temper of my troops. None but the Irish will stand by me, and the Irish are not in sufficient force to resist the enemy. A Parliament would impose on me conditions that I could not endure. I should be forced to undo all that I have done for the Catholics and to break with the King of France. As soon therefore as the Queen and my child are safe I will leave England and take refuge in Ireland, or with your master."

Even though the proposals put forward by William in his message to the King were moderate, as even James admitted, the King had already arranged for his Queen and the Prince of Wales to escape to France, and it was suspected by all save the moderate Papists that he would soon follow them. Whilst the Commissioners were in Hungerford, the Prince of Wales arrived at Westminster. Macaulay says that it had been intended that he should come over London Bridge, and some Irish troops had been sent to Southwark to meet him, but they were received by a great multitude with such hostility, hooting and execration that they thought it advisable "to retire with all speed." The Prince of Wales then crossed the Thames at Kingston, and was brought secretly into Whitehall from Portsmouth, where the King had earlier sent him, expecting him to be safe there, where there was a garrison manned by Roman Catholic officers. Lord Dartmouth was in command of the fleet there. One of the most loyal of the Protestant Tories, he had, to the King's utter disbelief, refused a royal order to take the infant prince to France, saying that it was no longer possible nor desirable to carry out this course of action. He was to receive a bitter letter from James on December 14th, but by that time he had chosen to support William, and had surrendered the fleet to the Prince:

"My affairs are, as you know, in so desperat a condition that I have been obliged to send away the Queen and the Prince, to secure them at least, what so ever becoms of me, that I am resolued to ventur all rather than consent to anything in the least prejuditial to the crowne or my concience, and hauing been basely deserted by many officers and souldiers of my troups, and finding such an infection gott amongst very many of those who still continu with me on shore, and that the same poysone is gott among the fleett, as you yourself owne to me in some of your letters, I could no longer resolue to expose myself to no purpose to what I might expect from the ambitious Prince of Orange and the assosiated rebellious Lords, and therefore haue resolued to withdraw till this violent storme is over . . . I know not whether any of the fleett vnder your command are free to continu seruing me; if they are, their best course will be to go to Ireland, where there are still some that will stick to me. If any are free to go order them thither to follow such orders as they shall receue from Lord Tryconnel. If they will not there is no remedy, and this I may say, never any Prince took more care of his sea and land men as I haue done, and been so very ill repayd by them."

The King discovered that it was not easy to find an Englishman of rank and honour who would take the responsibility of placing the heir apparent of the English throne in the hands of the King of France. Finally he arrived at a solution to his problem. He remembered that there was living in London a French nobleman, Antonine, Count of Lauzun, who had been a favourite of Louis XIV, but who had fallen into disgrace. He had then been forgiven for his misdemeanours and although not allowed at Court, was free to enjoy his liberty. He was well received at Whitehall, where his courage and his sense of honour were recognised. When asked if he would escort the royal refugees to France he felt that he might return with honour to his own country as the guardian of the Queen of England and the Prince of Wales, and he readily accepted the responsibility.

Arrangements were to be made for the royal party to go to Gravesend, where a boat would be waiting for them, but this was more easily said than done. The city was in an uproar. A crowd would assemble at the slightest excuse, and no foreigner could appear on the street without being apprehended and taken to a magistrate on suspicion of being a Jesuit in disguise. At the palace, every precaution was taken to give the appearance of normality. On the night of 9 December the King and Queen retired as usual. When all was quiet James rose and summoned his servant. "You will find," said the King, "a man at the door of the antechamber. Bring him hither." The servant duly returned with Lauzun, and led him into the King's bedchamber. "I confide to you," said James, "my Queen and my son. Everything must be risked to carry them into France." Lauzun thanked him for the dangerous honour which he had conferred upon him, and begged permission for his trusted friend Saint Victor, a gentleman of Provence, to help him, to which the King readily agreed.

Lauzun took Mary by the hand, and wrapped the baby prince in his warm cloak, then they crept down back stairs to the Thames and embarked in an open skiff. It was a miserable voyage. "The night was bleak, the rain fell, the wind roared, the water was rough. At length the boat reached Lambeth, and the fugitives landed near an inn, where a coach and horses were waiting. It took some time for the horses to be harnessed, and Mary, afraid that she might be recognised, would not enter the inn, but cowered with her child under the tower of Lambeth Church. She was terrified whenever the ostler came near her with his lantern. There were two foreign women attending her, but they were of little use to the Queen, for they could hardly speak any English, and they hated the cold English climate. All through this nightmare the baby lay quietly in his mother's arms, and uttered no sound. At last the coach was ready, and they set off, with Saint Victor following on horseback. At Gravesend a yacht awaited them, with Lord Powis and his wife on board together with three Irish officers to guard them. All but Saint Victor went aboard, and the yacht cast off and sailed away down the river with a fair wind, while Saint Victor sped back to Whitehall with the good news.

Monday, 10 December:

At about the same time that James was informed that his wife and son were on their way to France, and that there seemed every hope of the voyage being successful, a courier arrived at the palace with the despatches from Hungerford. Macaulay observes; "Had James been a little more discerning, or a little less obstinate, those despatches would have induced him to reconsider all his plans. The Commissioners wrote hopefully. The conditions proposed by the conqueror were strangely liberal. The King himself could not refrain from exclaiming that they were more favourable than he could have expected.

"But it soon appeared that William had perfectly understood the character with which he had to deal, and in offering those terms which the Whigs at Hungerford had considered too indulgent, had risked nothing. The solemn farce by which the public had been amused since the retreat of the royal army from Salisbury was prolonged during a few hours. All the lords who were still in the capital were invited to the palace that they might be informed of the progress of the negotiations which had been opened by their advice."

Halifax reports on the happenings of that day:

"During the day the King had held a variety of private interviews. About midnight the Earl of Ailesbury, a Gentleman of the Bedchamber, obtained an audience, and, taxing his Majesty with his intention of flight, implored him in moving terms to rescind so fatal a resolution. James, after a vain attempt at prevarication, at length begged the Question. 'If I should go, who can wonder after the treatment I have found? My daughter hath deserted me, my army also, and him that I raised from nothing. . . I knew not who to speak to, or who to trust.' Lord Ailesbury with passionate vehemence implored him to march on Nottingham; pressed upon him protestations of fidelity from the remaining officers, which he had been charged to deliver; and, when argument appeared useless, implored his Sovereign at least to await the report of his Commissioners. On retiring from the presence, Ailesbury met Lord Middleton with the despatches, and asked him, what news from the Commissioners? 'As far as I remember,' records Ailesbury, 'his answer was neither good nor bad.' In the Court at large, however, their arrival inspired some transient cheer; it was understood 'that they expressed his Highnesse's inclination to treat and gave more hope of the situation'. James said aloud, 'that is very good, my Lord; tomorrow, at nine o'clock, I will return an answer to your office'. A few minutes later he retired, and as he stepped into bed observed in a whisper to Lord Mulgrave 'that his Commissioners had newly sent him a very hopeful account of some good accommodation with the Prince of Orange'. He owned, however, that the Prince still approached London—an expression which must refer either to the Prince's intention of repairing to the capital for the session, or to the fact that Hungerford is more than thirty miles beyond the prescribed radius. A few minutes later the King silently rose, and having cancelled the writs for that Parliament, concerning which the treaty was even then in progress, he despatched a letter to the Earl of Feversham, commanding in chief, which that officer interpreted as a direction to disband his men. About three o'clock in the morning his Majesty left the palace by a secret door; and carrying with him, in the avowed intention that anarchy might succeed his flight, that mystic legal talisman, the Great Seal, he took the road to Sheerness."

James had instructed his Lord of the Bedchamber, Northumberland, not to open the door of his bedroom until the usual hour the next morning. On slipping secretly away he was met by Sir Edward Hales with a hackney coach and taken to Millbank, where he crossed the Thames in a small wherry. As he passed Lambeth, popular belief has it that he flung the Great Seal into the river. He landed at Vauxhall, where a carriage and horses awaited him, and he set off for Sheerness, where a boy from the Custom House had been ordered to await his arrival.

There is considerable doubt about the true fate of the Great Seal. That James dropped it into the Thames, from where it was recovered by chance some months later when a fisherman hauled it up in his net, is one legend. On the other hand, Barillon, the French Ambassador to England at this time, is quoted in Mavure's *Histoire de la Révolution* as having said that it was taken away by a Father Peters, who left the country a day or two before the King. It would normally have been in the keeping of Jeffreys, the Lord Chancellor, but James, in conversation with Barillon, is reported to have said: "The meeting of a parliament cannot be authorised without writs under the Great Seal, and they have been issued for fifteen counties only; the others are burned. The great seal is missing; the Chancellor had placed it in my hands eight days before I went away. They cannot make another without me." In the confusion following the King's flight, the loss of the seal does not seem to have had the disruptive effect for which James had hoped. Little more is heard of it.

Northumberland, of the King's Bedchamber, obeyed his master's orders implicitly, and did not open the doors of the royal apartments until broad daylight. Macaulay says, "The antechamber was filled with courtiers who came to make their morning bow, and with Lords who had been summoned to Council. The news of James's flight passed in an instant from the galleries to the streets, and the whole capital was in commotion. It was a terrible moment. The King was gone. The Prince had not arrived. No

Escape of James II from Whitehall.
The King took with him the Great Seal of England; at least that is how this Dutch engraver related events.
Print courtesy the BBC Hulton Picture Library.

regency had been appointed. The Great Seal, essential to the administration of ordinary justice, had disappeared."

The Prince had certainly not arrived. After the Commissioners had handed him their reply on December 10th he went on to "Newberry", and from there on the next day he progressed to Abingdon on his way to Oxford. It was on this journey that news reached him of the King's sudden departure from London, and he decided at once to make his way there.

Wednesday, 12 December:

Clarendon states in his diary that William arrived at Wallingford and dined at Schomberg's quarters. "He was very cheerful, and could not conceal his satisfaction at the King's being gone."

Thursday, 13 December:

"We went to Henley: the Prince came hither likewise tonight, and lay at Mr. Whitlock's. The Earl of Pembroke, the Lords Weymouth and Culpepper, and the Bishop of Ely came hither with a declaration from the Peers, who had assembled at Whitehall upon the King's withdrawing himself. The Bishop of St. Asaph came with them, though not sent. There came likewise addresses from the City and Lieutenancy of London, brought by Sir Robert Clayton and other Aldermen. The Lords supped with the Prince: after supper the Prince went into his chamber. He took those lords and gentlemen with him who came with him, and ordered the addresses to be read. He seemed much pleased with those that came from the City, but not at all with that from the Lords. Somebody told the Prince how Lord Feversham had disbanded the King's army; and that the soldiers were all running up and down, not knowing what course to take. at which the Prince seemed very angry at Lord Feversham, and said, I am not to be thus dealt with. I told the Prince, if he had no commands for me, I would go to-morrow to town: the truth is, I am weary of my company, and long to be at home. The Prince said he would go to-morrow to Windsor, and stay there a day or two: he desired me to be there on Sunday.'

Friday, 14 December:

The Prince, on his white charger, commander of a well-disciplined and formidable army of men and artillery, set out for Windsor. This powerful force was very different from Monmouth's small group of loyal followers of 1685, and posed a massive threat to the King. No wonder, then, that in his vacillating weakness, James fled from Whitehall.

The letter which James had sent to Lord Feversham, his Commanding Officer, on December 10th, the night he fled from his palace, was understood by Feversham to be orders to dismiss the royal army. This letter was read aloud to the troops, and is said to have made a deep impression upon them. A council of war was held at which it was resolved to obey the King and disband the army, and accordingly some four thousand men then serving under under the Earl were dismissed. The Earl and three other officers sent a letter to the Prince announcing this proceeding. William was disappointed to receive this news, because he was looking to the future, and had hoped that he could have amalgamated these troops with his own to form a strong force to help "in the prosecution of his designs against France".

The dismissing of the royal army had a marked effect on the mind of Lord Halifax. He liked to call himself "The Trimmer", and he had certainly trimmed his sails adroitly to the various winds which had blown since William landed at Brixham. He was not among those who had welcomed the Prince then and joined him. Instead, he had adopted the role of a go-between, without favour to either side. Now, however, he saw that with the King's troops disbanded, the Prince had become complete master of the military situation. Further, in Halifax's view it was unforgivable of James to have abandoned the kingdom to the reign of terror to which the excesses of roaming bands of licentious soldiers would lead, and so, to the chagrin of his Tory colleagues, he threw in his lot with William, and associated mainly with the Whigs. During the critical days which followed the flight of the King he became the acting head of government, and presided over the council which undertook to keep order during the crisis.

At this time of potential chaos the political instinct so characteristic of the English came into play. Order must be preserved at all costs. James had already summoned the Peers to assemble that morning to assist the working of the Privy Council, and the urgency of the crisis temporarily united all who were concerned for the public safety. Rochester, Lord Clarendon's brother, until that day had firmly supported the King. Now he saw only one way to avert general disorder.

"Muster your troop of guards," he said to Northumberland, "and declare for the Prince of Orange." This advice was immediately acted upon. Those chief officers of the army who were in London met at Whitehall and "resolved that they would submit to William's authority, and would, till his pleasure should be known, keep their men together and assist the civil power to keep order".

The extreme danger of the situation "drove Sancroft from his palace, and the Archbishop joined the Assembly of Peers and the Magistrates of the City in the Guildhall". Foxcroft describes the proceedings: "Archbishop Sancroft took the chair. The assembly did not indeed invite the Prince to London, nor did it request him to assume a provisional authority; but in a declaration laudatory of his undertaking, which was drafted by four High Churchmen, it promised to co-operate with him in obtaining a settlement by means of a free Parliament. It directed that Lord Feversham should remove his troops (who, since the King's letter had not seen the light, were of course regarded as still in arms) to distant quarters, and gave orders to prevent collision between the Dutch and English fleets."

Night of Riot and Terror

THE NIGHT was one of riot and terror; the "mobile vulgus", only just degraded to the cant appellation of "mob", felt the reins were loose, and amid scenes of great excitement the Popish chapels and the houses of several foreign ministers were sacked or burnt. Severe measures appeared evidently necessary when, on the morning of the 12th, the Lords reassembled in the Council Chamber at Whitehall. Sancroft did not appear; the meeting voted Lord Halifax (the only member of the Commission who attended) to the chair; and passing an order which threatened such as pulled down or defaced houses, especially those of foreign Ministers, with the rigour of the law, it commanded all officials being Protestants to exercise their functions and if necessary call out the Militia.

On the following night the disorders revived, and the confusion was intensified by a rumour that the disbanded Irish regiments were marching upon London. Next morning [13 December] the Lords, once more under the presidency of Halifax, issued instructions to the Trained Bands that they should fire on the rabble, if necessary, with bullet; that cannon should be "planted in the Park, Charing Cross, at the entrance into Piccadilly from Hyde Park side, and other proper places, that the foot guards should stand to their arms in St James's Park, and the horse guards the same, with other necessary orders".

While they were deliberating, a countryman arrived bearing a letter without address, but in the hand of James, which intimated that he had fallen into the hands of the mob at Faversham, and implored assistance. The messenger lingered unnoticed by the Council door until Mulgrave indignantly called the attention of the assembly to this neglect. Lord Halifax (with a by no means unnatural desire of obtaining some respite for the consideration of this fresh and bewildering revolution) attempted to adjourn. But Mulgrave insisted; the letter was read; and Lord Feversham—who, a General without an army, had returned to his duties as Chamberlain to the Queen Dowager—received directions to wait upon the King, accompanied by several officials. He insisted that the words "To receive his commands and protect his person" should be added to the order, and, having obtained this satisfaction, left on the following day for Kent.

The declaration drawn up by Sancroft and his assembly is described by Macaulay: "By this instrument they declared that they were firmly attached to the religion and constitution of their country, and that they had cherished the hope of seeing grievances redressed and tranquility restored by the Parliament which the King had lately summoned, but this hope had been extinguished by his flight. They had therefore determined to join with the Prince of Orange in order that the freedom of the nation might be vindicated, that the rights of the Church might be secured, that a just liberty of conscience might be given to Dissenters, and that the Protestant interest throughout the world might be strengthened."

The Peers committed themselves to Prince William in the following terms: "We do therefore unanimously resolve to apply ourselves to his highness the Prince of Orange, who, with so great kindness to these kingdoms, such vast expence, and so much hazard to his own person, has undertaken, by endeavouring to procure a Free Parliament, to rescue us, with as little effusion as possible of Christian blood, from the imminent dangers of Slavery and Popery. And we do hereby declare that we will, with our utmost endeavours, assist his highness in the obtaining such a parliament with all speed, wherein our Laws, our Liberties and Properties may be secured, and the Church of

England in particular, with a due liberty to Protestant Dissenters; and in general, that the Protestant religion and interest over the whole world may be supported and encouraged, to the glory of God, the happiness of the established government in these kingdoms, and the advantage of all princes and states in Christendom, that they may be herein concerned. In the mean time we will endeavour to preserve, as much as in us lies, the peace and security of these great and populous cities of London and Westminster, and the parts adjacent, by taking care to disarm all Papists, and secure all Jesuits and Romish priests, who are in or about the same. And if there be anything more to be performed by us, for prompting his highness's generous intentions for the public good, we shall be ready to do it, as occasion shall require." A deputation was instantly sent to lay this declaration before the Prince, and to inform him that he was impatiently expected in London.

News of the advance of the Prince's army and of the events in London is recorded by Whittle: "Our Army was now advanc'd far towards the City of London, The first line being marched from Newberry to Reading, Tylehurstone, and the adjacent places: The second line advanc'd to Newberry, and the third line to Hungerford. The Prince rode to Henl[e]y, attended with his Nobility and Gentry; sundry Regiments of the first and second Line being marched thither, and the Rear Line was come to Newberry. Here we received the first positive News of the late King James being gone away. As soon as it was certainly known about the City of London, that the late King was withdrawn, in order to his departure out of this Kingdom, the Lords Spiritual and Temporal assembled at Guildhal, Decemb. 11. and there agreed upon, and signed a Declaration, Entituled, The Declaration of the Lords Spiritual and Temporal in and about the Cities of London and Westminster, assembled at Guildhal, &c. The substance of which being to show, that the late King James was gone away, and to declare that they would assist his Highness with their uttermost Endeavours in the obtaining a Free Parliament with all speed, and in preserving, as much as in them lay, the Peace and Security of the Cities of London and Westminster; by taking care to disarm all Papists, and secure all Jesuits and Romish Priests, and in all things endeavour to promote his Highness's generous Intentions. This Declaration they ordered to be presented to his Highness, by the Earl of Pembrook, the Lord Viscount Weymouth, the Lord Bishop of Ely, the Lord Culpeper. The same Day the Lieutenancy of the City of London met there also, and agreed upon and signed an humble Address to be presented to his Highness by a committee appointed, viz. Sir Robert Clayton, Sir William Russel, Sir Basil Firebrass, Kts. and Charles Duncome Esq.

"The substance of which address was, to acknowledg the great Danger his Illustrious Highness had expos'd himself to, both by Sea and Land, for the Preservation of the Protestant Religion, and the Laws and Liberties of this Kingdom, and the happy Relief he had brought us; and therefore they humbly desired that his Highness would be pleased to repair unto the City of London with all the convenient speed he could, for perfecting the great Work He had so happily begun, to the general Joy and Satisfaction of all. The same day the Lord Mayor, Aldermen and Commons of the City of London, in Common Council assembled, agreed on and signed an Address to be presented to his Highness the Prince of Orange; the contents whereof was, To acknowledg the Peril his Highness had exposed himself to, both by Sea and Land, and the happy Deliverance he had brought to our Nation; and therefore they, in the name of their Capital City, did implore his Highness's Protection, and did humbly beseech his Highness to vouchsafe to repair to the City, where his Highness should be received with universal Joy and Satisfaction. All which Addresses were presented to his Highness the Prince of Orange, by the persons appointed, the 14th of December, at Henl[e]y, being accompanied with a great number of Citizens."

William sent a message accepting the invitation to London "which the City Magnates, more forward than the Peers, had despatched to him". He also took steps to take control of the royal army, and on 13 December he issued orders to call together "by beat of drum" or otherwise, those officers who had been disbanded by Lord Feversham, and to keep them under firm control. Churchill and Grafton were entrusted with the task of bringing discipline and order back into the army. "The English soldiers," writes Macaulay, "were invited to resume their military character. The Irish were commanded to deliver up their arms on pain of being treated as banditti, but were assured that, if they would submit quietly, they should be supplied with necessities." Most of the king's regiments obeyed the orders, but some units melted away and ceased to figure in the army records again.

Halifax comments that "the City magnates may have also received intelligence that the Prince on the 13th had ordered the officers of the King's army, on his own responsibility, to recall the disbanded men to their standards. In any case, the peers on this day required all Irish officers and soldiers to rejoin their respective bodies and surrender their arms, promising them substance in case of compliance, and directing their arrest as vagabonds in the event of disobedience."

There was scarcely any opposition to the Prince's orders, except that one of the Irish soldiers who were garrisoned at Tilbury "snapped a pistol at Grafton," which fortunately misfired. The would-be assassin was instantly shot dead.

The night of 12 December was long remembered throughout the capital and beyond as "Irish Night", a time of terror and confusion. It began with the arrival from the country of a number of rustics, who spread frightening rumours in the suburbs that bands of disbanded Irish soldiers were coming to murder the Protestants, rumours that "children would be compelled by torture to murder their parents; babes would be stuck on pikes, or flung into the blazing ruins of what had lately been happy dwellings" and similar highly coloured horror. As a result, armed crowds gathered together, and some began to pull down bridges and erect barricades. A stately home built for Lord Powis was attacked. At one in the morning the drums of the Militia beat to arms. Everywhere terrified women were weeping, and the men were arming. Candles blazed in the windows and public places were as bright as noon-day. More than twenty thousand pikes and muskets lined the streets.

Then the excitement died down, for there was not a Popish soldier in sight except for straggling bands of Irish soldiers demanding food. Some Roman Catholic gentlemen were attacked. Parks were ravaged and deer were slain, and much property was destroyed, but there were no reports of anyone being killed.

Many years later responsibility for having instigated "Irish Night", and "prompted the rustics to raise London" was claimed by the same man who had achieved notoriety by promoting the same kind of terror at Yeovil in the West Country earlier; none other than Hugh Speke, a man capable either of perpetrating such a hoax or of "falsely boasting that he had committed it".

On the next day, 13 December, a new story spread through London which astonished all who heard it, to the effect that the King had been captured, and was still in England, and this time it was no idle rumour. Macaulay describes how James had made his journey with relays of coaches along the southern bank of the Thames, and on the morning of the 12th had reached Emley Ferry, near the Isle of Sheppey.

"There lay the hoy in which he was to sail. He went on board, but the wind blew fresh, and the master would not venture to put to sea without more ballast. A tide was thus lost. Midnight was approaching before the vessel began to float. By that time the news that the King had disappeared, the country was without a Government, and that London was in confusion, had travelled fast down the Thames, and wherever it spread it produced outrage and misrule. The rude fishermen of the Kentish coast eyed the hoy with suspicion and with cupidity. It was whispered that some persons in the garb of gentlemen had gone aboard her in great haste [the King and Hales had exchanged roles as a disguise, James acting as Hales's servant]. Perhaps they were Jesuits: perhaps they were rich! Fifty or sixty boatmen, animated at once by hatred of Popery and by love of plunder, boarded the hoy just as she was about to make sail. The passengers were told they must go on shore and be examined by a magistrate. The King's appearance excited suspicion. 'It is Father Petre!' cried one ruffian; 'I know him by his lean jaws.' 'Search the hatchet-face old Jesuit!' became the general cry. He was rudely pulled and pushed about. His money and watch were taken from him. He had about him his coronation ring, and some other trinkets of great value, but these escaped the search of the robbers, who indeed were so ignorant of jewellery that they took his diamond buckles for bits of glass."

The prisoners were put on shore and taken to an inn. James, disguised in a wig of different shape and colour from his usual one, was, even so, instantly recognised by the crowd around him, who were somewhat overawed when they discovered who their prisoner was. But the sight of Hales, whom they knew and abominated, inflamed their anger. Even at that moment his park in the neighbourhood was being vandalised, and his deer were being shot. The King was assured that they would not harm him, but they would not release him.

The Earl of Winchelsea, a Protestant loyalist and a relation of Nottingham, happened to be in Canterbury at the time, and as soon as he heard the news of the King's detention, he and some Kentish gentlemen quickly travelled to the coast. They made sure that the king was removed to better lodgings, but he was still a prisoner. The mob kept constant guard round his lodging, and some even slept at his bedroom door.

He was a broken man, and at times irrational, having been subjected to such indignities. He abhorred being searched by the mob. At one time he spoke with such hauteur to the rustics that he provoked the men to insolence; at another he begged them, pleadingly, "Let me go. Get me a boat. The Prince of Orange is hunting for my life. If you do not let me fly now it will be too late. My blood will be on your heads. He that is not with me is against me." He was convinced that William was determined to kill him from the very beginning of his campaign.

He then preached for half an hour on the subjects of disobedience, disloyalty, and on "the virtues of a piece of the true cross which he had unfortunately lost". Referring to his son-in-law's actions he compared them to those of Herod. "Arise, and take the young child and his mother, and flee into Egypt, and be thou there until I bring thee word: for Herod will seek the young child to destroy him."

When details of the ill-treatment of the unfortunate King emerged, a surge of compassion for him was felt generally, in spite of his past conduct. He assumed a dignity of behaviour which impressed the common people, who forgot that he had brought this fate on himself, or they hoped that he might repent of "the errors which had brought him so terrible a punishment". The King's return under such circumstances turned him into something of a martyr, whereas had he escaped successfully, his actions would have been seen in their true light.

Whilst London adjusted to this sudden twist of fate, the invaders were making their way towards Windsor. The army met with little resistance after the skirmish at

The wooden Maidenhead Bridge.
Over the millstream branch of the River Thames, as it looked about 1582. Drawing by Michael Bayley [from the *Story of Maidenhead* by Luke Over].

Reading, although one or two incidents along the way were faithfully recorded by the Chaplain, the Reverend Whittle. "At Maidenhead," he writes, "(as we heard there from a Worthy Divine) The Irish perceiving the Army of the Prince of Orange advancing so fast, and with such speed towards London, perswaded the late King James to fortify Maidenhead-Bridg, it being the ready Road, and a difficult Post to be taken. Therefore in a new Brick House which is built between the Bridg and Town, they made sundry Port-holes for their great Guns, and put new Pales to blind them, and sundry places above to shoot with Musquets: And on the middle of the Bridg, they planted a great Gun or two, and here they were resolved to maul the Prince's Army, as they said. Indeed, those that understand Fortification well, have presumed, that the Passage there might be so fortified, that thousands of Men should not win it, because the Water ran in the Road-way a considerable length, or some hundred Yards; and the Bridg is so narrow, that a Man can hardly go along without falling, except he hold by the Rails; the Water too being up to a Man's middle here in the Road at the lowest Ebb: So the Irish bravadoing here at this Post, what they would do, certain worthy Persons there consulted together how to disperse the Irish, or cause them to go away, for they perceived well the Hearts of all Protestants were set upon his Highness, their Deliverer, under God, and by his Blessing; and the End of their Consultation was this: Sundry Persons of Courage and Resolution should go in the Dark, about Midnight, having each of them an old Barrel, or an old Kettle, standing at a certain equal distance from each other, they should beat the Dutch March: Which Stratagem took good effect, for these Men being got within a small distance of the Irish, began to beat a Dutch March; They no sooner heard it, but were prodigiously surprized, crying, Hark, Hark; and another presently made answer, God damn my Blood if it be not the Dutch come upon us; and forthwith they began to run and hasten away, without minding their great Guns, or taking away any thing; nay, happy was that Man that could get before his Comrade; and whither they went, no Man could tell. So the Souldiers belonging to his Highness, coming to Maidenhead, hearing of this Exploit, highly commended both the Contrivers and Actors in it, brought away the Guns, and all that was left, to Windsor Castle. And so I have done with both the Armies, in relation to Skirmishes or Actions.

"His Highness being now at Windsor, with all his Nobility and Gentry about him, the Citizens of London flock'd mightily to visit him, and congratulate his safe Arrival so far.

"The Army being now all about Windsor, and the adjacent Towns and Villages, the Souldiers, through the perswasions of the Country People, kill'd and destroy'd hundreds of Deer in the Forest; and hundreds more had been destroy'd, if so be his Highness had not given out his Royal Order to the contrary.

"The Irish Tories much abused the worthy Minister of Tylehurston, stripping his Rings off his Fingers, with the Skin and Flesh; threatning his Wife in Bed; and undoubtedly had murder'd the whole Family, if so be the Maid had not leap'd out of a Window, and call'd the Neighbours speedily to assist them, for they broke open the Door with an Iron made for the same purpose, which they forgot and left behind them, with their Dark Lanthorn, both which I saw. They swore divers times by St. Patrick, they would cut them all into pieces, if they would not give them Mony, for they must shortly be gone, and the late King had not paid them: So hearing the Neighbours coming, they took their Horses and rode away, having above thirty Pounds in Mony, Plate and Rings, for they took the old Gentlewoman's Rings off her Fingers."

Friday, 14 December:
Whilst his army was encamped round Windsor, William was visited by two "gentlemen of Kent" who were directed to Dr. Burnet. They told him of the events at Faversham, and wished to know what further action should now be taken. Burnet went to Bentinck and awakened him with the news. He was concerned for James's safety in the hands of a mob who had said that they would obey orders only directly from the Prince. Bentinck went to the Prince, who ordered Zuylestein, the son of his old tutor, to go down to Faversham where the King was being held "and to see the king safe, and at full liberty to go withersoever he pleased".

In the meantime, as Macaulay relates, "Some Whig gentlemen of the neighbourhood [of Faversham] had brought a large body of militia to guard him. They had imagined most erroneously that by detaining him they were ingratiating themselves with his enemies, and were greatly disturbed when they learned that the treatment which the King had undergone was disapproved by the Provisional Government in London, and that a body of cavalry was on the road to release him. Feversham soon arrived. He had left his troops at Sittingbourne, but there was no occasion to use force." The King was allowed to go without any opposition, and was taken to Rochester, where he rested. He sent Feversham with a letter to the Prince to say that he was on his way back to Whitehall, and asking for a private meeting with him. He also said that he wanted St. James's Palace prepared for William. For the moment James seemed to contemplate resistance, but William was determined that he should retire from London. Feversham returned to the Prince, and to his dismay was placed under arrest, as he had come without a passport, and had commanded an army against the Prince.

William's chief concern now was "how to dispose of the king's person", as Burnet puts it. "Some," he writes, "proposed rougher methods: the keeping him a prisoner, at least till the nation was settled, and till Ireland was secured. It was thought, his being kept in custody, would be such a tie on all his party, as would oblige them to submit, and be quiet. Ireland was in great danger; and his restraint might oblige the earl of Tyrconnel to deliver up the government, and to disarm the papists, which would preserve that kingdom, and the protestants in it. But, because it might raise too much compassion, and perhaps some disorder, if the king should be kept in restraint within the kingdom, therefore the sending him to Breda was proposed . . . The Prince said, he could not deny but that this might be good and wise advice; but it was that to which he could not hearken: he was so far satisfied with the grounds of this expedition, that he could act against the king in a fair and open war; but for his person, now that he had him in his power, he could not put such a hardship on him, as to make him a prisoner; and he knew the princess's temper so well, that he was sure she would never bear it: nor did he know what disputes it might raise, or what effect it might have upon the Parliament that was to be called. He was firmly resolved never to suffer anything to be done against his person: he saw it was necessary to send him out of London; and he would order a guard to attend upon him, who should only defend and protect his person, but not restrain him in any sort."

"Zulestein came to Faversham too late to prevent the King, who had already gone to Rochester, from returning to London. He followed him there, and found him at Whitehall, where the King gave him audience. Zulestein told his Majesty that the Prince of Orange could not appear in London without enough troops to protect him, and to this James replied: 'He may bring as many as he will; I will have myself even only those he may think necessary; or rather, not being sure of my own troops, I would as lieve have none at all'."

The King gave orders to put St. James at the disposal of the Prince of Orange. Meanwhile Lord Craven, who commanded the Coldstream Guards at Whitehall, was involved in a confrontation with Count Solmes, commander of the élite Dutch Blue Guards. Solmes called upon Craven to order his men away, but Craven was not disposed to agree except under James's personal order. This was finally forthcoming. James gave orders to Lord Craven to stand down the Coldstreams and to prepare quarters for the Dutch troops. At the same time he expressed his surprise and indignation at the arrest of Lord Feversham, which, he said, was a direct violation of the law of nations.

That evening, after supper, the King held a conversation with M. Barillon. "The Prince of Orange," he said, "would much rather I had gone away; and will find himself very much embarrassed what form of government to establish. The meeting of Parliament cannot be authorised without writs under the great seal. They cannot make another without me; all this will create difficulties and incidents which afford me to take suitable measures." Barillon, in his account of this conversation, adds, "I see that he is still determined to seek the means of saving himself: he had intended it at Rochester. He puts no trust in the acclamations which he received yesterday, and the few bonfires which were lighted in the City".

It was midnight by the time Solmes was settled at Whitehall with his Dutch Guards, but despite the lateness of the hour, a deputation from the Prince of Orange consisting of the lords Halifax, Shrewsbury and Delamere, who had arrived in London, "sent to the Earl of Middleton," says Burnet, "to desire him to let the king know that they had a message to deliver to him from the Prince. He went in to the King, and sent them word from him that they might come with it immediately. They came, and found him a-bed. They told him, the necessity of affairs required that the Prince should come presently to London," and they quoted their letter of authorisation from William: "We desire you, the Lord Marquis of Hallifax, the Earl of Shrewesbury, and the Lord Delamere, to tell the king: That it is thought convenient, for the greater quiet of the City, and for the greater safety of his Person, that he do remove to Ham, where he shall be attended by his guards, who will be ready to preserve him from any disturbance. W. P.De Orange, Given at Windsor the 17th day of December 1688."

Burnet goes on: "The king seemed much dejected, and asked if it must be done immediately. They told him, he might take his rest first; and they added, that he should be attended by a guard, who should only guard his person, but should give him no sort of disturbance. Having said this, they withdrew. The earl of Middleton came quickly after them, and asked them, if it would not do as well, if the king should go to Rochester; for since the prince was not pleased with his coming up from Kent, it might be perhaps acceptable to him if he should go thither again. It was very visible that this was proposed in order to a second escape. They promised to send word immediately to the prince of Orange, who lay that night at Sion, within eight miles of London. He very readily consented to it."

Before eight the next morning a letter came from M. Bentinck by the Prince's order, agreeing to the King's proposal to go to Rochester, providing the Dutch Guards should attend him. He left Whitehall at 11 a.m.

Tuesday, 18 December:
"The King's barge, with the Coaches and pads being ready, the King embarked and reached Gravesend the same day, and Rochester the next day." A quotation in Clarendon's Diary draws a pathetic picture of the King at the time. "The King was carried down the river in a very tempestuous day, not without some danger. And while the poor old King was thus exposed to the mercy of the elements, and an actual prisoner under the guard of Dutchmen, that very moment his daughter Denmark, with her great favourite [Lady Churchill] both covered with orange ribbons, in her father's coaches, and attended by his guards, went triumphant to the playhouse."

A prominent figure of King James's reign was Judge Jeffreys, his Lord Chancellor. He it was who, as Lord Chief Justice, sedulously carried out his master's cruel and vindictive vengeance after the Monmouth Rebellion, and so created such hatred of himself and of James throughout the West Country which contributed significantly to the welcome which the Prince of Orange received when he landed there. Jeffreys must have realised the danger to which the flight of James exposed him, and he thought that he, too, had better follow his master's example, and on 12 December he disguised his appearance and made his way to Wapping, where he took temporary refuge in an alehouse, with his eyebrows shaved off, dressed as a common sailor from Newcastle, and black with coal-dust.

It was unfortunate for him that as he stood peering out at the alehouse window, there passed by one who had suffered as a victim of his harshness in judgement, and who, as he tottered half dead with fright from Jeffreys's court, had vowed, "While I live I shall never forget that terrible countenance." Now he saw that terrible countenance, disguised, perhaps, but savage as ever of eye and mouth, looking out of an alehouse window, a face he would have known anywhere. He knew it as the face of the Lord Chancellor, and raised the alarm. In the shortest possible time the inn was surrounded by a raging, cursing mob, flourishing bludgeons and demanding his life. He was saved from the mob by the arrival of a company of militia, who cleared a way through the melée and secured him, taking him from thence before the Lord Mayor.

It was all too much for the Mayor. He was a simple man, quite overwhelmed by the recent events and disorders in his city, and now he was confronted by the famous and terrible Judge, before whom the whole kingdom had quailed. Furthermore, the great man was begrimed and dressed in sailor's clothing, half dead with fright, and followed into the courtroom by a raging multitude. The mayor collapsed. He "fell into fits," and was carried to his bed, from which he never arose again, but died soon after. The fury of the rabble was unabated, and the crowds grew greater. Jeffreys, terrified, begged to be sent to prison, and word getting to Whitehall, where the Lords were sitting, an order came that he was to be taken to the Tower.

The two regiments of militia ordered to escort him found the duty difficult. Repeatedly they were compelled to form up as though to repel a cavalry charge, presenting a forest of pikes to the mob, which followed the coach to the gates of the Tower, "brandishing cudgels and holding up halters full in the prisoner's view". The wretched man meantime was in convulstions of terror. He wrung his hands; he looked wildly out, sometimes at one window, sometimes at the other, and was heard even above the tumult crying, "Keep them off, gentlemen! For God's sake, keep them off!" At length, having suffered far more than the bitterness of death, he was safely lodged in the fortress where some of his most illustrious victims had passed their last days, and where his own life was destined to close in unspeakable ignomy and horror. Jeffreys died in great agony of "the stone", a disease for which no remedy was then known. Macaulay adds that the mobs which rioted freely after the abdication of James showed "no inclination to blood, except in the case of Jeffreys".

Saturday, 15 December:
The Halifax papers record that the Provisional Government was principally occupied in examining Lord Jeffreys as to the fate of the writs and the Great Seal, with a view to ascertaining whether legal arrangements had already been made under which Parliament might meet in due course. Naturally, however, nothing was forthcoming.

Tuesday, 18 December:
At about three o'clock of the same day that King James left for Rochester, the Prince of Orange came to the Court of St. James. Whittle reports, "December the 18th, his Highness parted from Windsor, dined at Sion-House, and came that Evening to St. James's, amidst the loud Acclamations of a vast number of People of all Sorts and Ranks, the Bells everywhere ringing; the Evening concluded with vast Bonfires, and such general Joy as can scarce be parallel'd."

It happened to be a very rainy day, typical of the climate of this country, but with the optimism usually inherent in the English character the crowds came from miles around London, determined to make the best of the occasion whatever the weather. Many wore orange ribbons, and twirled oranges on sticks, and all rejoiced at the arrival of their champion.

Macaulay writes: "Whilst the King's barge was slowly working its way on rough waves down the river, brigade after brigade of the prince's troops marched into London from the West. It had been wisely determined that the duty of the capital should be chiefly done by the British soldiers in the service of the States General. The three English regiments were quartered in and around the Tower, and three Scotch regiments in Southwark.

"In defiance of the weather, a great multitude assembled between Albemarle House and St. James's Palace to greet the Prince. Every hat, every cane, was adorned with an orange riband. The bells were ringing all over London. Candles for an illumination were disposed in windows. Faggots for bonfires were heaped up in the streets. William, however, who had no taste for crowds and shouting, took the road through the park."

Burnet comments, "And even this trifle set the people's spirits on the fret."

The Prince entered St. James's accompanied by Schomberg, and in a short time all the rooms and the staircases in the palace were thronged by those who came to pay court. Such was the press that men of the highest rank were unable to elbow their way into the presence chamber. As Lord Clarendon wrote of the occasion, "I went to court, but the crowd was so great I could not see the Prince . . ."

While Westminster was in this state of excitement, the Common Council, that is,

St James's Palace, Westminster.
The Prince of Orange took up residence on 18 December 1688.

the council which manages the affairs of the City of London, was preparing an address of thanks and congratulation. The Lord Mayor was unable to preside. He had never risen from his bed since the day the Lord Chancellor had been dragged before him, but the aldermen and other officers of the corporation were in their places.

Burnet sums up this memorable day: "The revolution was thus brought about with the universal applause of the whole nation."

The concerns of the Prince of Orange were not confined to those occasioned by his invasion of England. On learning of his expedition, France had taken advantage of the situation and declared war against the Government of the Netherlands, the States General; and the Prince of Waldeck, who was in command of the forces left to defend Holland, needed troops, which England was required by treaty to provide. In a letter dated "St. James's, Dec. 18-28" William wrote regretting that he could send him no cavalry, but that he thought he would in a short time be able to spare him five or six regiments of infantry. He could not do this now because of the unsettled state of the Government of England. He said he could easily take over the crown, and so probably expedite matters, but he would not do so. He concluded, "If my disposition were not so scrupulous as it is, I should not be so embarrassed, and could finish the matter soon; I have more trouble than you can imagine. I hope that the good God will guide me as He has done up till now."

Halifax was encouraging. It was reported that on the evening of the day that William took up residence in St. James's, "the Marquis of Hallifax told the prince he might be what he pleased himself; . . . for as nobody knew what to do with him, so nobody knew what to do without him".

Wednesday, 19 December:

"The magistrates of the City went in state to pay their duty to their deliverer," continues Macaulay. "Their gratitude was eloquently expressed by their Recorder, Sir George Treby. Some princes of the house of Nassau, he said, had been the chief officers of a great republic. Others had worn the imperial Crown. But the peculiar title of that illustrious line to the public veneration was this, that God had set it apart and consecrated it to the high office of defending truth and freedom against tyrants from generation to generation."

On the same day all the prelates who were in town, Sancroft excepted, waited on the Prince in a body. [Since James had returned to London a number of the leaders of the Church and other men of influence had, for different reasons, changed their attitude to him, and preferred to regard him as a poor ill-used victim, and even though he had left Whitehall, many Tories of few principles, like Clarendon, swung to James's support, for they saw that there was not much to their advantage in the Revolution, and they began to give out that William had forced him out. Others, like Sancroft, were genuine in their support of James, although earlier he had been in favour of William's campaign.]

Then came the clergy of London, the foremost men of their profession in knowledge, eloquence and influence, with their Bishop at their head. Mingled with them were some eminent dissenting ministers, whom Compton, much to his honour, treated with marked courtesy. A few months earlier, or a few months later, such courtesy would have been considered by many churchmen as treason to the Church. Even then it was but too plain to a discerning eye that the armistice to which the Protestant sects had been forced would not long outlast the danger from which it had sprung.

About a hundred nonconformist divines resident in the capital presented a separate address. They were introduced by Devonshire, and were received with every mark of respect and kindness. The lawyers, too, paid their homage headed by Maynard, who, at ninety years of age, was alert and clear headed. "Mr. Serjeant," said the prince, "you must have survived all the lawyers of your standing." "Yes Sir," said the old man, "and but for your Highness I should have survived the Law itself."

Whittle, the army chaplain, writes: "Most of the Nobility congratulated his Highness's safe arrival at St. James's, and on the 20th the Aldermen and Common Council of the City of London attended his Highness upon the same account, and the Lord Mayor being disabled by Sickness, Sir George Treby, Kt. Recorder of the Honourable City of London, made an Oration to his Highness to this effect: 'Great Sir, When we look back to the last Month, and contemplate the swiftness and fulness of our present Deliverance, astonish'd, we think it miraculous. Your Highness led by the hand of Heaven, and call'd by the Voice of the People, has preserved our dearest interest, the Protestant Religion, which is Primitive Christianity restored. Our Laws, which are our ancient Title to our Lives, Liberties and Estates, and without which this World were a Wilderness. But what Retribution can we make to your Highness? Our hearts are full charged with Gratitude. Your Highness has a lasting Monument in the Hearts, in the Prayers, in the Praise of all good Men amongst us. And late Posterity will celebrate your ever-glorious Name, till Time shall be no more."

On the same day, 20 December, the Prince summoned those Peers in town to his presence. At 10 o'clock they duly assembled, and William informed them that he intended to retain control of military affairs, and would leave the Lords to carry out the civil administration and the arrangements for the calling of a free Parliament. Later, their Lordships drew up a vote of thanks to the Prince, but it was very carefully worded so as to avoid too much humility, and it was reported that "the formula of offering to stake Lives and Fortunes in his favour was omitted, as worn out".

Saturday, 22 December:

During the interregnum caused by the flight of King James the Assembly met again in the House of Lords, and Halifax was elected to the Chair. A contemporary account relates that "their lordships ordered five lawyers to attend, and give their opinion whether the Act for Triennial parliaments applied to the existing crisis; and came, moreover, to the following conclusions: (1) That all Papists should be banished from London. (2) That all Irish officers in England should be arrested, as hostages for the safety of their Protestant compatriots; and that Tyrconnel should be threatened with reprisals. (3) That the King shall be sent to desire his concurrence and for calling a New Parliament." The writer of this report discerned three parties in the Assembly: the Commonwealth party, which desire a Stadtholder rather than a King: the party that would depose the King in favour of his nephew: and the party that would make "all ye offers in ye world" to James in order to induce his return. "My Ld. Delamere" (adds our informant) "appears like a fury, and my Lord Hal. Trims it like himself. The 'Association' was signed by all present, excepting the Bishops, Lord Nottingham, Lord Wharton, and two inconsiderable Peers. The assembly adjourned over Sunday."

In an interesting sidelight on these proceedings, and how word of them was received by the populace at large, Green writes of the people of Somerset: "On December 22nd, when the nobility declared in favour of the prince and against the late king's proceedings, 'as rendering the laws a nose of wax,' the streets were thronged with people all rejoicing at being redeemed from 'popery and slavery'. Thus the revolution was complete. How Somerset men sang we learn from a ballad entitled: 'The Courageous Soldiers of the West, or, The Undaunted Countrymens Resolution in taking up arms in defence of King William and Queen Mary, together with the Protestant Religion.' Tune is: 'Lilli Borlero'. Woodcut: soldiers marching.

> Now to maintain the Protestant cause,
> All the whole West does loyally stand,
> For our lives, religion and laws,
> Roman shall never reign in this land.
> Stout lads brisk and airy, for William and Mary,
> They'll valiantly fight their rights to maintain.
>
> Bridgewater boys I need must commend,
> Freely they to the wars did repair,
> Parents and wife, nay, every friend,
> They recommend to Heaven's great care;
> Life and fortune freely venter,
> Nothing alive true courage can stain.
> Stout lads brisk and airy, for William and Mary.
> They'll valiantly fight their rights to maintain.
>
> As for the town of brave Taunton-dean,
> Their loyalty shall ne'er be forgot,
> Four our most gracious king and his queen,
> They will engage with thundering shot.
> Noble true souls came flocking amain.
> Stout lads brisk and airy, for William and Mary,
> They'll valiantly fight their rights to maintain.

124

George Savile, first Marquis of Halifax.
Prominent statesman of the time of James II and William III; "Trimmer Halifax" he was dubbed. Print based on his portrait by Arnold Houbracken.

Swallenfield, Berkshire.
The seat of Henry Hyde, second Earl of Clarendon. From an engraving of 1827.

The real troubles now begin

HAVING SUCCEEDED in reaching Whitehall from his landing point at Brixham in under fifty days with relative ease, William realised that his real troubles were now beginning. He had at once to grapple with the complexities of English politics and also to avoid the pitfalls of religious prejudice with which his path was scattered, problems which were very different from any he had faced as supreme commander of an army in the field. A false step could be disastrous, and yet it seemed to be impossible to take any step without offending susceptibilities and rousing angry passions.

During the interval between the sitting of the Assembly on the Saturday and that due on the Monday there were anxious moments. One group of Peers led by Archbishop Sancroft still hoped that the constitution and religion of England could be secured without deposing the King, and this royalist party resolved to send letters to the King imploring him to renounce, even at this late hour, his previous intentions so hated by his people, and assuring him that if he could do this he would be strenuously defended by his loyal followers. The Earl of Clarendon in his diary writes of this time: "In the evening Mr. Keightley was with me . . . I told him I wished he would go to Rochester, and assure the King of my humble duty; that I would serve him to the utmost of my power; that he should tell the King his enemies wished he would be gone, and that his friends feared it, though they hoped he would not leave us; that he should let the King know the opinions of several lords and others, of whom I gave him the names; that there would certainly be addresses made to him, and therefore to beseech him not to leave Rochester till he saw what the Lords did."

Mr. Keightley journeyed in vain on the Earl's behalf. Clarendon continues: "Dec. 23. Sunday. In the morning I sent Richards to Rochester, with a letter from the Bishop of Ely to Mr. Keightley. In the afternoon I went to St. James's: the Prince took me into his bed-chamber. He asked me if the peers met again tomorrow? I told him, yes. He then asked what I thought we should do? I said I could only tell him my own mind; and that I should endeavour that we might proceed upon his Highnesses declaration; which I hoped he would keep to, as the only foundation upon which to make the King and kingdom happy. The Prince heard me with great patience; and very calmly said, (when I expected he would make me some answer) 'My Lord, the King is gone from Rochester'. 'Whither, Sir?' said I: 'I know not,' replied the Prince: 'he went away about one or two this morning.' I was struck to the heart; and, without saying one word, I made my leg, and went home as fast as I could. I had not been long in my chambers, when Mr. Belson and Mr. Keightley came to me. They told me that as soon as they got yesterday to Rochester, Keightley went presently to the King, and told him that Mr. Belson was come to speak with him from several of his old friends, upon matters of the greatest importance. The King was going to supper: when he had done, he told Keightley that he was going in to write letters, and that he would speak with Mr. Belson this morning. That when he went this morning to wait on him, he found his Majesty was gone privately away in the night; that he had left a letter upon his table for my Lord Middleton; and this was all they could tell me. Good God! What will become of this poor, distracted and distempered nation? In the evening the Bishop of Ely and Sir Thomas Clarges were with me, full of astonishment, as everybody was, at the King's being again withdrawn. It is like an earthquake."

The Prince had received the news of the King's flight just a few hours after he had gone. It appeared that James, having told "some of the gentlemen who had brought intelligence and advice" that he would meet them again the next day, escaped from

Rochester that night, 22 December.   Attended by Lord Berwick and Mr. Biddulph, loyal friends, he had left in a waiting skiff, and soon after dawn on Sunday they boarded a smack which took them down the Thames to the open sea.

Reactions to this abrupt change of fortune were predicatable.   The Royalists were dismayed and the Whigs delighted.   James's final flight had relieved the Prince of a great embarrassment.   He took a bold step immediately, and signed an order deporting M. Barillon, the French Ambassador, who he knew to be an active agent hostile to him. This by no means suited the purposes of the Ambassador, who was most reluctant to leave London at that time, and went to considerable lengths to show support for William.   He threw money from his coach to the hostile crowds in the streets, and made a great show of publicly drinking the health of the Prince of Orange, but William was unmoved by this pretence.   He took great care not to exert regal authority, but as a general, he would not tolerate the presence in his occupied territory of one whom he regarded as a spy.   "Barillon, in his last letter to Louis XIV," Clarendon writes, "says that the Prince commanded in London as if in a camp, that his troops mounted guard every where, not without some murmurs on the part of the English regiments at seeing the Tower and other places of strength in the hands of the Dutch; and he speaks of the agitations which troubled the Assembly at Westminster, where the King's cause found defenders."

Barillon begged for even a short respite, but the order was firmly repeated, and so he set off for Dover, escorted by one of his Protestant countrymen who had suffered persecution at home and had taken refuge in London!   The English so bitterly resented French ambition and arrogance that even those who were not William's supporters praised him for so spiritedly rejecting the insolence with which for years Louis had treated all the courts of Europe.

Monday, 24 December:

On the day after the news of the King's flight had broken, the Lords met again, and Lord Halifax was again asked to preside.   Again, the Primate was absent.   "The Bishop of Ely and I sent to him," says Clarendon, "But the King's being gone had cast such a damp upon him, that he would not come; which many of us were sorry for.   His declaring himself at this time would have been weight among us."   Clarendon goes on to detail the arguments which raged and the motions moved, and concludes: "At last, after many things had been started, the result of all was that an address should be made to the Prince of Orange to take the Administration of the Government, and to write circular letters to all the counties, cities, and universities, and cinque ports, to choose Representatives to meet in a Convention at Westminster on the 22d of January next."

The Lords, who tended to disregard the House of Commons, presented their address to the Prince, but he wisely decided to make no decisions until he had tested the feelings of those gentlemen who had been elected by the counties and towns of England.   In fact, the Commons came to conclusions similar to those of the Lords, having no different opinions on any serious questions.   When both Houses had presented the findings to the Prince, he agreed to comply with their joint request, and on their advice he sent out letters summoning a Convention of the "Estates of the Realm".

Tuesday, 25 December:

Whittle records: "The Lords Spiritual and Temporal assembled at the house of Lords, Westminster, and there agreed upon and signed an Address, wherein they humbly desired his Highness in this Conjuncture to take upon him the Administration of Publick Affairs, both Civil and Military, and the Disposal of the Publick Revenue, for the preservation of our Religion, Rights, Laws, Liberties and Properties, and of the

Peace of the Nation; and that his Highness would take into his Care the Condition of Ireland, and endeavour, by the most speedy and effectual Means, to prevent the Danger threatening that Kingdom. All of which the Lords Spiritual and Temporal make their requests to his Highness, to undertake and exercise till the Meeting of the intended Convention, Jan. 22. next." This, says Whittle, was signed by all the Lords then assembled, "and presented to his Highness the Prince of Orange the same day at St. James's. All which his Highness was pleased to do according to their Desires".

In the County Archives at Taunton there is an original copy of the Prince of Orange's directions for electing the Convention in 1688 which was sent to the magistrates of Minehead in Somerset. It is signed by William of Orange, and the full contents are as follows:

"Directions for electing the convention, 1688.

Whereas the Lords Spiritual and Temporal, the Knights, Citizens and Burgesses, heretofore Members of the Commons House of Parliament, during the reign of King Charles the Second, residing in and about the City of London, together with the Aldermen, and divers of the Common-Council of the said city, in this extraordinary Conjuncture at our Request, severally assembled, to advise us the best Manner how to attain the Ends of our Declaration, in calling a free Parliament, for the Preservation of the Protestant Religion, and Restoring the Rights and Liberties of the Kingdom, and Settling the same, that they may not be in Danger of being again subverted, have advised and desired us to cause our Letters to be written and directed, for the Counties, To the Coroners of the respective Counties or any One of them, and, in default of the Coroners, To the Clerks of the Peace of the respective Counties; and for Universities, To the respective Vice-Chancellors; and for the Cities, Boroughs and Cinque-Ports, To the Chief Magistrate of each respective City, Borough and Cinque-Port; Containing Directions for the choosing, in all such Counties, Cities, Universities, Boroughs and Cinque-Ports, within Ten Days after the Receipt of the said respective Letters, such a Number of Persons to represent them, as from every such Place is or are of Right to be sent to Parliament: Of which Elections, and the Times and Places thereof, the respective Officers shall give Notice; the Notice for the intended Election, in the Counties, to be published in the Market-Towns within the respective Counties, by the Space of Five Days, at the least, before the said Election; and for the Universities, Cities, Boroughs and Cinque-Ports, in every of them respectively, by the Space of Three Days, at the least, before the said Election: The said Letters, and the Execution thereof, to be returned by such Officer and Officers who shall execute the same, to the Clerk of the Crown in the Court of Chancery, so as the Persons, so to be chosen, may meet and sit at Westminster the Two-and-Twentieth Day of January next.

We, heartily desiring the Performance of what we have in our Said Declaration expressed, in pursuance of the said Advice and Desires, have caused this our Letter to be written to you, to the Intent that you, truly and uprightly, without Favour or Affection to any Person, or indirect Practice or Proceeding, do and execute what of your Part ought to be done, according to the said Advice, for the due Execution thereof; the Elections to be made by Such Persons only, as, according to the ancient Laws and Customs, of Right, ought to choose Members for parliament: and that you cause a Return to be made, by Certificate under your Seal, of the Names of the Persons elected, annexed to this our Letter, to the said Clerk of the Crown, before the said Two-and-Twentieth Day of January.

Given at St. James's, the Nine-and-Twentieth Day of December, in the Year of our Lord 1688.

"To the Chief Magistrate or such others of the Borough of Mynehead [Minehead] in the County of Somerset who have right to make returns of members to serve in the Parliament according to the ancient right of the said Borough before the Sovereign and on Surrender of Charter made in the time of King Charles the Second.

(Signed) Wm of Orange"

William's directions for electing the Convention, 1688.
Final paragraphs and William's signature, on the copy sent to magistrates at Minehead, Somerset. Courtesy of Somerset Record Office, from the manuscripts deposited by Lieutenant Colonel Walter Luttrell MC [document DD/L 1/59/2].

With all the concerns in England pressing upon him, William was at the same time obliged to remain in touch with affairs in the Netherlands, and to answer the letters which the Prince of Waldeck continued to send, all of them appealing for troops. He wrote at this time giving Waldeck an account of what had taken place, and assuring him of help. "If I accept the government, I can send you immediately the help which in case of war England is obliged to give to Holland, which I believe amounts to 6,000 men, and I can prepare everything to make a considerable diversion next spring, when the Convention or a Parliament will have given money."

On Christmas Day, after a difficult journey, James landed in France at Brest, "whither the Queen, and supposed, Prince of Wales, was gone before, where," says Whittle, "'I'll leave him'". James travelled to St. Germains, where he was met by Louis XIV, who invited both James and Mary to meet him in Versailles the next day.

Now that the King had abandoned the throne and fled abroad, William had a legitimate claim to the crown. Carefully he set about the work of controlling the civil government with which he had been entrusted whilst the country awaited the outcome of the elections. Throughout this time he was at pains to make it clear that he did not in any way influence the course of the elections. His troops were removed from the enfranchised districts, and voting for the Convention was quite free of pressure. Dr. Burnet makes this clear. He writes:

"The Sitting of the Convention was now very near. And all men were managed fairly all England over. The Prince did in no sort interpose in any recommendation, directly or indirectly . . ."

But order had to be brought to the administration of the country. The Justices of the Peace had abandoned their duties; taxes remain uncollected; the remnants of the late royal army were in confusion and verging on mutiny; the Fleet was in disarray; great arrears of pay were owing to the civil and military servants of the Crown, and there remained only forty thousand pounds in the Exchequer.

Energetically the Prince set about the tasks facing him. A proclamation was issued requiring all magistrates to remain in office, and another ordered that revenues be collected. The remodelling of the army continued, and many nobles and gentlemen who had been relieved of their command in the English army were reinstated. The Irish soldiers could not be allowed to remain in England because of their religion, and the anger felt towards them by the people, and neither could they be allowed to return and so reinforce Tyrconnel's forces in Ireland, so they were deported to the Continent to serve under the banner of the house of Austria, "where they might render indirect but effectual service to the cause of the English Constitution and of the Protestant religion". Lord Dartmouth was relieved of his command, and the navy was assured that the sailors would soon receive their pay.

The City of London undertook to finance the Prince. The Common Council promised to raise two hundred thousand pounds. "It was thought a great proof," says Macaulay, "both of the wealth and of the public spirit of the merchants of the capital that, in forty-eight hours, the whole sum was raised on no security but the Prince's word. A few weeks before, James had been unable to procure a much smaller loan, though he had offered to pay higher interest, and to pledge valuable property."

In a short time affairs began to return to normal, and the country felt a general sense of security. William's opponents were able to walk in safety in the streets, and even offered themselves as candidates for the seats in the Convention. Feversham was released, and was permitted to resume office as Chamberlain to the Dowager Queen. The Roman Catholics were treated in a prudent and humane way, and although it would not have been safe to "rescind formally the severe resolutions the

Peers had passed against the professors of a religion generally abhorred by the nation . . . those resolutions were practically annulled'. William had said on his march from Torbay that no outrage should be committed on the Papists, and he now renewed these orders. He told the kindly and warm-hearted Burnet to see that his orders were obeyed. In fact, the Spanish Minister told his government, and they informed the Pope, that there was "no need for Roman Catholics to fear the Prince, and that no Catholic need feel any scruple of conscience on account of the late Revolution in England, that for the dangers to which the members of the true Church were exposed, James alone was responsible, and that William alone had saved them from a sanguinary persecution".

The French were disturbed by the news of the success of this great Revolution. They hated William, but at the same time, respected him for his bravery and his achievement.

In the Netherlands the united Provinces were exhilarated by the news. Ever since William had set out on his expedition there had been intense anxiety among the Dutch people. They had followed each step of the Prince's progress, and when they heard that the Lords had invited him to take over the administration of the country they were overjoyed. They sent Dykvelt, who knew intimately the peculiarities of English politics, as Ambassador, and Nicholas Witson, Burgomaster of Amsterdam, to congratulate William on his success.

Tuesday, 8 January:

Dykvelt and Witson came to Westminster. "Well," said William, "and what do our friends at home say now?", and he was moved by the warmth shown by his native country. He was less impressed by his immense popularity in England, and forseeing the reaction to come said: "Here, the cry is all 'Hosannah' today, and will, perhaps, be 'Crucify' tomorrow."

During the elections for the Convention popular support for William decreased somewhat. The majority of the nation had backed his invasion, united in a general detestation of James and his works, but by now, three parties had formed. One, consisting chiefly of Tories, wanted to recall the King, for they felt they had little to gain under William, who seemed to them to favour the Whigs and Dissenters rather than the Tories and Anglicans. This party, however, after much discussion, joined with a second party which inclined to the notion of creating a Prince Regent, "so that the right of sovereignty should be owned to remain still in the King, and that the exercise of it should be vested in the Prince of Orange as Prince Regent".

The third party wished to ignore the King and put the Prince firmly on the throne in his stead. Those of this mind were Whigs, who hoped for favours in return, and foresaw a permanent Whig supremacy in office, so turning the tables on the Tories.

Amidst these mixed fears and feelings the election of the members of the Convention was carried out. The followers of the King had hoped that the elections would sink into confusion and fail, but they went smoothly forward. The City of London elected, unopposed, four rich Whig merchants, and in the counties many gentlemen who had been nominated in defiance of the King and the Lord Lieutenant were similarly returned uncontested. A great majority of the shires and boroughs appointed Whig members, and there were no grounds for any accusation that unfair pressure was exerted, for on the Prince's express order, not a soldier was to be seen in any town where the election was proceeding.

The Convention met on 22 January 1689, and as Whittle says: "They agreed upon and Ordered, that the Thanks of both Houses should be returned to his Highness in the behalf of the whole Nation, for his Highness happy Deliverance of this Kingdom from

Popery, Slavery, and Despotick Power; and for the Preservation of the Protestant Religion and the Laws, Rights, Priviledges, and Customs of our Land, &c. And moreover to beseech his Highness to continue the Administration of publick Affairs Civil and Military, and the Disposal of the Publick Revenue, until such time as farther Application be made to his Highness: All which his Highness was pleased to do and exercise according to their desire."

A letter from the Prince of Orange was then read to the assembly. In it "he recommended to the notice of the Convention the entire political situation. He exhorted to union, and to that speedy decision which the critical state of Ireland and Continental politics alike demanded; nor was a clear intimation wanting of his hope that England, in return for assistance lent by the Dutch States, would join in the war with France, which had been already declared by the latter power."

More important at this stage than Irish or French politics, it was essential to resolve the question of the crown. The general belief was that the House of Lords favoured a Regency, while the Lower House preferred a stronger solution. Dr. Burnet reports intense discussion of the question. A minority of Jacobites argued for the recalling of James, but the majority of Tories did not wish this course of action to be taken unless James would agree unequivocally to adhere to very strong terms which they would put before him. Others favoured the idea that William should take the crown by right of conquest. Some mentioned the "so-called Prince of Wales," and suggested his return, with Princess Mary ruling as Regent during his infancy, and there were those who went further, promoting the idea that since Mary was legally next in line for the succession if the claim of the "so-called Prince of Wales" were ignored, she should be invited to become the ruler in her own right.

Each of the two Houses appears to have been waiting for the other to resolve the matter first. Sir Thomas Clarges, who strongly advocated a Regency, moved and carried in the Lower House that the "Debate on the State of the Nation"—i.e. the entire political outlook—should be "deferred four days, thus affording to the Peers an opportunity of assuming the initiative". Sir Thomas was a close friend of Lord Halifax, the Speaker of the House of Lords, but his motion would seem to have annoyed the noble lord, for, as Clarendon records, "the next day Halifax, with some warmth, told Sir Thomas it was very strange he had made such a motion; that it was just so much time lost; for the Lords should not proceed upon any public business till they saw what the Commons did." Foxcroft reports that some of the Tories in the Lords endorsed Clarges's policy by moving that they should proceed to consider the State of the Nation on the 25th, but Lord Devonshire, acting in the Whig interest, proposed an adjournment of the debate until the 29th in expectation, as he candidly expressed it, of "Light from below," and supported by Halifax, Winchester and others he carried the motion.

While the Upper House awaited the "light" in question, Lord Halifax sent to all those Lords who had been absent from the House on the 25th a strongly worded exhortation to attend on the 29th, which concluded, "The Lords doe therefore earnestly require yor Lordshipp (all excuses sett apart, but such as are Absolutely indispensable) To come up with all convenient sped to attend the publique Service in the house not doubting but that yor Lordshippes Zeale for the publique good will be a more powerfull argument to perswade you to comply with this desire of the House than any penalty that could be imposed upon the omission of it."

The debate in the Commons on 28 January is reported in detail in *A Journal of the Convention at Westminster Begun the 22 of January 1688/89*, which sets out all the arguments put forward on that momentous occasion. Speaker after speaker advanced his complaint against King James, with constant reference to the conflict between his Roman Catholic religion and the Protestant religion of the country. It was resolved that "A Popish King had been found by experience inconsistent with a Protestant Government". It was further argued that, by his flight, James had left the throne vacant, and in spite of differing opinions, a second resolution was finally agreed by a majority: "That King James the 2nd by endeavouring to subvert the constitution of the Kingdom by breaking the Originall compact between King and people, and by the Advice of Jesuits & other wicked persons having violated the fundamentall Laws both of Church & State by withdrawing himself, has thereby abdicated the Government & left the Throne Vacant."

Mr. Hampden was ordered to take the vote to the Lords immediately and ask for their agreement on it.

Tuesday, 29 January:

Lord Clarendon records that during a debate in the Lords on the question of establishing a Regency, a motion which was defeated by two votes, there was received "a message from the House of Commons by Mr. Hampden, with the vote, that the throne was vacant". The resolution from the Commons was read, and then, it being eight o'clock in the evening, the House adjourned until the afternoon of the next day.

Wednesday, 30 January:

The Commons motion was debated in detail in the House of Lords. The term "abdicated" was not approved, "deserted" being substituted, and this and other amendments were sent back to the Commons.

So the debate continued. The chief difficulty to be overcome was the completely new idea that the succession should now become elective, and not hereditary, but Halifax argued that although this might appear to be the case on this occasion, the Crown would become hereditary again thereafter. Clarendon records that on Wednesday, 6 February, "under one pretence or other, several Lords who had always voted in favour of the King were not in the House today," but "All imaginable pains were taken to bring other Lords to the House, who never used to come; as the Earl of Lincoln, who, to confirm the opinion several had of his being half mad, declared he came to do whatever my Lord Shrewsbury and Lord Mordaunt would have him. The Earl of Carlisle was brought upon his crutches: the Lord Lexinton, who came into England but three days ago; and the Bishop of Durham, who had been at the House but twice before, came today to give his vote against the King, who had raised him. These four all voted against the King. And now the throne being declared vacant, the next business was to fill it; and to that end it was proposed that the Prince and Princess of Orange might be declared King and Queen."

So the matter was finally decided, and without any intervention from the Prince of Orange himself, whose behaviour was quite irreproachable. Burnet describes his comportment at this time. "During all these debates, and the great heat with which they were managed, the prince's own behaviour was very mysterious. He stayed at St. James's: he went little abroad: access to him was not very easy. He heard all that was said to him, but seldom made any answers. He did not affect to be affable, or popular; nor would he take any pains to gain any one person over to his party. He said, he came over, being invited, to save the nation; he had now brought together a free and true representative of the kingdom; and, when things were once settled, he should be well satisfied to go back to Holland again. Those who did not know him well, and who imagined that a crown had charms which human nature was not strong enough to resist, looked on all this as an affectation, and as a disguised threatening, which imported, that he would leave the nation to perish unless his method of settling it was followed. After a reservedness that had continued so close for several weeks, that nobody could tell certainly what he desired, he called for the marquis of Halifax, and the earls of Shrewsbury and Danby, and some others, to explain himself more distinctly to them.

"He told them, he had been till then silent, because he would not say, or do, any thing that might seem in any sort to take from any person the full freedom of deliberating and voting in matters of such importance: he was resolved neither to court nor threaten anyone; and therefore he had declined to give out his own thoughts. Some were for putting the government in the hands of a regent; he would say nothing against it, if it was thought the best means for settling their affairs; only he thought it necessary to tell them, that he would not be the regent; so, if they continued in that design, they must look out for some other person to be put in that post: he himself saw what the consequences of it were likely to prove; so he would not accept of it: others were for putting the princess singly on the throne, and that he should reign by her courtesy: he said no man could esteem a woman more than he did the princess; but he was so made, that he could not think of holding any thing by apron-strings; nor could he think it reasonable to have any share in the government unless it was put in his person, and that for term of life: if they did think it fit to settle it otherwise, he would not oppose them in it;but he would go back to Holland, and meddle no more in their affairs. He assured them that whatsoever others might think of a crown, it was no such thing in his eyes, but that he could live very well, and be well pleased without it. In the end, he said that he could not resolve to accept of a dignity, so as to hold it only for the life of another; yet he thought that the issue of princess Anne should be preferred in the succession to any issue that he might have by any other wife than the princess. All this he delivered to them in so cold and unconcerned a manner, that those who judged of others by the dispositions that they felt in themselves, looked on it all as artifice and contrivance.

"This was presently told about, as it was not intended to be kept secret; and it helped not a little to bring the debates at Westminster to a speedy determination."

The conference of the Houses of Lords and Commons considered a full report of this audience which the Prince gave, and after his views on the subject of the accession to the throne were known, and with the throne declared vacant, it was agreed that the Prince and Princess of Orange be offered a "double bottomed Monarchy," namely that they be invited to accept joint rule as equal partners on the throne.

Then there followed one of the most important events in the growth of true democracy in this country, one which laid the foundation-stone of a new constitution, and set out clearly the future relationship between the Monarch and the people. The "Declaration of Right", which later was embodied in the Bill of Rights, and passed into the law of the land in December 1689, was conceived.

Thursday, 7 February:
"The Commons," says Macaulay, decided that "the instrument by which the Prince and Princess of Orange were called to the throne, and by which the order of succession was settled, should set forth in the most distinct and solemn manner the fundamental principles of the constitution. This instrument, known by the name of the Declaration of Right, was prepared by a committee of which Somers [an up and coming young barrister] was chairman. In a few hours the Declaration was framed and approved by the Commons. The Lords assented to it with some amendments of no great importance.

"The Declaration began by recapitulating the crimes and errors which had made a revolution necessary. James had invaded the province of the legislature; had treated modest petitioning as a crime; had oppressed the Church by means of an illegal tribunal; had, without the consent of Parliament, levied taxes and maintained a standing army in time of peace; had violated the freedom of election and perverted the course of justice. . . He, by whose authority these things had been done, had abdicated the government. The Prince of Orange, whom God had made the glorious instrument of delivering the nation from superstition and tyranny, had invited the Estates of the Realm to meet and to take counsel together for the securing of religion, of law and of freedom. The Lords and Commons, having deliberated, had resolved that they would first, after the example of their ancestors, assert the ancient rights and liberties of England. Therefore it was declared that the dispensing power, as lately assumed and exercised, had no legal existence; that, without grant of Parliament, no money could be exacted by the sovereign from the subject; that, without consent of Parliament, no standing army could be kept up in time of peace. The right of subjects to petition, the right of electors to choose representatives freely, the right of the legislature to freedom of debate, the right of the nation to a pure and merciful administration of justice according to the spirit of our mild laws, were solemnly affirmed. All these things the Convention claimed as the undoubted inheritance of Englishmen."

Extract from the original black-letter text of the Bill of Rights.
It would pass into law in December 1689. Courtesy the Clerk of the Records, at the House of Lords, Westminster.

Lords and Commons Resolved

HAVING THUS vindicated the principles of the constitution, the Lords and Commons, in the entire confidence that the deliverer would hold sacred the laws and liberties which he had saved, resolved that William and Mary, Prince and Princess of Orange, should be declared King and Queen of England for their joint and separate lives, and that, during their joint lives, the administration of the government should be in the Prince alone. After them the crown was settled on the posterity of Mary, then on Anne and her posterity, and then on the posterity of William.

The Declaration clearly set out the vital religious qualification. It stated that no Catholic could become King or Queen of England, and extended the ban to any who was the wife or husband of a Catholic. A new oath of allegiance was also devised and included.

The Declaration of Rights—which became the Bill of Rights in December 1689—did little more than restate the principles of freedom and religion which James had trampled underfoot, and which William had come to restore, but it is significant that in it lay the seeds of future discord, and of bitter resentment on the part of William at his treatment by Parliament which, by its control of the state revenue, was enabled to exercise more and more power, and the Monarch correspondingly less. During 1689, Parliament refused to award William a sufficient revenue for life, limiting his income to a regular sum for civil administration, the "Civil List," whilst Parliament held control of other expenditure, particularly for the waging of war. In this way it ensured that it would continue to meet frequently and regularly, and the royal power to summon and dismiss Parliament would be limited. A furious William told Halifax that "the Commons used him like a dog," but he was powerless to change matters.

The Princess of Orange had been kept in Holland by unfavourable winds, but now the weather changed, the winds went round into the east, and she sailed for England. On 11 February her ship lay off Margate, and on the following morning it made its way up the Thames and anchored at Greenwich.

Tuesday, 12 February:
The Prince had previously written to Mary asking her to behave happily and cheerfully when she arrived in England, and she was to overplay this part for a time, although she felt far from cheerful. She was concerned that attempts had been made to separate her interests from those of William; she naturally regretted the plight of her father: "I cannot forget my father and I grieve for his misfortune," she said; and she was miserable at leaving the country where "I had the esteem of the inhabitants, and where I had led a life so suitable to my humour and, as I think, not unacceptable to my God; where, in a word, I had all earthly content."

William and Mary greeted each other with real affection, but the Princess was concerned at her husband's appearance. The stress of the campaign together with the subsequent events in London had taken their toll, and his health, never robust, was poor. Mary made an effort to appear bright and buoyant, and she entered Whitehall "laughing and jolly as to a wedding, so as to seem quite transported".

Shrove Tuesday, 12 February:
The Princess was up early in the morning, before her ladies-in-waiting were about, and ran about her new home from fine room to fine room. She peeped into cupboards "with girlish delight," and "lay in the same apartment where the queen lay" seemingly without a thought for the previous occupant. She even shocked some of the die-hards

after a few nights by playing basset as the Queen used to do, and moved the Duchess of Marlborough to criticism, her ladyship observing that Mary was "wanting bowels," and that her behaviour on arriving at Whitehall was "very strange and unbecoming". Evelyn in his Diary wrote; "She seems to be of good nature, and she takes nothing to heart; whilst the prince her husband has a thoughtful countenance, is wonderful serious and silent, and seems to treat all persons alike gravely, and to be very intent on affairs".

One of the last entries in Whittle's Diary refers to the outcome of the debate in the Lords and Commons, and then to the Banqueting House where Lords and Commons were received by William and Mary: "And with all expedition on the 12th of February, the Lords and Commons consulted about the Settlement of our Government: and agreed that the late King James the Second having endeavour'd to subvert and extirpate the Protestant Religion, &c., and having abdicated the Government, the Throne was thereby become vacant, They did resolve that William and Mary, Prince and Princess of Orange, be, and be declared King and Queen of England, France and Ireland, and the Dominions thereunto belonging, &c.

"On the 12th of February, Her Royal Highness the Princess of Orange arrived at Whitehall, the welcome news whereof was received with Ringing of Bells, Bonfires, and other Publick Demonstrations of Joy. The next day the Lords and Commons assembled at Westminster, attended their Highnesses at the Banqueting-house with their Resolve, and received their Consent thereto, and about 11 of the Clock proclaimed William and Mary, Prince and Princess of Orange, King and Queen of England, France and Ireland, and the Dominions thereunto belonging. After that their Majesties were Proclaimed before Whitehall, And the Lord Mayor and Aldermen of the Famous City of London, together with the Sheriffs met the Lords and Heralds at Arms at Temple-Bar, and there Proclaimed their Majesties King William and Queen Mary, &c. And so proceeded to the Royal Exchange, where the same was done a third time.

"The day concluding with Ringing of Bells and Bonfires, to the General Satisfaction of all.

"After their most excellent Majesties were proclaimed all over England, there was great preparation made in order to their Majesties Coronation."

Wednesday, 13 February:
A more detailed account of the Proclamation Ceremony is given by Macaulay, who describes the preparation of the magnificent Banqueting House. The Yeoman of the Guard lined the walls, and near the Northern Door on the right-hand side the Peers had assembled, whilst the Commons with their Speaker attended by the Mace were on the left. "The Southern Door opened," he continues, "and the Prince and Princess of Orange, side by side, entered and took their place under the Canopy of State.

"Both Houses bowing low, William and Mary advanced a few steps. Halifax on the right and Powle on the left stood forth, and Halifax spoke. The Convention, he said, had agreed to a resolution, which he prayed their Highnesses to hear. They signified their assent, and the Clerk of the House of Lords read, in a loud voice, the Declaration of Right. When he concluded, Halifax, in the name of all the Estates of the Realm, requested the Prince and Princess to accept the Crown.

"William, in his own name and in that of his wife, answered that the Crown was, in their estimation, more valuable because it was presented to them as a token of the confidence of the nation. 'We thankfully accept,' he said, 'what you have offered us.' Then for himself he assured them that the laws of England, which he had once already vindicated, should be rules of his conduct, that it should be his study to promote the welfare of the Kingdom, and that, as to the means of doing so, he should constantly

Reading the Declaration of Rights to the Prince and Princess of Orange.
In the Banqueting House, an Inigo Jones building in Whitehall, on 13 February 1689. They were then jointly offered, and accepted, the Crown of England. Courtesy the BBC Hulton Picture Library.

recur to the advice of the Houses, and should be disposed to trust their judgement rather than his own [a new concept of kingship]. These words were received with shouts of joy, which were heard in the streets below, and were instantly answered by huzzas from many thousands of voices.

"The Lords and Commons then reverently retired from the Banqueting House and went in procession to the great gate of Whitehall, where the heralds and pursuivants were waiting in their gorgeous tabards. All the space as far as Charing Cross was a sea of heads. The kettledrums struck up; the trumpets pealed; the Garter King of Arms, in a loud voice, proclaimed the Prince and Princess of Orange King and Queen of England, charged all Englishmen to bear, from that moment, true allegience to the new Sovereigns, and besought God, who had already wrought so signal a deliverance for our Church and Nation, to bless William and Mary with a long and happy reign."

The Coronation would be held on 11 April, 1689. The English Revolution had come to a glorious moment in its devolution. The wishes of the Convention had been amicably received.

The people of London welcomed the proclamations, and cheered and cheered again. Every window from Whitehall to Piccadilly was ablaze with light. The Staterooms of the Palace were thrown open and a dazzling crowd of courtiers filled them as they waited to kiss the hands of the King and Queen.

There were celebrations throughout the country. For three weeks afterwards the Gazettes reported "cavalcades of gentlemen and yeoman, processions of sheriffs and bailiffs in scarlet gowns, musters of zealous Protestants with orange flags and ribands, salutes, bonfires, illuminations, music, balls, dinners, gutters running with ale and conduits spouting claret".

Abroad, there were rejoicings in Holland that the First Minister of the

Commonwealth had been raised to a throne. On the day after accepting the Crown William had written to Waldeck: "I wished not to delay in informing you that after the petition which Parliament has made to ask me to be their King, I have accepted and we have just been proclaimed. I assure you it is no light burden, and I considered it thoroughly, but could not exempt myself.

"I imagine you know me well enough to believe that the lustre of the crown does not dazzle me. If it had not been absolutely necessary I should not have accepted it—as those who have been here can witness—and unless I was willing to lose everything I could not have acted otherwise."

*   *   *   *

It was obvious to William that he could not engage the power and resources of England in his great plan to gain independence for Europe from France, and free his own country of Holland from the threat of French domination, unless he accepted the Crown of England. This was his consuming ambition, and he had now taken the first great step towards its fulfilment; although even on the throne there were many problems to face and difficulties to overcome, not the least being the continuing threat of the resurgence of James's power, particularly in Scotland and Ireland, and also the obstinate temper of the English Parliament.

At least the Prince was now able to keep his promises to Waldeck, and he sent several regiments back to Holland.

Saturday, 23 February:

The King approved a Bill which made the Convention into a Parliament, and so began the difficult but vital task of gaining the goodwill of the members, and endeavouring to bring together into some harmony the differing factions of a disorganised and demoralised people. The two great parties, the Whigs and the Tories, were at the time, as a result of the actions of James, momentarily united, but this condition would not survive for long now that James had gone and there was a prospect of a settled monarchy and smooth government under William and Mary. William wished to be above party politics, but this could only be if he were independent of Parliament, and by the very nature of the revolution this was impossible. His natural allies were the Whigs, who had for the most part instigated the revolution, but the political principles of the Whigs included the lessening of the power of the sovereign. The Tories were the royalists, who by tradition and inclination always supported the monarch, but in this case, which monarch? Most Tories at this time in their hearts supported James. They saw little profit for themselves in the new order, and were not inclined to give their allegience to a king whose title they were not prepared to acknowledge.

Whilst William had been in his favourite position as a military leader, and the champion and deliverer of the English nation, his popularity and success were assured, but with the deliverance achieved, the throne accepted, and the need now to turn from military matters and grapple with English politics, difficulties arose on all sides.

It was noticed that during all the celebrations of the Proclamation, two important groups took little part in the festivities. Seldom was there either a priest or a soldier to be seen in the crowds which gathered to hear the new King and Queen proclaimed. Both the clergy and the army had suffered injury to their professional pride, and they took little part in the general rejoicing.

The clergy had great difficulty in reconciling the abdication of James, and the accession in his stead of William and Mary, with all that they had been in the habit of preaching to their flock at great length in the past about the duty of the subject to his king. As Burnet wrote, "The truth was, the greatest part of the clergy had entangled themselves so far with those strange conceits of the divine right of monarchy, and the unlawfulness of resistance in any case; and they had so engaged themselves, by asserting these things so often and so publicly, that they did not know how to disengage themselves in honour, or conscience." Some managed it, and gave their support to William and Mary, but the far greater part of the clergy held aloof.

The attitude of the army, who also stood apart, discontented, silent and surly, is, perhaps, easier to understand. As individuals, the soldiers hated popery as much as the rest of the populace, and had little time for James II, but as a professional army they were resentful and ashamed of the role which they had been compelled to play in the campaign. Their army, the regular army, whose equal had never marched under the English standard, had ignominiously retreated before the invader, and had been withdrawn without ever attempting a trial of strength, or even striking a blow. This great force "had done nothing towards keeping William out and none towards bringing him in". The troops felt that Lovelace and his train of rustics armed with pitchforks had taken a bigger part in the Revolution than their own splendid Household Troops, with their "plumed hats, embroidered coats and curvetting chargers in Hyde Park," which had drawn such admiration from the Londoners.

During his campaign, and when he was in London, William had detailed the British regiments serving under him for all duties which, given to the foreigners, might have caused offence; but in spite of his discretion he could not appease the royal army. The troops felt disgraced, and their feelings were further aggravated by the taunts of the foreigners. An increasing irritation was occasioned by the admirable discipline of the Dutch soldiers, and the public lost no time in making comparisons between the smart conduct of the newcomers and that of the redcoats. Discontent spread rapidly among the troops, to such a degree that during the celebrations at Cirencester, a battalion doused the bonfires, cheered for King James, and "drank confusion to his daughter and his nephew". At Plymouth the garrison rioted at the festivities of the county of Cornwall and there was fighting in which a man was killed.

The ill-humour of the clergy and the soldiers provoked an angry outburst by a Whig in the Commons, who declared: "Black coats and red coats are the curses of the nation!"

On the day that the Commons agreed to the repayment to the United Provinces in Holland of the expenses which had supported William's campaign in England, a sum of no less than six hundred thousand pounds, alarming news reached Westminster, which convinced Parliament that the services of the foreign troops could not be dispensed with. France had declared war against the States General, and England, bound by the Treaty of Nijmegen, had to provide troops for their defence.

Friday, 8 March:

Lieutenant General Lord Marlborough was ordered to embark four battalions of guards and six of the line, including the First Battalion Royal Scots, the Seventh and Twenty-first Buffs, Collier's and Fitzpatrick's, for Holland.

Among the Royal Scots, smouldering resentment was ready to flame into open mutiny on two accounts:

First, with the best possible motives, William had appointed the Duke of Schomberg, acknowledged the greatest soldier in Europe, Colonel of the Royal Scots. Although he had previously fought alongside the Royal Scots in the cause of the

Protestant religion, and had in fact sacrificed his Marshal's baton to do so, he was not, of course, a Scot. This rankled with the fiercely Scottish regiment, whose colonels had only ever been a Mackay, a Hepburn or a Douglas.

Second, the Convention in London, which was not a Scottish assembly, had with reference to none transferred the allegience of the Regiment from King James II to William of Orange-Nassau. If they had to serve William, they should be so ordered by the Estates at Edinburgh, and not by the Convention at Westminster.

The forces were ordered to assemble at Harwich in order to embark for Holland. Truculent and complaining, the Scots marched to Ipswich, and here, in the market place, two Jacobite officers gave the signal to revolt, the men mutinied, and utter chaos ensued, with pikemen and musketeers running wildly, and muskets discharged at will. Officers who tried to quell the riot and restore order were attacked and disarmed, whilst the rebellious officers seized the army chest containing a considerable amount of money, and four cannon. Turning northwards, the mutineers advanced by forced marches in the direction of Scotland.

The Government was seriously alarmed, and both in the Commons and in the Lords immediate pursuit was counselled, and messengers were ordered to be sent to the King with this advice. William received the messengers with his customary courtesy, and informed them that he had already despatched Ginckel, one of his best officers, with a substantial force, after the mutineers.

The Scots made good progress, and were near Sleaford in Lincolnshire when they learned that Ginckel was on their trail. Their leaders urged them to give battle, and they took up a position on a knoll almost surrounded by swamps, with the cannon placed to cover the vulnerable approach. Ginckel ordered an attack out of the range of the artillery. His dragoons forded the swamps and swam their horses across the watercourses, and the insurgents, overwhelmed and helpless to resist, surrendered their arms.

Despite the enormity of their offence—not only mutiny, but waging war against the Crown—William dealt mildly with the men, and having picked out some of the ringleaders for punishment, ordered the remainder to return to duty, and the Royal Scots Guards duly embarked for Holland.

For William, good came from this episode. The Commons in particular had had a real scare, and not only did they approve the expenses of William's expedition and pay the United Provinces of Holland without further ado, but they were also frightened into passing the first Mutiny Act on 12 April 1689, which recognised that civil law was not competent to deal with military offences, and which, most important of all, "gave the army more or less a statutory right to exist". It would be re-enacted annually for the next two hundred years.

* * * *

A few days before the mutiny, Tyrconnel, the Lord Deputy of Ireland, who had built up a formidable Catholic force in that country, had called the Irish to arms in support of King James. Having prevailed upon King Louis XIV of France to provide him with the aid he needed, James landed at Cork on 14 March with several hundred officers to organise the enrolment of the Irish troops. Tyrconnel had been preparing for this day since before the Revolution, and had already mustered a number of regiments of Irish troops. Some of these went over to James in their entirety, whilst others split into groups of "Irish" (the Catholics) and Protestants, and were on opposite sides.

William and the Government of England were in no doubt that nothing less than the re-conquest of Ireland lay before them, as nearly the whole of that country was in the hands of James.

By this time several regiments had been sent to Flanders, and it was evident that the army must be increased in size for the campaign in Ireland. Fortescue, in his *History of the British Army* gives some details. Estimates were prepared for the cost of raising "Six Regiments of Horse, Two of Dragoons, Twenty-five of Foot". Among the Irish Corps which James brought over to England during William's march from Tor Bay was the 1st Lord Forbes's Regiment, which was made up entirely of Protestants; and William did not disband this unit on his accession. On 8 March 1689, Major Erle, of Charborough Park in Dorset, was appointed Colonel of a new regiment of foot, and he continued in command throughout the campaign in Ireland.

Possibly because of the attractive colour of the uniform of King William's own Dutch Blue Guards, three of the new regiments wore blue coats instead of the usual scarlet.

So in the spring of 1689 no less than ten thousand more men were needed for enlistment into the army, and all had to be equipped, trained and drilled. In addition, a rot had spread through the whole military system. Fortescue comments that it was not long before William and Schomberg made the discovery that the old regiments would need as much watching as the new. Rumours of false muster-rolls and other embezzlement and fraud were rife, and reports were received of the ill-treatment of the English in Flanders. Waldeck sent disquieting news. He said that the English regiments were below standard, the officers ill-paid, and the men sickly and listless; "nonchalants" was the word he used.

William immediately sent his best officer, John Churchill, Earl of Marlborough, to bring order to this unruly and dispirited army, and Marlborough soon earned praise from Waldeck both for his own capabilities and for the qualities of his men after his first encounter with Marshal d'Humières at Walcourt.

In addition to the troubles in Flanders and in Ireland, the Revolution in Scotland was proving far more stormy than in England, largely because it was conducted by a number of separate chiefs, without any central direction. John Graham of Claverhouse, Viscount Dundee, known as "Bluidy Claverhouse" from his brutal and relentless repression of the free-thinking Covenanters, was an ardent supporter of James II and the Stuart cause, and rushed into rebellion, stirring up those Highland clans who were loyal to James. Ironically, he was an old comrade of William, and was reputed to have saved his life at the battle of Seniff in 1674. William had consented to call a Convention in Scotland similar to that at Westminster, and this body, known by its Scottish title of the "Estates", was an assembly of the representatives of the various orders or "states" of men with political power. It met on 14 March in the Parliament House in Edinburgh. It was clear from the beginning that here there were two bitterly opposed factions again, Whigs and Tories, the former for William and the latter, at heart if not overtly, for James. The Duke of Hamilton, for the Whigs, was elected President of the Assembly, defeating by forty votes the rival candidate, the Jacobite Marquess of Athol.

The Assembly was uncomfortably reluctant to proceed to business whilst the Parliament House where they sat was threatened by the batteries of Edinburgh Castle, held by the Duke of Gordon for James, and a delegation was sent to Gordon to order him to evacuate the Castle within twenty-four hours. He asked for a night in which to consider the situation, and used the time in secretly consulting Dundee, who still lurked in Edinburgh. His eventual reply to the Estates was that whilst he would not think of harassing them, neither would he "resign his command at such time". The Estates threatened him with trial for high treason, and posted guards at the approaches to the castle, but Gordon remained.

A letter to the Estates from William was read, a "well weighed and prudent letter". This was followed by the reading of a letter from James, which brought despair to the Jacobites. "It was plain," says Macaulay, "that adversity had taught James neither wisdom nor mercy. All was obstinacy, cruelty, insolence . . . Not only was no sorrow expressed for past offences, but the letter itself was a new offence. The hall was in a tumult. His friends, angry with him and ashamed of him, saw it was vain to think of continuing the struggle in the Convention."

When the assembly met on the following Monday it was discovered that Dundee had left Edinburgh to raise insurrection in Stirling. There was uproar in the Parliament House, and the Assembly resolved to protect itself. The Jacobites became prisoners, and Protestants were ordered to be ready to take up arms at a moment's notice. Gordon was still in the Castle, but he adhered to his pledge not to fire upon the city.

William sent on board a squadron of warships a force of three Scottish regiments from his own army commanded by Hugh Mackay. They landed on the shores of the Firth of Forth, and Mackay was appointed General of the Forces by the Convention, who now felt able to offer the Crown of Scotland to William and Mary. This they did on the day of their coronation in England, 11 April, 1689.

Thursday, 11 April:

Whittle describes the coronation of William and Mary: "The Day being come, viz. April 11, 1689, Their Majesties came from Whitehall to Westminster, and the Nobility being put in Order by the Heralds, They came down in State into Westminster-Hall, where the Swords and Spurs were presented to them. Their Majesties being at Westminster-Abbey, the Right Reverend Father in God the Lord Bishop of Sarum [Burnet] preached the Sermon, his Text being 2 Sam.23, 3, 4. And after the Ceremonies of the Coronation were finished, about four of the Clock the Crowns were put upon their Royal Heads by the Right Reverend Father in God the Lord Bishop of London, assisted by several other Bishops. At the sight whereof the People shouted, the Drums and Trumpets sounded, the great Guns at the Tower &c. were discharged, and the Peers and Peeresses put on their Coronets."

Macaulay fills in the picture with rather more detail: "Mary, being not merely Queen Consort but also Queen Regnant, was inaugurated in all things like a King, was girt with the Sword, lifted up into the Throne, and presented with the Bible, the Spurs and the Orb. Of the temporal grandees of the realm and of their wives and daughters, the muster was great and splendid. None could be surprised that the Whig aristocracy should swell the triumph of Whig principles. But the Jacobites saw with concern that many Lords who had voted for a Regency bore a conspicuous part in the ceremonial. The King's crown was carried by Grafton, the Queen's by Somerset. The pointed sword, emblematic of temporal justice, was borne by Pembroke. Ormond was Lord High Constable for the day, and rode up the Hall on the right hand of the hereditary Champion, who thrice flung down his glove on the pavement, and thrice defied to mortal combat the false traitor who should gainsay the title of William and Mary."

Amongst the maids in waiting to the Queen was Henrietta Hyde, daughter of Rochester, who had voted against the resolution which had declared the throne vacant. There were few Bishops present, and the Primate was absent, so Compton took his place. On one side of Compton the paten was carried by Lloyd, Bishop of St. Asaph, and on the other, in charge of the chalice, was Sprat, Bishop of Rochester. Dr. Burnet, the junior prelate, preached well, and with greater delicacy than usual. "His grave and eloquent discourse was polluted neither by flattery nor malignity."

The coronation ceremony went off well, and it was a day of general rejoicing. Churches were full in the morning, and the afternoon was taken up with sport and festivities. At night bonfires were lighted and rockets set off, and all the windows were lit with candles. On this scene, the Reverend John Whittle brings his diary to a loyal close:

"Their Majesties being Crowned, returned to Westminster-Hall, And Dinner being ended, and the whole Solemnity perform'd with great Splendour and Magnificence, about Eight in the evening their Majesties return'd to White-Hall. Where I most humbly leave them, heartily beseeching Almighty God to bless and preserve their most excellent Majesties, that they may long Live and Flourish together, To the advancement of his Glory, the Good of his Church, the Safety, Honour and Welfare of their Majesties Kingdoms, and the exceeding Joy and Comfort of all good Protestants. As for all their Enemies let them (O God) be daily discover'd and brought to Shame and Confusion; but upon their Sacred and Royal Heads, let the Crowns of England, Scotland, France and Ireland long Flourish."

Honours were duly distributed after the coronation. Devon, Ormond and Schomberg were awarded the Garter; Prince George was created Duke of Cumberland; Danby became Marquess of Carmarthen; Churchill the Earl of Marlborough; and Bentinck was made Earl of Portland. The appointment of Mordaunt as Earl of Monmouth was not popular with those who still remembered fondly the Protestant Duke, and who had hoped that his title would be restored to his descendants. Halifax received no advancement, though no doubt he would have been honoured had he desired it. Macaulay suggests that he held such a gloomy view of the immediate future of the country and the new monarchy that he preferred to lie low. If the government could endure through the summer, he felt that it would probably survive.

No such gloom clouded the festivities which continued throughout London and across the country. A surviving broadsheet published in Bath claims to be "a true and perfect Relation of the great and splendid Procession and joyful Transactions" held in the City "on the 11th day of April; being Coronation-day of their most sacred Majesties William and Mary, King and Queen". The broadsheet goes on to detail the various groups which made up the Procession, including "a hundred young men in holland shirts, richly adorned, and carrying naked swords in their hands as a protection to the succeeding train of two hundred virgins . . . with crowns on their heads and sceptres in their hands. They carried also two flags: on one, 'God save King William and Queen Mary: Let their enemies perish' and on the other, 'This is a joyful day.' . . . Then came the militia with drums and colours accompanied by acclamations of unforced joy exceeding anything ever seen. After marching twice round the city, they entered the Guildhall and attended a sumptuous banquet . . ."

A splendid send-off for the "double-bottomed" monarchy!

OVERLEAF: the Coronation of the Prince and Princess of Orange.
In Westminster Abbey, on 11 April 1689. From an engraving by R. de Hooghe.
Courtesy the Rijksmuseum, Amsterdam.

Vuirwerk voor Withall.

Haare Maiesteiten ontfangen het Heiligen Avondmaal.

Z. M. met de Keisers Kroon gehuldt voorts de Regalia gebeet.

KROONING VAN WILLEM DE III. EN MARIA, TOT KONING EN KO

Vuirwerk voor den Touwr

Z.M. Offerd de Gouden beur

Z.M. flaat Ridders; en doet Medalien onder het volk firoojen.

VAN ENGELAND, ENZ. IN WESTMUNSTERS ABDY DEN $\frac{11}{21}$ APRIL 1689.

The Crown of Scotland had yet to be accepted by William and Mary, and since these events took place before the Act of Union, a separate coronation had to be held to crown them King and Queen of Scotland. This ceremony took place at Whitehall on 11 May, 1689.

It differed in many respects from the English coronation. Three commissioners had been appointed by the Scottish Convention to bring the "Instrument of Government" to London. They were Argyle, Montgomery and Dalrymple. Argyle, though legally not strictly a Peer, represented the Peers. Sir James Montgomery represented the Commissioners of the Shires, and Sir John Dalrymple the Commissioners of the Towns. These representatives came to the Council Chamber at Whitehall, and attended by Scotsmen of note then in London, went to the Banqueting House.

William and Mary were seated under a canopy, and they were encircled by a splendid group of English Nobles and Statesmen. Macaulay describes what followed: "The Sword of State was carried by a Scottish Lord, and the oath of office was administered in the Scotch manner. Argyle recited the words slowly. The royal pair, holding up their hands towards heaven, repeating after him till they came to the last clause. Here William paused. That clause contained a promise that he would root out all heretics and all enemies of the true worship of God, and it was notorious that, in the opinion of many Scotchmen, not only all Roman Catholics, but all Protestant Episcopalians, all Independents, Baptists and Quakers, all Lutherans, nay all British Presbyterians who did not hold themselves bound by the Solemn League and Covenant, were enemies of the true worship of God. The King had appraised the Commissioners that he could not take this part of the oath without a distinct and public explanation, and they had been authorised by the Convention to give such an explanation as would satisfy him. 'I will not,' he now said, 'lay myself under any obligation to be a persecutor.' 'Neither the words of this oath,' said one of the Commissioners, 'nor the laws of Scotland lay any such obligation on Your Majesty.' 'In that sense, then, I swear,' said William, 'and I desire you all, my lords and gentlemen, to witness that I do so.' Even his detractors have generally admitted that on this great occasion he acted with uprightness, dignity and wisdom."

Insurrection in Scotland

AS KING of Scotland William soon discovered that he had as many problems there as he had in England. The insurrection there had begun to develop into a civil war, and the King had already sent Mackay with his small force to quell it, but skilful as Mackay had shown himself to be in battles on the fields of Flanders, he was no match for the canny Highland Scots, who were so difficult to bring to battle in their own wild country, pursue them how he would. He merely succeeded in wasting weeks of effort, and exhausting his men and horses in brief skirmishes, and in marching and counter-marching. At length he realised that the only way to subdue the Highlanders was to build a chain of fortresses at strategic points and garrison them. The first, he suggested, should be at Inverlochy, where the remains of an ancient castle stood. It was near the sea, and it was in the heart of the country occupied by the rebellious clans —the Macdonalds, the Camerons and the Macleans. They could be kept in check by a strong force stationed there, supported by warships.

At the same time Dundee, the leader of the rising, was beset with troubles of a different kind. Because he himself was no Highlander, he had moderate success at first in his efforts to combine the different clans into a disciplined force, but he was dealing with haughty, independent chiefs such as the Macdonald of Keppoch, or the Maclean of Duart; men who scarcely acknowledged the King as their superior, and who would certainly never accept an inferior position under the chief of another clan. Only by argument, flattery, bribery and supplication was the Commander able to bring harmony among them for a short time. So unreliable were his forces that Dundee might find at any time that "his right wing had fired on his centre in pursuance of some quarrel two hundred years old, or that a whole battalion had marched back to its native glen because another battalion had been put in the post of honour. Local jealousies and local interests had brought his army together; local jealousies and local interests dissolved it. The Gordons left him because they fancied he neglected them for the Macdonalds. The Macdonalds left him because they wanted to plunder the Campbells. The force which Dundee had thought enough to decide the fate of the kingdom faded away in a few days."

Dundee made another attempt to bring them together under the discipline of a regular army. In May and June he wrote to James II at Dublin asking for reinforcements to be sent to Lochaber. He received reassuring replies which led him to believe that the forces for which he asked would soon be sent from Ulster, and he decided to wait at Lochaber until they arrived.

Mackay's forces were resting in quarters spread out over the lowlands from Aberdeen to Stirling, and Mackay himself was at Edinburgh trying to persuade the King's Ministers to grant him the funds necessary to set up his chain of fortifications in the Grampians. He then found that the troops which should have been available to him were unwilling to enlist. He had decided that he must have fresh troops for his next campaign, and he had expected that Covenanters of Western Scotland, known for their hatred of "Bluidy Claverhouse" (Viscount Dundee), would have readily provided recruits, but the Covenanters had qualms about joining King William's army, ('wherein they might be set shoulder to shoulder with the immoral, and even worse, the unorthodox.) Even Mackay, a man of extreme piety ("the piousest man I ever knew" said Dr. Burnet) was suspected by them. At a turbulent gathering the majority proclaimed that "military service was a sinful association". Even so, there were sufficient volunteers for the Earl of Angus to form a body of infantry twelve hundred strong, which, "now numbered 26 of the line", says Fortescue in 1899, "is still best known by its first name of Cameronians".

The Covenanters had odd ideas about military organisation. "They desired that each company should furnish an elder, who with the chaplain should constitute a court for the suppression of heresy and immorality; and though the elders were never appointed, and the officers bore the usual titles of captain, lieutenant and ensign, yet the chaplain, a noted hill preacher, supplied in his own person fanaticism for all." So, in spite of the ranting of the majority, the red coat was once more donned by a true Puritan regiment, under Angus, a youth of eighteen, who was the youngest colonel since Henry Cromwell. The first lieutenant-colonel was Cleland, who had driven Dundee from the Convention. During this period the Duke of Gordon surrendered Edinburgh Castle, the garrison marched out and the keys were handed over.

Blair Castle in Athol, was of outstanding military importance. About five miles south of this stronghold is the Pass of Perthshire. The river Garry runs through it, and at the north end of the pass is Killiecrankie. The glen of Killiecrankie was in those days spoken of in fear by men of peace, for it was regarded as the most perilous of all the dark ravines where lurked the brigands of the Highlands, who ambushed and murdered their victims in such places. The steep, narrow and rugged pathway through the pass would barely accommodate two men abreast, and a horse could be led through only with great difficulty. In places the path ran dangerously close to the edge of a precipice.

At Blair Castle events were developing which would draw the two main forces in Scotland, under Mackay and Dundee respectively, into confrontation and battle.

The steward and confidential agent of the Marquess of Athol, Steward of Ballenach, together with the garrison within the Castle, had declared for James, whilst Lord Murray, the eldest son and heir of the Marquess, was for William, and had twelve hundred men to back him. The Marquess himself, a weak-willed man, who had at different times declared himself both for William and for James, had "retired to Bath to take the waters". Furious at being denied access to the family castle, which would be his own eventually, Murray clamoured at the gates, and clansman fought with fellow clansman.

Seeking aid, Ballenach sent to Dundee at Lochaber, whilst Murray called for assistance from Mackay at Edinburgh. Both messages provoked instant response, for both Dundee and Mackay saw the importance of Blair Castle. On it depended the fate of all Athol, and on Athol might depend the fate of Scotland. Mackay summoned his scattered forces and moved north at the head of three thousand men. Dundee called forth all the clans which he believed supported him, and "sent the fiery crosses in all haste through Appin and Ardnamurchan, up Glenmore and along Loch Leven," and he moved on Blair Castle with somewhat less than three thousand Highlanders, together with a small force of Irish foot which James had sent, "ill-armed, ill-clothed and ill-disciplined".

Meanwhile, Murray was in difficulties. His besieging army had begun to shrink and dwindle in numbers. His clansmen hated Whigs, whom they considered to be synonymous with the Campbells, their traditional enemies. Opposed to them were numbers of their kinsmen, commanded by one who represented the Marquess, and they began to find a number of reasons to defect. Some said plainly that they would not fight in such a dispute. Others pleaded the need to ensure the safety of the families and their cattle if war were to develop in this area. One other large group left for another reason altogether. Making for a nearby brook, they filled their bonnets with water and drank nosily to King James. They then dispersed and hid themselves among the rocks and shrubbery which overhung the river Garry, where they lay ready to plunder any corpses after battle, and steal what they could find.   Murray was finally left with three or four hundred men to face the oncoming Macdonalds and Camerons, and he decided to raise the siege of the castle and withdraw to the shelter of the Killiecrankie Pass.   Here he was shortly joined by a detachment of two hundred fusileers sent ahead by Mackay to hold the pass, and the main body of the Lowland troops followed on their heels.

Macaulay gives an account of the battle: On 27 July in the early morning Dundee reached Blair Castle, and when he knew that Mackay's troops were in the Pass he conferred with his chiefs.   The Saxon officers were against giving battle, but the fiery Celts Glengarry and Lochiel were ready to go to war.   "Fight, my Lord", said Lochiel with his usual energy: "Fight immediately: fight if you have only one to three.   Our men are in heart.   Their only fear is that the enemy should escape.   Give them their way; and be assured that they will either perish or gain a complete victory.   But if you restrain them, if you force them to remain on the defensive, I answer for nothing.   If we do not fight, we had better break up and retire to our mountains."

Dundee's countenance brightened.   "You hear, gentlemen," he said to his Lowland officers.   "You hear the opinion of one who understands the Highland war better than any of us."   It was determined to fight, and the clans advanced to meet the enemy.

Mackay's forces were resting from the arduous climb up the Pass.   It had been a long, wearisome struggle.   Even the foot soldiers had to climb in twos and threes, and the twelve hundred baggage horses could climb only one at a time.   The head of the column emerged onto the tableland whilst the rearguard was still on the plain.   At length, when they had completed the ascent, the troops found themselves in a valley of no great size.   Their right was flanked by rising ground, and on their left was the river Garry.   Wearied by their morning's exertions, they threw themselves on the grass to rest.

27 July, 1689 — the Battle of Killiekrankie:

The alarm was given in the early afternoon—the Highlanders were coming.   The regiments rose in order, for in a very short time the top of the Pass was covered with tartan-clad men as Dundee's troops emerged to confront them, and paused about a musket-shot away.   Fire was steadily exchanged, and the space between the two armies became clouded with smoke.   Some Highlanders were wounded, and the clans became impatient for battle, but Dundee waited until the sun was setting before giving the order to prepare for action.   His men raised a great cheer, which was answered only feebly by Mackay's exhausted troops.   "We shall do it now", said Lochial.   "That is not the cry of men who are going to win."

Just after seven o'clock Dundee ordered the attack.   The Highlanders flung away all their encumbrances and advanced in bare feet; men remembered after, in Lochaber, how Lochiel took off what probably was the only pair of shoes in his clan and charged barefoot at the head of his men.   They fired as they ran, and Mackay's army returned the fire, and caused many casualties.   Suddenly, as they closed, the Highlanders threw away their muskets, drew their swords, and with the most bloodcurdling yells rushed upon the enemy.   Whilst the Lowlanders were still awkwardly fitting their bayonets to the muzzles of their guns a torrent of Macleans, Macdonalds and Camerons poured over them, and within a few minutes the battle was over.   The Lowland regiments broke before the Highland charge.   Of the three Scottish regiments which William had originally sent north under Mackay, with Balfour and Ramsay, Balfour was hacked down in the melée and his men scattered; Ramsay's men turned and threw down their arms, and Mackay's own infantry were swept away by the fierce charge of the Camerons.   His brother and his nephew both tried in vain to rally the men.   His

Duart Castle, Isle of Mull: home of the Macleans.
The Macleans joined James's Highlanders for their victory at Killiecrankie, Perthshire, on 17 July 1689. The present Lord Maclean is the twenty-seventh Chief of the Clan Maclean.

brother was struck down and killed, and his nephew sustained eight wounds as he struggled through the frenzied troops to his uncle's side.

Mackay retained his customary self-possession, hoping that it was still not too late for a cavalry charge to save the day, but he called on the mounted troops in vain. Belhaven stood his ground, but his troopers, terrified by the rout of the infantry, turned and galloped off in disarray. Annandale's men followed suit, and "the mingled torrent of red coats and tartans went raving down the valley to the gorge of Killiecrankie".

Mackay, with a trusty servant by his side, rode gallantly through the thickest part of the battle and stopped at a spot where he might survey the field. His army had disappeared, with the exception of some Borderers held together by Leven, and the one regiment which had stood firm, the English regiment, the third Light Infantry under Hastings. They had kept up a murderous fire to the end, and they retired calmly and in good order. Yet this was their first action, and Hastings, their colonel, was known as "one of the most unscrupulous scoundrels".

The General gathered his remaining few hundred men and speedily led them across the river Garry, where he paused to review the situation. He was surprised to have been given a moment's respite, but it seemed that the Celtic warriors had spent their energy in that one frenzied onslaught. The Pass was choked by the twelve hundred animals which had carried the baggage of the defeated army, and the Highlanders were busy plundering.

Dundee, at the beginning of the attack, was leading his small band of cavalry into battle when the troopers hesitated. He turned in the saddle, stood up in his stirrups, and waving his hat, urged them on. As he lifted his arm his cuirass rose and exposed the lower part of his left side, and here he was struck by a musket ball. "His horse sprang forward," writes Macaulay "and plunged into a cloud of smoke and dust, which hid from both armies the fall of the victorious general. A person named Johnstone was near him, and caught him as he sank down from the saddle. 'How goes the day?' said Dundee. 'Well for King James,' answered Johnstone, 'but I am sorry for your Lordship.' 'If it is well for him', answered the dying man, 'it matters the less for me'. He never spoke again . . . The body, wrapped in two plaids, was carried to the Castle of Blair." Dundee was buried in the church of Blair Athol, a building which is no longer there.

Mackay, who was ignorant of Dundee's fate, expected to be pursued by the victors. Retreat through the Pass was impossible, since it was held by the Highlanders, so he decided to cross the mountains towards the Tay Valley, and he soon came upon two or three hundred of his deserters. A lesser man might have given way to despair in his situation. He had suffered a humiliating defeat, and a triumphant enemy was probably even then hunting him down. His loved brother was dead, and his nephew was dying of his wounds at his side. He had to provide safety for his utterly demoralised men in the dark of the night, and he had very little idea of his whereabouts. But Mackay was sustained by his firm belief in God and his devotion to his duty to the State, and holding his head high, he inspired all around him with his courage.

He had to make sure of his way, and soon he saw a light shining through the darkness, which guided him to a small cottage. The inhabitants could speak only Gaelic, but Mackay remembered enough of the tongue from his childhood, and with the aid of this, and of a rough map of the mountain tracks which he had, he was able to follow their directions, and he and his men came eventually to Weem Castle. The owner was friendly to the new government, and he gave them generous hospitality. They marched all the next day over moors and mountains, and arrived that night at Castle Drummond, which was held for King William by a small garrison. The next day they reached Stirling.

The news of Mackay's defeat spread rapidly, and its importance was at first greatly exaggerated. Scotland was in a ferment, and Edinburgh verging on panic, but the news of the defeat was rapidly followed by tidings of the death of Dundee, and such was his reputation that the fact of his death appeared to turn victory into defeat. A message to the King in London, "Dundee is killed: Mackay has got to Stirling," put London's mind at rest.

The final battle of the Scottish insurrection took place less than a month later. Victory at Killiecrankie brought hundreds more clansmen to the Jacobite forces, although it did not diminish the rivalry between the Highland chiefs, nor soothe their quarrels with the Irish officers sent by James.

Mackay had rebuilt his army largely with men who had not been at Killecrankie, and he included the new regiment of the Puritan Covenanters, the Cameronians, under Lieut.-Colonel Cleland and Major Henderson. Against his own judgment and advice, he was sent by the Scottish ministers of the Crown to garrison the open and vulnerable town of Dunkeld, and he took with him his new force of Cameronians.

The Highlanders had massed near the town in numbers considerably greater than those of the garrison, and within two days, under their General, Clandon, they fell upon Dunkeld in fury, and Mackay's raw soldiers were desperately fighting their first battle. The struggle lasted four hours, by which time many of the houses were ablaze, Colonel Cleland and Major Henderson were dead, and the Cameronians were reduced almost to their last flask of powder, but they continued to fight with undiminished fury. Then the assault slackened as the Highlanders began to fall back in disorder, whole groups of them making for the hills despite their general's exhortations to return to the attack, and the mocking jeers of the Puritans. Macaulay writes, "In a short time the whole

Gaelic army was in full retreat towards Blair. Then the drums struck up: the victorious Puritans threw their caps into the air, raised, with one voice, a psalm of triumph and thanksgiving, and waved their colours, colours which were on that day unfurled for the first time in the face of an enemy . . . The Cameronians had good reason to be joyful and thankful; for they had finished the war."

After Dunkeld, the Highland confederation fell apart, and the clans returned to their hills and their homes. Mackay entered the Castle of Blair, and a chain of military outposts extending as far north as Inverness was established to keep the peace. Within a year Inverness was firmly under control, and on the western coast Fort William, erected by Monk at Inverlochy in 1655, was rebuilt by Mackay.

An interesting consequence of Killiecrankie, where the difficulty of fitting bayonets into the barrels of muskets was an important factor contributing to Mackay's defeat, was his order that in future bayonets should be made to screw on to the barrels of the muskets without impeding their fire, so that the troops could receive a charge immediately after firing. "So finally was accomplished the blending of pike and musket into a single weapon," says Fortescue, "a great era in the art of war." He adds that the French had introduced this improvement some time before.

In the aftermath of the Jacobite insurrection in Scotland William realised the importance of supporting the Presbyterians, who were by now the main religious force in that country. He saw that without them he could not hold the throne, and so Presbyterianism was re-established as the religion of the State.

The Royal Family Tree

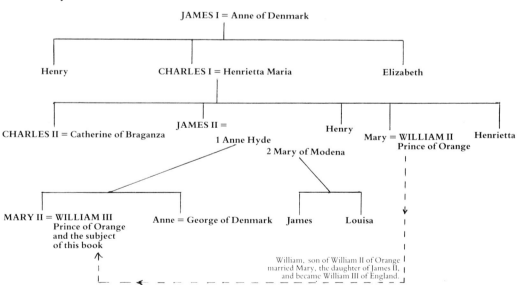

Derry Under Siege

IRELAND WAS the sole base of power remaining to James II. It was predominantly a Roman Catholic country, and he had replaced Protestant officers and other important figures with Roman Catholics. Lord Clarendon had been recalled to England and Richard ("Roaring Dick") Talbot, Earl of Tyrconnel, was appointed Lord Deputy of Ireland. Clarendon said of Tyrconnel that he was "a man of monstrous vanity as well as pride and furious passion," and in February of 1687 he came to Ireland. The diarist Evelyn wrote: "Lord Tyrconnel gone to succeed the Lord Lieutenant in Ireland, to the astonishment of all sober men, and to the evident ruin of Protestants in that kingdom." Many merchants shared Evelyn's view, and found refuge in England, whilst a good number of the officers who were thrust out of the army because they were Protestants went to join the Prince of Orange. The fear and despondency which the appointment caused was reflected in the words of a song sung to the tune *Lillibulero,* which caught the imagination of the people throughout England and Scotland as well as Ireland, and many different versions were used to reflect the mood of the times:

> Ho brother Teague dost thou hear de decree,
> Lillibulero, bullen-a-la,
> Dat we shall have a new deputy?
> Lillibulero, bullen-a-la,
>
> Ho by my soul it is a Talbot,
> Lillibulero, bullen-a-la,
> And he will cut all de English throat!
> Lillibulero, bullen-a-la.

James had the entire support of Tyrconnel, who had sent Irish troops to England when the Prince of Orange landed at Brixham. This had the effect of weakening the forces remaining, especially in the North. Londonderry was the chief stronghold of Protestantism in Northern Ireland, and troops from this town had been withdrawn. Now, on 7 December, Jacobite troops were sent back there, but they were refused admission, and thirteen apprentices closed the town gates in their faces. Protestant forces united with the local gentry to defend the town from James's troops, and they did the same in the town of Enniskillen, which was another Protestant refuge.

January 1689 saw the Protestants of Ulster raising forces for their own defence. They set up societies in local areas from which nominees were sent to a central Commission. A representative was sent to England to ensure that the Prince knew of their operations, and the Ulster Protestants showed their loyalty to William by proclaiming William and Mary King and Queen on their accepting the Crown of England. "Roaring Dick" Tyrconnel had stirred up the Irish Catholics to such a pitch that they supported James with wild enthusiasm, and now he set about restoring Jacobite authority in the north, where James's men still held important strongholds such as Carrickfergus and Charlemont. He first offered favourable terms of surrender to the Protestant forces, but when these were spurned he sent his wild troops into Ulster in great force, and on 14 March there was frightful slaughter at Dromore, and the surviving Protestants retreated to the North in disorder, pursued by the "Irish", who slew their victims indiscriminately, irrespective of age or sex. Some families escaped by sea from the Belfast area, and made for Scotland, whilst those fugitives in the North and West crowded into Londonderry or Enniskillen, the sole remaining fortified places in Ulster left in Protestant hands.

William, encumbered with affairs at home, could give his loyal subjects in Ireland little immediate help, although he did try to negotiate with Tyrconnel without success, and even called on the rebellious Irish to surrender, but to no effect.

12 March, 1689:

James landed in Ireland to find that nearly the whole of the island was in his hands. Burnet records: "Upon King James's landing in Ireland, he marched his army from Kinsale to Ulster; and when it was all together, it consisted of 30,000 foot, and 8,000 horse. It is true the Irish were now as insolent as they were undisciplined; and they began to think they must be masters of all the king's counsels. A jealousy arose between them and the French; they were soon on very bad terms, and scarcely ever agreed on their advices . . . But the first thing that was to be done was to reduce Londonderry. In order to this, two different advices were offered. The one was, to march with great force, and to take it immediately; for the town was not capable of resisting if vigorously attacked. The other was to block it up so that it should be forced in a little time to surrender; and to turn to other more vigorous designs. But, whereas either of these advices might have been pursued with advantage, a third advice was offered, but I know not by whom, which was the only bad one which could be proposed; and yet, by a sort of fatality which hung over that king, it was followed by him; and that was, to press the town by a slow siege which, as was given out, would bring the Irish into the methods of war, and would accustom them to fatigue and discipline. And this being resolved on, King James sent a small body before it, which was often changed; and by these he continued the siege above two months, in which the poor inhabitants formed themselves into great order, and came to generous resolutions of enduring the last extremities. They made some sallies, in which the Irish always ran away and left their officers; so that many of their best officers were killed. Those within suffered little, but by hunger, which destroyed nearly two-thirds of their number. One convoy, with two regiments and provisions was sent to their relief, but looked on the service as desperate, being deceived by Lundy, who was the governor of the place [Londonderry], and had undertaken to betray it to King James; but he finding them jealous of him, came to the convoy and persuaded them that nothing could be done; so they came back, and Lundy with them." These were the 9th and 17th Foot which Lundy persuaded to return and leave Derry to its fate. Their colonels Cunningham and Richards were both suspended on their return to England. Lundy escaped in the guise of a private soldier. He is remembered as "Lundy the traitor", and his effigy is burnt by the Apprentice Boys' Clubs at the commemoration of the closing of the gates each year.

The town's watchword was "No surrender," and Dr. George Walker, "a fierce minister of the gospel," was elected, together with Major Baker, governor of the town. Preparations for the defence were re-organised immediately.

20 April:

Major Baker became Commander-in-Chief of the military forces, and Dr. Walker's responsibility was "to preserve internal tranquillity and to dole out supplies from the magazine". All able inhabitants who could carry arms were formed into eight regiments, and everyone joined forces against the common enemy. Claude Hamilton, Lord Strabane, a Roman Catholic peer, came to the gates under a flag of truce, and was met by Murray, commander of one of the newly-formed regiments. According to Macaulay, Strabane had been instructed to offer terms for the surrender of the town, which included free pardons for the citizens together with a colonel's commission and a

OVERLEAF: 'No Surrender' – the Siege of Londonderry.
The besieged Protestant town was finally relieved by William's forces after it had held out against James's army for a hundred and five days. Engraving from a contemporary Dutch work, courtesy of the Mansell Collection.

thousand pounds for Murray. Murray's answer was short. "The men of Londonderry," he said, "have done nothing that requires a pardon, and own no sovereign but King William and Queen Mary. It will not be safe for your Lordship to stay longer, or to return on the same errand. Let me have the honour of seeing you through the lines."

James, now leading the besieging troops, had been assured that the town would surrender as soon as he appeared outside the walls. Finding that this was not the case, he retired immediately to Dublin with Rosen, who commanded these forces, leaving Maumont, a French Lieutenant General, to continue the siege, with Richard Hamilton and Major General Pusignam to support him. The town was now subjected to a continuous barrage of cannon, so that fire took hold and houses collapsed, crushing the defenders. The defenders were dismayed by these new horrors, but they were encouraged by their commanders to take the offensive.

21 April:

Murray led a sally from the gates in force. The Irish stood firm, and a "furious and bloody contest took place". Maumont, leading the Irish cavalry, advanced to the centre of the battle, but was shot in the head and fell dead, and the Irish lost many officers and some two hundred men before the Protestants were driven back. Murray's horse was killed under him, and he had to fight his way back to the gates, where he was rescued by Walker.

Richard Hamilton, "who had never in his life seen a siege," now took command of the Irish army, and Pusignan found himself second in command, but not for long. He died in another sally made by the garrison on 6 May.

18 June:

General Kirke from England sailed into Lough Foyle with the 2nd, 9th and 11th Foot, but incredibly, he would not move until he had received repeated firm orders from England to relieve Londonderry. For weeks the defenders held firm, defying the calls to surrender, and constantly encouraged by their leader Walker with, it is said, a bible in one hand and a sword in the other. They suffered the agonies of all besieged communities as food became ever more scarce, and famine, disease and battle took their toll. Their ammunition ran so low that they were firing lead-covered bricks from their cannon. All the time, the masts of the relieving ships could be seen in the Lough. By the time Kirke received his orders from England, the Irish had fortified the River Foyle, and a stout boom of tree-trunks was in position across it.

Enter Le Count de Schomberg.

He was Friedrich Hermann, Europe's leading soldier of fortune – the veteran commander of Portugal's defence against Spain in the war of 1662. William created him the first Duke of Schomberg in 1689. He arrived in Ireland two weeks after the end of the siege of Londonderry and took charge of William's expanding army.

28 July:

At sunset on 28 July the guards on the wall saw the white sails of three ships sailing up the Foyle, bringing food for the starving people and troops for their defence. The leading merchant ship was the Mountjoy, laden with provisions, commanded by Micaiah Browning, a native of Londonderry who had volunteered to bring help to his people. Next came the *Phoenix,* another merchant ship, and both were under the protection of the *Dartmouth,* a frigate whose captain John Leake engaged the Irish guns on the bank of the river with constant fire. The *Mountjoy* struck the boom, but with insufficient force to break through, and she was forced back to the bank. Men from the *Dartmouth,* in a long boat, began hacking away at the obstacle, and it was not long before the *Phoenix* was able to pass through. The *Mountjoy,* which had enjoyed the protection of the *Dartmouth's* guns whilst aground in a dangerous situation, managed to float off on the rising tide, and the resouceful men in the longboat towed her in to the town behind the *Phoenix.* Browning, her master, was killed by a shot from the shore batteries in sight of Londonderry, his birthplace, which his devotion and courage had helped to save.

By ten o'clock at night the ships were tied up at the quay, and the entire population flocked to greet them. There were bonfires all night along the fortifications. The people received rations of "three pounds of flour, two pounds of beef and a pint of pease," their first good meal for 105 days. The Irish guns fired ceaselessly all night, and all night the bells rang in "joyous defiance". For three more days the Irish continued their firing, and on the third night they burned their camp.

1 August:

Smoke was still rising from the ruins of their camp the next day as the Jacobite army retreated along the banks of the Foyle and away towards Strabane.

Meanwhile the other Protestant stronghold in Ulster, Enniskillen, or Inniskilling, which was inundated with refugees from Munster and Connaught, was the centre of operations against the Jacobites. The men of Enniskillen, with amazing energy, organised a force of cavalry and another of infantry and maintained constant harassment of the insurgent Irish by raiding their lines of communication, and they carried the warfare dangerously near to Dublin. When these Protestants heard that Kirke had arrived they asked him for reinforcements. He could not spare troops, but he did send them two good officers, namely Colonel Wolseley and Lieutentant Colonel Berry, with supplies of arms and ammunition. These officers came by sea round the coast of Donegal and up the river Erne, and on Sunday, 29 July the entire population turned out to welcome them.

31 July:

On the same day that the siege of Londonderry was raised, the men of Enniskillen under Colonel Wolseley encountered an Irish force under Macarthy at Newton Butler. Macaulay describes how Wolseley had marched out against Macarthy, who had "over 5000 men and several pieces of artillery," with a small army of under three thousand recruits "made up of gentlemen and yeoman fighting, not for pay, but for their lands, their wives, their children and their God. The ranks were drawn up under arms, and the question was put, 'Advance or retreat?' The answer was a universal shout of 'Advance!' Wolseley gave out the word, 'No Popery!' It was received with loud applause."

The army, having made contact with the enemy, advanced on the retreating Jacobites in well-disciplined order through the small town of Newton Butler. Then the Irish turned and faced their pursuers. They had the advantage of a superior position on the top of a hill rising from deep bogs. There was a narrow hard pathway across the bog which was the sole road for the sturdy Enniskillen horsemen, but the Irish cannon dominated this approach. Wolseley attacked with his infantry, and the men floundered through the bog to seize the guns. There was a short, desperate fight during which the Irish gunners stayed gallantly by their guns to the last man, but were cut down. Then the Enniskillen cavalry, freed from the artillery fire, galloped furiously up the causeway, so terrifying the Irish dragoons by the fierceness of their approach that they fled in panic without a fight, and the rest of the cavalry followed suit, riding their horses so hard and so clumsily that many of them fell. Throwing away their guns, swords, and even their coats, the dismounted riders fled on foot, and the infantry, seeing this, dropped their muskets and pikes, and they, too, ran for their lives. The Enniskillen force slew about fifteen hundred of their enemies, and five hundred more, strangers to that country and hotly pursued by the Protestants, fleeing along the Lough Erne road, plunged into the waters and drowned. Macarthy, deserted by his troops, ran into the midst of his adversaries and fell to the ground, wounded, but he was recognised, and saved from death. The Enniskillens lost only twenty men killed, and fifty were wounded. They took "400 prisoners, seven pieces of cannon, fourteen barrels of powder, all the drums and all the colours of the vanquished army".

William was much impressed by the demeanour and the military prowess of the men of Enniskillen, and came to rely upon them later. They gave their name subsequently to a number of regiments in the British Army, as Fortescue, writing in 1899, records. He says that the Protestant forces of Newton Butler were re-organised into two regiments of dragoons and three of foot, which were later represented as the Fifth Royal Irish Dragoons, now Lancers, the Sixth Enniskillen Dragoons, now Lancers, and the 27th Enniskillen Regiment of the Infantry of the Line.

When the news of the defeat at Newton Butler reached the retreating Jacobites at Strabane they flung their stores into the river, left their sick and wounded to the Protestants, and fled to Omagh and Charlemont. Sarsfield, commander of the forces at Sligo, abandoned the town, and a unit of Kirke's troops immediately occupied it.

These reverses for the Jacobite cause brought dismay to Dublin, and James actively considered retreating to France. The Dublin Parliament, overwhelmingly Catholic in composition, completely alienated the Protestants remaining in Southern Ireland, and gave James no chance to reconcile them in any way. The right of the Dublin Parliament to legislate for Ireland was re-established, and any control exercised by the English Parliament was rejected. An Act of Attainder was threatened, by which 2,400 Protestant landowners in the island would be dispossessed, but James and his followers could see that the progress of events was now destroying his hopes of victory, and in the event of his failure any legislation by the Dublin Parliament could not be implemented.

The relief of Londonderry and the victory at Newton Butler had saved the North for William, and whilst Mackay had been labouring to put down the Highland insurrection in Scotland, and the Irish Protestants were gallantly withstanding the Jacobite troops at Londonderry and Enniskillen, English recruiting sergeants were beating their drums throughout English market towns. Preparations for the re-conquest of Ireland had been continuing for months, and it was time for the expedition to sail to that country whilst the Protestant victories in Ulster were uppermost in the minds of the people.

The investigation which followed the failure of the expedition led by Colonels Cunningham and Richards to effect the relief of Londonderry in the April had led to the suspension of both of these incompetents. More important, however, it revealed a mess of corruption, deceit and mismanagement in matters concerning the supply of provisions for the men, and in the accommodation provided for them which, it was feared, extended throughout the armed forces. Conditions for the troops aboard the ships had been so cramped that the men could not even lie down, and their food had been putrid and often inedible. Even the beer was foul and undrinkable, so that they preferred to drink water.

A great effort was now made to improve transport and victualling, and to stamp out the associated cheating and corruption by those who supplied the forces. The enquiries had concerned two battalions. Only time would show how the military would cope with the organisation of the movement and supply of a whole army.

It was planned to establish a force of nineteen thousand men in Ireland, and of these about five thousand were already there. Marshal Schomberg, a veteran over eighty years of age and still active and fit for duty, was put in charge of the campaign.

13 August:

Two weeks after the seige of Londonderry was raised, Schomberg made landfall at Bangor, and having disembarked his troops, marched at the head of twelve regiments to the Jacobite stronghold of Carrickfergus and besieged the town. Within a week the garrison had surrendered, and was allowed to retreat to Newry, whilst Schomberg went on to take Lisburn. He was, however, far from contented with his army. He found that the officers were ignorant and slack, and the newly-recruited troops were merely ill-disciplined boys. Their weapons were so badly made and so carelessly handled that practically every regiment had to be re-armed. The artillery officers were found to be dilatory and cowardly. Their guns, as was usual in European forces then, were poorly constructed, and became unserviceable after a week's use in battle. Many of the guns used at Carrickfergus were Dutch.

In spite of the lessons which should have been learned from the Cunningham/Richards enquiry, the officers in the higher ranks of command were insufficiently qualified, and the Commissary General had failed to provide enough victuals for the men. Even the transport ships were so badly handled that when crossing St. George's Channel a whole regiment of the Queen's Bays lost every charger and troop horse on the way. Such was the chaos among the troops that the Marshal himself had to investigate and supervise every department, a most aggravating and time-wasting procedure for the Commander-in-Chief.

Fortunately for William's army, the Irish forces under James were so demoralised by their adverse fortunes and by the news of Schomberg's advance that they offered little opposition. The officer commanding the Jacobite forces in Belfast evacuated the town, and the Marshal immediately garrisoned it and marched on Newry. As Schomberg approached, the Duke of Berwick, who was defending the road, retreated to Drogheda, where James had a strong force of twenty thousand men. The Marshal followed him down the coast as far as Dundalk without meeting much resistance, and there entrenched his forces. James tried to tempt him out of his position by advancing to within three miles of his camp, but Schomberg would not take the bait, although at that time he could probably have reached Dublin with little trouble because of the demoralised and debilitated state of James's troops. He preferred not to take risks, however, with his unseasoned troops, and decided to await further support from William. It was now the middle of September, and all was not well with the English army, although the first stage of Schomberg's campaign was successfully completed.

The men were dispirited and demoralised by the lack of provisions, and were on the brink of starvation. Their camp was in "a low, moist ground under great hills". Shales, the Commissary General in charge of stores at Belfast was an experienced man who had been responsible for provisioning James's forces at Hounslow. He had plenty of stores in Belfast, but had neglected to make arrangements for transporting them with the army. He had bought a number of horses in Cheshire, but instead of having them sent to Ireland he had hired them out to local farmers there for use in harvesting, and pocketed the proceeds. The artillery could not be moved for lack of the horses which Shales should have provided, but he, conveniently, said that the artillery had nothing to do with him. Even had there been horses there were no shoes for them. Provisions were so scarce that one of the chaplains, George Story, in his *Impartial History* on which Macaulay relies heavily for the details of this campaign, had to dig potatoes for his dinner, and he was lucky to find any, for the Jacobites left little on the land which they passed over.

Macaulay's account of the miserable conditions which the men endured, entrenched in that boggy ground, is a sad one. The September rains were heavier than usual, and the whole countryside was flooded. The Enniskillen men were used to the climate, and the Dutch troops also were accustomed to wet, lowland conditions. They kept the huts which they had built dry and clean: but the English, raw recruits, many of them peasants from Yorkshire and Derbyshire, were quite unaccustomed to such conditions in time of war, when their survival depended on their own resourcefulness. Weakened by sickness, lacking food and adequate clothing, with barely a greatcoat among the infantry, and the cavalry lacking cloaks, boots, belts and horseshoes, they lacked the stamina to build themselves huts, or cover the boggy earth with carpets of fern as their Dutch and Huguenot comrades had done. They became incapable almost of obeying orders, and succumbed to dysentry and other diseases, perishing by the hundred: "Exertion had become more dreadful to them than death." They could not help themselves, and nor did they then help each other. They neither gave nor asked compassion. There was no medical help of any kind except for lint and plasters for wounds. Surgeons were rare, and there was no hospital.

By one unscrupulous scheme and another, many officers, principally of the rank of colonel and above, diverted army funds, and even the pay of their men, into their own hands. Fictitious units existed on paper, and muster rolls were regularly falsified. At the top, Harbord, Treasurer of the Army and a member of Parliament, misappropriated huge sums to his own use. Shales, the Commissary General was also busy lining his own pockets. Schomberg, who found he could rely only upon his Dutch and Huguenot troops, informed William of his difficulties, and of Harbord and Shales's dishonesty.

Jacobite troops had pushed Kirke's men out of Sligo, and secured Galway for James, but no attempt had been made on the army at Dundalk, and on 5 November, 1689 the English army went into winter quarters. Six thousand of them had perished through sickness. They had ceased to fire a volley over the grave when they buried a man as the frequency of doing so merely served to encourage the enemy. They retired to Ulster, with the General's headquarters at Lisburn.

During the autumn of 1689 William was faced with his second session of Parliament at Westminster. The House of Commons, suddenly aware of the state of the English Army in Ireland, petitioned the King for the arrest of Shales, to be informed by William that the arrest had already been made. He managed, however, to avoid retribution with the help of his corrupt colleagues. William then took the unprecedented step of requesting the appointment of seven members of Parliament to oversee the preparations for the coming campaign in Ireland. This was not acceptable to the Commons, but a committee was appointed to look into the expense of the war. A new Mutiny Act was passed with power to deal with such offences as falsifying musters, and other dishonest practices. Not that existing laws were the basic problem. "It was not legislation that was wanted," says Fortescue, "but enforcement of existing laws! William appears to have abandoned in despair the hope of finding an honest man in England."

This session of Parliament was bedevilled by continual violent quarrelling between the two parties over the Corporation and Indemnity Bills, the former designed to ensure that local government was in the hands of non-Papists, the latter to absolve those who had unwittingly offended the new regime. This strife and discord so exasperated William that he threatened to quit England, and it took the combined diplomacy of Shrewsbury and Nottingham to persuade him to remain. He ended the quarrelling over the Indemnity Bill by issuing an Act of Grace, which was an Act originating from the throne which does not pass through the usual Parliamentary procedures, but is accepted or rejected by a single vote in each House. William's Act received unanimous approval, and so was enacted. It was an Act of Grace for political offences, absolving all from retribution. "The Act of Grace the nation owed to William alone," says Macaulay, "and it is one of his noblest and purest titles to renown."

After the Act was passed, on 20 May, 1690, the King told both Houses of Parliament that he could no longer delay going to Ireland himself, and that he would prorogue Parliament. He would not recall them until the next winter unless some unforseen emergency made it necessary. "Then," he said, "I hope by the blessing of God we shall have a happy meeting."

William and Schomberg had together planned for the campaign of 1690. Schomberg was adamant that this time he would not use regiments of "miserable English and Irish boys," but that twenty-seven thousand seasoned men should be transported to Ireland. Of these, seventeen thousand were British, and the rest were Dutchmen and Danes from the forces of England and Holland, to be commanded by the Duke of Würtemberg-Neustadt. Cannon and small arms were brought over from Holland. The King took the providing of clothing out of the hands of the colonels, and this time the transport of the troops was very carefully organised.

The Secretary for Northern Ireland was given the responsibility for working out a plan of campaign, and this he, Sir Robert Southwell, did with imagination. His main idea was to attack simultaneously in the north and the south of the country, for to leave the ports of Munster and the south coast unprotected would be to invite the French to use them to bring in supplies and reinforcements. Schomberg was to advance from the north, and at the same time an attack would be made on the south, Cork being the objective.

There was no doubt that the English forces in Ireland felt the effects of William's organisation, and there was an upsurge of confidence and renewed activity amongst government and troops. The King's influence was apparent in every military department. Plentiful supplies of food and clothing, ample stocks of medicine, and stores of all kinds, all of vastly better quality than anything Shales had ever supplied, were shipped across St. George's Channel. Fresh troops from Scotland, Cheshire, Lancashire and Cumberland had landed in Belfast Bay, and by the end of May there was a strong English force in Ulster. Macaulay puts the strength of the army there at thirty thousand men, with a thousand baggage waggons streaming across England towards the ports for Ireland. More troops and an immense quantity of military stores were on board a fleet which lay in the estuary of the Dee, ready to weigh anchor as soon as the King was on board.

The administration at the court of James in Dublin was very different. During the six months from November to May the opportunity to bring the slack and feckless Jacobite troops up to some kind of standard of training and discipline had been lost. "The Court of Dublin was, during that season of inaction," says Macaulay, "busied with dice and claret, love letters and challenges. . . The whole number of coaches which could be mustered there, those of the King and the French Legation included, did not amount to forty. But though there was little splendour there was much dissoluteness. Grave Roman Catholics shook their heads and said that the Castle did not look like the palace of a King who gloried in being the champion of the Church. The military administration was as deplorable as ever. The cavalry indeed was, by the exertions of some gallant officers, kept in a high state of efficiency. But a regiment of infantry differed in nothing but name from a large gang of Rapparees [wild Irish plunderers]. Indeed a gang of Rapparees gave less annoyance to peaceable citizens, and more annoyance to the enemy, than a regiment of infantry."

Jean Antoine de Mesmes, Count of Avaux, a foremost diplomat at the court of Louis XIV, who had been the French Ambassador at The Hague, attended James on his Irish expedition. His correspondence was a chief source to Macaulay of information about Irish military affairs during 1689 and 1690. He was a man of perception and great wisdom, and James would have done well to listen to his advice. Macaulay continues: "Avaux strongly represented, in a memorial which he delivered to James, the abuses which made the Irish foot a curse and a scandal to Ireland. Whole companies, said the ambassador, quit their colours on the line of march and wander to right and left, pillaging and destroying: the soldier takes no care of his arms: the captain never troubles himself to ascertain whether the arms are in good order: the consequence is that one man in every three has lost his musket, and that another man in every three has a musket that will not go off. Avaux adjured the King to prohibit marauding, to give orders that the troops should be regularly exercised, and to punish every officer who suffered his men to neglect their weapons and accoutrements. If these things were done, His Majesty might hope to have, in the approaching spring, an army with which the enemy would be unable to contend. This was good advice: but James was so far from taking it that he would hardly listen to it with patience. Before he had heard eight lines read he flew into a passion, and accused the ambassador of exaggeration. 'This paper, Sir,' said Avaux, 'is not written to be published. It is meant solely for your Majesty's information; and, in a paper meant solely for your Majesty's information, flattery and disguise would be out of place: but I will not persist in reading what is so disagreeable.' 'Go on,' said James, very angrily; 'I will hear the whole.' He gradually became calmer, took the memorial, and promised to adopt some of the suggestions which it contained. But his promise was soon forgotten."

William R.
William's signature as King – now of England, lowland Scotland and the Protestant north of Ireland.

James's man in southern Ireland.
Richard Talbot, Earl of Tyrconnel – the Lord Deputy of Ireland. He was to be tasked with the defence of the passes over the River Boyne after James's army had retreated from Dundalk. Painting of the French School, courtesy the National Portrait Gallery.

Base Metal Sovereignty

JAMES'S FINANCIAL situation was as bad as his military affairs. His revenue had dwindled, and in desperation he reduced the value of the coinage by substituting base metal. Even this "brass money" was at risk, because there was a shortage of brass in Dublin, and James was forced to apply to Louis for help. The benevolence which he extended to his ally was limited to "an old, cracked piece of cannon to be coined into crowns and shillings". Matters became worse, as the people refused to accept the new coinage, and James was reduced to ordering the direct robbery of all those Protestants who had remained in Southern Ireland "by the simple process of taking money out of their strong-boxes, drink out of their cellars, fuel from their turf-stacks and clothes from their wardrobes".

James had little faith in his Irish infantry, placing the blame for their failings on the men themselves instead of on the disgraceful lack of training and discipline to which he should have addressed himself, and he accepted the suggestion from the French King, who was aware of the potential of these sturdy Irish peasants as infantrymen, given "the best discipline then known in the world," of an exchange of some four thousand Irish troops for between seven and eight thousand excellent French infantry, "who were likely in a day of battle to be of more use than all the kernes [Irish foot soldiers] of Leinster, Munster and Connaught together".

Even here James, "by a sort of fatality which hung over that king," as Burnet wrote earlier, made the error, prompted by his Queen, of insisting, against all advice—even that of Louis XIV—that Lauzun should command his forces. It was Lauzun who had escorted the Queen on her escape from London to France. There were generals of far greater ability in France, and there was enmity between him and Avaux which would effectively prevent them from working together. In addition, as Macaulay observes, "it would have been an affront to the old general [Rosen] to put him under the orders of Lauzun". Tyrconnel was disturbed by this change in events, and did not welcome the idea of Lauzun taking command. He wrote to Mary of Modena and told her of his feelings. He preferred Louvois's influence on the troops, and said that the appointment of Lauzun was not acceptable to the French. However, James had his way. Avaux and Rosen were recalled to France, and Lauzun arrived in Cork in March, 1690. He took up quarters in Dublin Castle, and the troops he brought with him were billeted in Protestant households.

Meanwhile Schomberg had begun the campaign by taking Charlemont, the last important stronghold occupied by the Jacobites in Ulster, but before continuing he waited for the coming of William, who was still busy in London making preparations for the defence of England against a possible Jacobite rising during his absence in Ireland.

Burnet writes that in Ireland, "King James and his Court were so much lifted up with the news of the debates in Parliament, and of the distractions of the City of London, that they flattered themselves with false hopes that the King durst not leave England, nor venture over to Ireland." They were due to be disappointed. There was still much to do, however, before he could safely depart. According to an Act of Parliament which provided for William's absence from England, Mary was lawfully entrusted with the administration of the government of the kingdon "in his name and her own," but during his absence "he should nevertheless retain all his authority". Burnet records that before William left for Ireland, "The king named a cabinet council of eight persons, on whose advice she was chiefly to rely: four of them were tories and four were whigs: yet the marquis of Caermarthen and the earl of

Nottingham, being of the first sort, who took most upon them and seemed to have the greatest credit, the whigs were not satisfied with the nomination. The queen balanced all things with an extraordinary temper, and became universally beloved and admired by all about her." Thomas of Wilton, the 8th Earl of Pembroke, who carried the Sword of Justice at the Coronation, was also appointed to advise the Queen during the King's absence in Ireland, so there were nine privy councillors eventually.

"On the day before William's departure," writes Macaulay, "he called Burnet into his closet, and, in firm but mournful language, spoke of the dangers which on every side menaced the realm, of the fury of the contending factions, and of the evil spirit which seemed to possess too many of the clergy. 'But my trust is in God. I will go through with my work or perish in it. Only I cannot help feeling for the poor Queen;' and twice he repeated with unwonted tenderness, 'the poor Queen'. 'If you love me,' he added, 'wait on her often, and give her what help you can. As for me, but for one thing, I should enjoy the prospect of being on horseback and under canvas again. For I am sure that I am fitter to direct a campaign than to manage your Houses of Lords and Commons. But though I know that I am in the path of duty, it is hard on my wife that her father and I must be opposed to each other in the field. God send that no harm may happen to him. Let me have your prayers, Doctor.'

"Burnet retired, greatly moved, and doubtless put up, with no common fervour, those prayers for which his master had asked." Burnet records: "I acquainted the queen with this; and I saw in her a great tenderness for her father's person: and she was much touched with the answer the king had made."

4 June,1690:

The King finally left London for Ireland, travelling in the royal coach with Portland as a companion, and accompanied by Prince George. They arrived at Chester on the 8 June and found the fleet awaiting them. On 11 June William embarked, and was convoyed across the sea by a squadron of men-of-war under the command of Sir Cloudesley Shovel, disembarking with his forces at Carrickfergus on 14 June. He was heartily welcomed by the population which had turned out to meet him, but he did not remain among them. As soon as he could he mounted his white charger and set off for Belfast. Close to a lone white house on the shore of the Lough he was met by Schomberg. Later there grew up a village here, and a cotton mill rose where the white house once stood.

Belfast at that time was a small English settlement, says Macaulay. There were "about three hundred houses, commanded by a Castle which has long since disappeared, the seat of the noble family of Chichester. In this mansion, which is said to have borne some resemblance to the palace of Whitehall, and which was celebrated for its terraces and orchards stretching down to the riverside, preparations had been made for the King's reception. He was welcomed at the North Gate by the magistrates and burgesses in their robes of office; the multitude pressed towards him with shouts of 'God save the Protestant King!' for the town was one of the strongholds of the Reformed Faith; and when two generations later the inhabitants were, for the first time, numbered, it was found that the Roman Catholics were not more than one in fifteen."

That night a royal salute was fired from the Castle, and Schomberg's guns roared in echo, and passed the signal from post to post, proclaiming the news of William's arrival wherever the sound was heard. By midnight bonfires were blazing on the heights of Antrim and Down, and their brilliance was seen at Carlingford and Dundalk, giving notice to the enemy "that the decisive hour was at hand. Within forty-eight hours after William had landed James set out from Dublin for the Irish camp, which was pitched near the northern frontier of Leinster."

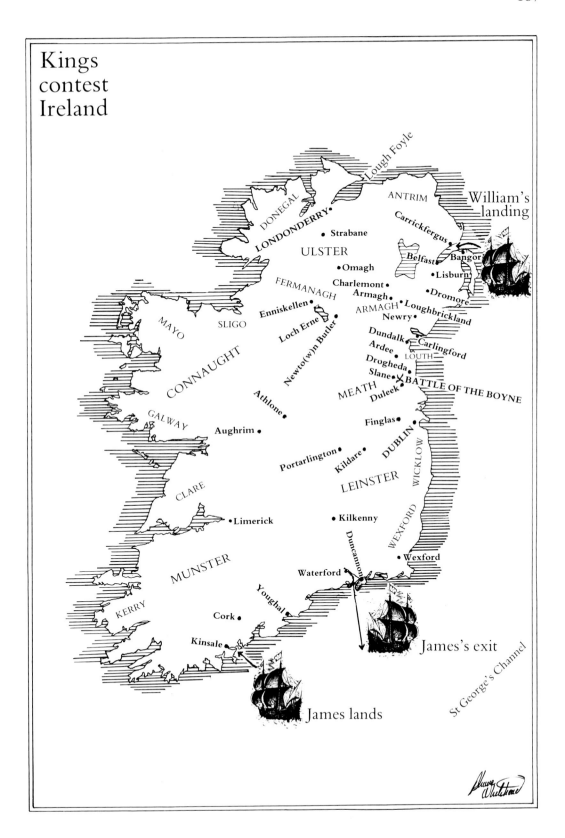

Kings contest Ireland

Mary – William's Queen.
Painted in Holland by Willem Wissing. Reproduced by gracious permission of Her Majesty Queen Elizabeth II.

Dublin was in confusion. Simon Luttrell, in charge of the city, became the embodiment of the repressed hatreds and passions. The Protestants were put under curfew, and even Dr. William King, a mild cleric of the Established Church, was taken prisoner. Colleges and parish churches were taken over and packed with those who were arrested solely because of their faith.

Son-in-law and father-in-law, the two royal Princes were equally occupied in assembling their forces. William named Loughbrickland, some ten miles east of Armagh, as a rendezvous for all his scattered units, and whilst they were gathering he conscientiously and tirelessly went about improving the lot of his men. He had brought with him two hundred thousand pounds in cash as well as great quantities of ammunition and provisions. Looting was banned under severe penalties, and on the other hand liberal supplies were distributed, and regimental paymasters were instructed to send in their claims immediately. Thomas Coningsby, a Whig Member of Parliament for Leominster, accompanied the King and acted as Paymaster General. William instituted an annual payment by the Collector of Customs at Belfast of twelve hundred pounds to the principal dissenting ministers of Down and Antrim, "who were to be trustees for their bretheren". The king said that he had awarded this amount to the nonconformist clergy in recognition of their loyalty to him, and partly as compensation for their recent losses.

Burnet gives some detail of the planning which was going on in the Jacobite camp. He says that as soon as James knew that William had arrived in Ireland, "he immediately passed the Boyne, and lay on the south side of it. His army consisted of twenty-six thousand men; his horse were good; and he had five thousand French foot, for whom he had sent over in exchange five thousand Irish foot. He held some councils of war to consider what was fit to be done; whether he should make a stand there, and put all to the decision of a battle; or if he should march off and abandon that river, and, by consequence, all the country on to Dublin.

"All his officers, both French and Irish, who disagreed almost in all their advices, yet agreed in this, that though they had there a very advantageous post to maintain, yet their army being so much inferior, both in number and in everything else, they would put too much to hazard if they should venture on a battle. They therefore proposed the strengthening their garrisons, and marching off to the Shannon with the horse and a small body of foot till they should see how matters went . . ."

William was re-vitalised. After enduring eighteen months of waning popularity, and the discouraging wranglings of Parliament, he was stimulated and refreshed to find himself once again at the head of an army, a position in which he revelled. In spite of his obvious bad health, his army was inspired by the close interest which he took in their conditions and his determination to share their hardships. It was clear that he was more concerned for their well-being than his own. He would rather his common soldiers were well provisioned than that he should have any luxuries. In the field, he never set up his headquarters in a house or a palace. He had commissioned no less a personage than Sir Christopher Wren to design and construct for him a wooden 'travelling hut'. When dismantled, this could be easily transported on two supply waggons, and it was designed for speedy erection on any chosen site, and became his headquarters in that camp. Although he breathed at times with great difficulty,so that when in London he would take any opportunity to escape to the countryside for relief from the smoky atmosphere, with the army he rode with his men through the choking dust of a hot summer's day without hesitation. His troops became accustomed to hearing his voice and seeing him amongst them as he inspected them, their regiments and the conditions in which they existed with minute attention. His kind and courteous manner to the lowliest of his men was recalled by one who brought to him a basket of the first cherries of the year, and it is recorded that "his pleasant looks and sayings were long remembered". His animated conversation at the supper table contrasted sharply with his dour, retiring manner when dealing with his Court at Whitehall, and it was obvious that he was happy and relaxed in the company of his military associates.

24 June, 1690:

Ten days after he had landed in Ireland William marched his entire force southwards from Loughbrickland. Schomberg and other officers advised him to move more slowly, with greater caution, but the King replied that "he had not come to Ireland to let the grass grow under his feet". He knew that England was unhappy with the progress of the war and he decided that a speedy and successful end to the campaign would revive the spirits of the people and the government at home. He was impatient for battle.

As he went through the country towards Dundalk William was sickened by the devastation which he saw on every hand. The land had been laid waste by James's soldiers and by the wild bands of Irish bandits, the Rapparees. "The cattle had been slaughtered; the plantations cut down; the fences and houses were in ruins. Not a human being was to be found near the road, except a few naked and meagre wretches who had no food but the husks of oats, and who were seen picking these husks from amidst dust and cinders. Yet even under such disadvantages, the natural fertility of the country, the rich green of the earth, the bays and rivers so admirably fitted for trade, could not but strike the King's observant eye . . . 'The country,' he was heard to say, 'is worth fighting for.' "

James's mind was in a ferment of indecision, not assisted in any way by the conflicting advice which he received from his French and Irish officers. The French view was that he should burn Dublin. Tyrconnel, on the other hand, urged that they must fight rather than lose the city, and then vacillated, and advised against fighting. James hesitantly ordered an advance to the North. Meanwhile it was rumoured that he had sent a message to Waterford to prepare means for him to return to France, and some said that part of his belongings and some guns had been sent back to Dublin. When he reached Dundalk he heard that William was advancing towards him, and he ordered a rapid retreat, so that by the time William's advance guard reached Dundalk, all that could be seen of their enemies was "a great cloud of dust which was slowly rolling southwards towards Ardee".

The English encamped for one night at the spot where they had been a year earlier, near the never-to-be-forgotten bog, "the sepulchre of thousands of brave men". On 29 June William reached Ardee, and found that James had retreated to Drogheda, and was established on the southern bank of the River Boyne once more. The English army continued its march from Ardee, and on Monday, 30 June, William and his forces breasted the heights overlooking the valley of the Boyne, which there forms the boundary between the counties of Louth to the north and Meath to the south. They moved down to the northern bank of the river, and made their camp a ten-minute ride from Drogheda to the east. Macaulay describes the appearance of the vicinity at the time. There were few ships on the river, but there were coracles of wickerwork covered with leather which the local peasants used in fishing for trout and salmon. Drogheda itself was made up of a "small knot of narrow, crooked and filthy lanes encircled by a ditch and a mound". The houses were built of wood, with high gables and projecting upper storeys. Outside the encircling mound scarcely a dwelling was to be seen except at a place called Oldbridge. Here, the river was fordable, and at the southern end of the ford were a few mud cabins, and a single house built of more solid materials.

William was very contented when he saw that the Jacobite army was making a stand, and that he would be able to get to grips with them. In a long survey of the enemy position he observed that James had pitched his tent on the high ground, and that the walls of Drogheda were flying the flags of the House of Stuart and the House of Bourbon. "All the southern bank of the river was lined by the camp and batteries of the hostile army. Thousands of men were moving about among the tents, and every one, horse soldier or foot soldier, French or Irish, had a white badge in his hat. The colour had been chosen in compliment to the House of Bourbon. "I am glad to see you, gentlemen," said the king as his eye surveyed the Irish lines. "If you escape me now, the fault will be mine."

James held the stronger defensive position behind the Boyne, and the majority of his troops were drawn up on the heights overlooking Oldbridge and the ford over the river, with a small force holding Drogheda, but he had fewer troops - about 25,000 in all, and although the French infantry and the Irish cavalry were fine, well-trained fighting men, the rest were cowardly and inefficient.

The Boyne from King William's position presented an extremely difficult and dangerous barrier to be crossed under fire, but his army was altogether more powerful and formidable than that of the enemy. It numbered in the region of 36,000 men, and was made up of well-equipped, seasoned forces from several countries, "which a strange series of events had brought to fight for the Protestant religion in the remotest island of the West". English troops accounted for half their number. "Ormond was there with the Life Guards," says Macaulay, "and Oxford with the Blues. Sir John Lanier, a prudent and experienced officer, was at the head of the Queen's Regiment of Horse (later the First Dragoon Guards). There were Beaumont's Foot, who had, in defiance of the mandate of James, refused to admit Irish Papists amongst them, and Hastings's Foot, who had, on the disastrous day of Killiecrankie not long before, maintained the military reputation of the Saxon race. There were two Tangier Regiments, hitherto known only by deeds of violence and rapine, but destined to begin on the following morning a long career of glory. Two fine English regiments, which had been in the service of the States General, and had often looked death in the face under William's leading, followed him in this campaign not only as their general, but as their native King. . . The Scotch Footguards marched under the command of their countryman James Douglas. Conspicuous among the Dutch troops were Portland's and Ginckel's Horse, and Solmes's Blue Regiment, consisting of two thousand of the finest infantry in Europe. Germany had sent to the field some warriors sprung from her noblest houses. Prince George of Hesse Darmstadt, a gallant youth who was serving his apprenticeship in the military art, rode near the King. A strong brigade of Danish mercenaries was commanded by Duke Charles Frederic of Würtemberg. It was reported that of all the soldiers of William these were most dreaded by the Irish, for centuries of Saxon domination had not effaced the recollection of the violence and cruelty of the Scandinavian sea kings; and an ancient prophecy that the Danes would one day destroy the children of the soil was still repeated with superstitious horror. Among the foreign auxiliaries were a Brandenberg regiment and a Finland regiment. But in that great array so variously composed, were two bodies of men animated by a spirit peculiarly fierce and implacable, the Huguenots of France thirsting for the blood of the French, and the Englishry of Ireland impatient to trample down the Irish. . . Mitchelburne was there with the stubborn defenders of Londonderry, and Wolseley with the warriors who had raised the unanimous shout of

'Advance!' on the day of Newton Butler. Sir Albert Conyngham had brought a regiment of dragoons which still glories in the name of Enniskillen.

"Walker, notwithstanding his advanced age and his peaceful profession, accompanied the men of Londonderry. He was now a great prelate. William, on his march through Louth, learned that the rich see of Derry was at his disposal. He instantly made choice of Walker to be the new Bishop. The brave old man was overwhelmed with salutations and congratulations. Unhappily he had, during the siege in which he had so highly distinguished himself, contracted a passion for war; and he easily persuaded himself that, in indulging this passion, he was discharging a duty to his country and his religion . . . The Bishop elect was determined to be wherever danger was: and the way in which he exposed himself excited the extreme disgust of his royal patron, who hated a meddler almost as much as a coward. A soldier who ran away from a battle and a gownsman who pushed himself into a battle were the two objects which most strongly excited William's spleen."

Whilst exercising his mind on the foremost problem now confronting him, namely how to force a crossing of the Boyne in the face of the enemies' dispositions, William decided to engage in some investigation. He had time. It was early in the day, still, on 30 June, and it was a Monday, and keen though he was to engage the enemy and finish the job, it is said that William shared with his troops the feeling prevalent among most Nordic warriors that Monday was an inauspicious day for a battle, and he would prefer to wait until the morrow. Accompanied by Schomberg, Ormond, Solmes, Prince George of Hesse and other officers, he took stock of the Irish positions. He could be clearly seen by them, for there was at times a matter of a few yards only between the armies. "Their army is but small," said one of the Dutch officers. In fact, although only about 16,000 men were in view, many regiments, according to William's spies, were concealed from sight in folds in the ground. "They may be stronger than they look," said William, "but weak or strong, I will soon know all about them."

When the King reached a position facing Oldbridge he dismounted and decided to eat breakfast with his friends around him (an obelisk once marked this spot, but it is no longer there). William appears either to have tempted fate or to have had a complete disregard for danger, for he was now so close to the enemy that he was observed by horsemen who had gathered at the water's edge on the other side of the Boyne. Among them William's companions could recognise the youthful Berwick, the small, fair-haired Lauzun, Tyrconnel—bent by the years and crippled with gout—and overtopping all, the stately head of Sarsfield. It did not take long for these men to realise that it was William who was now remounting his horse.

As Burnet reports: "On the last of June, the king came to the banks of the river; and as he was riding along, and making a long stop in one place to observe the grounds, the enemy did not lose their opportunity, but brought down two pieces of cannon, and, with the first firing, a ball passed along the king's shoulder, tore off some of his clothes and about a hand-breadth of the skin, out of which about a spoonful of blood came; and that was all the harm it did him. It cannot be imagined how much terror this struck into all that were about him; he himself said it was nothing; yet he was prevailed on to alight till it was washed and a plaister put upon it; and immediately he mounted his horse again, and rode about all the posts of his army. It was indeed necessary to show himself everywhere, to take off the apprehensions with which such an unusual accident filled his soldiers. He continued that day nineteen hours on horseback; but, upon his first alighting from his horse, a deserter had gone over to the enemy with the news, which was carried quickly into France, where it was taken for granted that he could not outlive such a wound; so it ran over the kingdom that he was dead. And upon it there were more public rejoicings than had been usual upon their greatest victories; which gave that court afterwards a vast confusion, when they knew that he was still alive; and saw that they had raised in their own people a high opinion of him by this inhuman joy when they believed him dead."

On that same day a fierce encounter between a combined English and Dutch fleet under Torrington and a great French fleet under the Count of Tourville off Beachy Head, in which the English Admiral made sure that the Dutch bore the full brunt of the fighting, and consequently were largely destroyed, resulted in a disastrous defeat for Torrington and an ignominious flight along the coast of Kent and into the Thames estuary by the English and the remaining Dutch ships. This left the French complete masters of the Channel, and laid the entire south coast of England open to invasion. Macaulay comments: "It may be doubted whether our country has ever passed through a more alarming crisis than that of the first week of July 1690." The effect was to unite the country. "The words, 'The French are coming,' like a spell, quelled at once all murmurs about taxes and abuses, about William's ungracious manners, and raised a spirit as high and unconquerable as had pervaded, a hundred years before, the ranks which Elizabeth reviewed at Tilbury. Had the army of Humières landed, it would assuredly have been withstood by every male capable of bearing arms."

22 July, 1690:

Tourville anchored in Tor Bay with a fleet now numbering one hundred and eleven ships, with a considerable number of troops aboard, and sent in a force to attack Teignmouth, chiefly to test the reaction of the people, he having been led to believe by James and his Jacobites that the French had but to land and the country would rise and join them to depose William and Mary and restore James to the throne. In fact, whilst Teignmouth was burning, a force of local militia had encamped by the shore, and the whole of the West Country had risen, so that the French were impatient to depart, and did so just as soon as the weather allowed. "The enemy had departed, after doing just mischief enough to make the cause of James as odious for a time to Tories as to Whigs." So the danger receded. Meanwhile, a strict inquiry was instituted into the causes of the disaster off Beachy Head, and Torrington, the feeble Admiral, "who indeed could not at that moment have appeared in public without risk of being torn to pieces, was sent to the Tower".

Macaulay continues: "During the three days which followed the arrival of the disastrous tidings from Beachy Head the aspect of London was gloomy and agitated. But on the fourth day all was changed. Bells were pealing: flags were flying: men were eagerly shaking hands with each other in the streets. A courier had that morning arrived at Whitehall with great news from Ireland."

174

Louis XIV, King of France.
He gave support and refuge to James. Painted by Jean de la Haye, courtesy the BBC Hulton Picture Library.

Crossing the Boyne

ON THE BANKS of the Boyne on the last day of June a continuous barrage of cannon fire was exchanged across the river all day, and William, who had been watching the effect of the firing on his untried English regiments was satisfied with the way they behaved under such conditions. His comment: "All is right; they stand fire well." The King made a final inspection of his troops by torchlight, and gave orders that everything should be ready for forcing a passage across the river on the morrow. Every soldier was to wear a green bough in his hat. The baggage and greatcoats were to be left under guard. The code word was, "Westminster".

Tuesday 1 July, 1690:
A brilliant, cloudless day dawned, "as if the sun itself had a mind to see what would happen". William opened the attack by sending Marshal Schomberg's son, in command of his right wing, to cross the river some miles higher up at Slane Bridge and to turn the Irish left wing. He was accompanied by Portland and Douglas. However, the bridge was broken, and on learning of this he decided to cross below Slane, at Rosnaree ford. James had anticipated this move, and had posted Sir Neil O'Neil with a regiment of dragoons to defend the crossing. He bravely held the English in check until he was killed in the battle, whereupon his troops fled before Schomberg's men, who crossed the Boyne and were joined by Douglas and his Scotch Footguards. As they approached the Dublin road the French, under Lauzun, turned to face them with infantry and Sarsfield's Horse, so the Irish alone were left to defend the ford at Oldbridge.

James, it seems, had assumed that William and his forces would join Schomberg and Douglas higher up the river, and, with the major part of his army, he made his way across to support Lauzun, leaving Tyrconnel, with Richard Hamilton and Antrim and about a third of the Jacobite forces, to defend the Oldbridge sector. The French engineers had fortified the area, and a breastwork had been thrown up close to the waterside. The Meath bank bristled with pikes and bayonets. At Oldbridge had been assembled the entire Irish army; foot, dragoons and horse, Sarsfield's regiment alone excepted.

William's plan of campaign had so far succeeded, and he then decided to attack at Oldbridge. The start of the battle was described by George Clarke, the Judge Advocate General accompanying William's forces: "About eight or nine o'clock our cannon began to fire upon two houses, with yards walled, that stood on each side of the road on the other side the Boyne just over against the ford where the Guards were to pass." By ten o'clock William, at the head of his left wing, composed entirely of cavalry, prepared to ford the river a little way above Drogheda. Meanwhile, his Dutch Blue Guards had advanced from their camp above the Boyne, sheltered by the pass which takes its present name of King William's Glen from that day, and approached the river.

Schomberg ordered an advance into the river. Solmes's Blues were in the van, and they marched with drums beating to the brink of the river. The drums ceased, and then the men, ten abreast, entered the water. Clarke continues: "The enemy had posted some foot in those houses, whose fire was silenced by our own cannon, but as the guards were got almost through the water they rose up from behind the walls and gave one fire upon them and ran away."

The Londonderry and Enniskillen men splashed in after the Guards, and a little to their left Caillemont crossed at the head of a long column of French refugees. To the left again the main body of the English infantry, up to their armpits in water, struggled across, and still farther down the stream the Danes found another ford. In a few minutes the Boyne, for a quarter of a mile, was alive with muskets and green boughs.

"It was not until the assailants had reached the middle of the channel that they became aware of the whole difficulty and danger of the service in which they were engaged. Now whole regiments of foot and horse seemed to start out of the earth. A wild shout of defiance rose from the whole shore; during one moment the event seemed doubtful, but the Protestants pressed resolutely forward. The King was watching the action from the other side of the river. He was deeply concerned for his Blue Guards, who had marched to the left between the two houses and the river and were forming as fast as they could to receive a body of Irish horse that was coming towards them upon a full trot."

"The King," continues Clarke, "was in a good deal of apprehension for them, there not being a hedge nor ditch before them, nor any of our own horse to support them, and I was so near his Majesty as to hear him say softly to himself: 'My poor Guards, my poor Guards, my poor Guards,' as the enemy were coming down upon them; but when he saw them stand their ground and fire by platoons, so the horse were forced to run away in great disorder, he breathed out, as people use to do after holding their breath upon a fright or suspense, and said he had seen his Guards do that which he had never seen foot do in his life."

William's men advanced steadily and forced the whole Irish line to give way, and the Irish foot soldiers to flee. "Tyrconnel," says Macaulay, "looked on in helpless despair. He did not want personal courage, but his military skill was so small that he hardly ever reviewed his regiment in the Phoenix Park [Dublin] without committing some blunder; and to rally the ranks which were breaking all round him was no task for a general who had survived the energy of his body and of his mind, and yet still had the rudiments of his profession to learn. Several of his best officers fell while vainly endeavouring to prevail on their soldiers to look the Dutch Blues in the face. Richard Hamilton ordered a body of foot to fall on the French refugees, who were still deep in water. He led the way, and, accompanied by some courageous gentlemen, advanced, sword in hand, into the river. But neither his commands nor his example could infuse valour into that mob of cowstealers. He was left almost alone, and retired from the bank in despair. Farther down the river, Antrim's division ran like sheep at the approach of the English column. Whole regiments flung away arms, colours and cloaks, and scampered off to the hills without striking a blow or firing a shot.

"It required many years and many heroic exploits to take away the reproach which that ignominious rout left on the Irish name. Yet, even before the day closed, it was abundantly proved that the reproach was unjust. Richard Hamilton put himself at the head of the cavalry, and, under his command, they made a gallant though unsuccessful attempt to retrieve the day. They maintained a desperate fight in the bed of the river with Solmes's Blues. They drove the Danish brigade back into the stream. They fell impetuously on the Huguenot regiments, which, not being provided with pikes, then ordinarily used by foot to repel horse, began to give ground. Caillemot, while encouraging his fellow exiles, received a mortal wound in the thigh.

"Four of his men carried him back across the ford to his tent. As he passed, he continued to urge forward the rear ranks which were still up to the breast in the water. 'On; on; my lads! To glory: to glory!' Schomberg, who had remained on the northern bank, and who had thence watched the progress of his troops with the eye of a general, now thought that the emergency required from him the personal exertion of a soldier. Those who stood about him besought him in vain to put on his cuirass. Without defensive armour he rode through the river, and rallied the refugees whom the fall of Caillemot had dismayed. 'Come on,' he cried in French, pointing to the Popish squadrons; 'come on, gentlemen: there are your persecutors.' Those were his last words. As he spoke, a band of Irish horsemen rushed upon him and encircled him for a moment. When they retired, he was on the ground. His friends raised him; but he was already a corpse. Two sabre wounds were on his head; and a bullet from a carbine was lodged in his neck. Almost at the same moment Walker, while exhorting the colonists of Ulster to play the men, was shot dead. During near half an hour the battle continued to rage along the southern shore of the river. All was smoke, dust, and din. Old soldiers were heard to say that they had seldom seen sharper work in the Low Countries. But just at this conjuncture, William came up with the left wing. He had found much difficulty in crossing. The tide was running fast. His charger had been forced to swim, and had been almost lost in the mud. As soon as the King was on firm ground he took his sword in his left hand, - for his right arm was stiff with his wound and his bandage, - and led his men to the place where the fight was the hottest. His arrival decided the fate of the day. Yet the Irish horse retired fighting obstinately. It was long remembered among the Protestants of Ulster that, in the midst of the tumult, William rode to the head of the Enniskilleners. 'What will you do for me?' he cried. He was not immediately recognised; and one trooper, taking him for an enemy, was about to fire. William gently put aside the carbine. 'What,' said he, 'do you not know your friends?' 'It is His Majesty;' said the Colonel. The ranks of sturdy Protestant yeoman set up a shout of joy. 'Gentlemen,' said William, 'you shall be my guards today. I have heard much of you. Let me see something of you.' One of the most remarkable peculiarities of this man, ordinarily so saturnine and reserved, was that danger acted on him like wine, opened his heart, loosened his tongue, and took away all appearance of constraint from his manner. On this memorable day he was seen wherever the peril was greatest. One ball struck the cap of his pistol: another carried off the heel of his jackboot: but his lieutenants in vain implored him to retire to some station from which he could give his orders without exposing a life so valuable to Europe. His troops, animated by his example, gained ground fast. The Irish cavalry made their last stand at a house called Plottin Castle, about a mile and a half south of Oldbridge. There the Enniskilleners were repelled with the loss of fifty men, and were hotly pursued, till William rallied them and turned the chase back."

Throughout that long, desperate day William continued to display great personal courage, and some of the Irish soldiers were heard to declare, "Had the Dutchman been our commander, we should have won." "James," continues Macaulay, "saw his rival, weak, sickly, wounded, swimming the river, struggling through the mud, leading the charge, stopping the flight, grasping the sword with his left hand, managing the bridle with a bandaged arm. But none of these things moved that sluggish and ignoble nature. He watched from a safe distance the beginning of the battle on which his fate and the fate of his race depended. When it became clear that the day was going against Ireland, he was seized with an apprehension that his flight might be intercepted, and galloped towards Dublin. He was escorted by a bodyguard under the command of Sarsfield, who had, on that day, had no opportunity of displaying the skill and courage which his enemies allowed that he possessed. The French auxiliaries, who had been employed the whole morning in keeping William's right wing in check, covered the flight of the beaten army. They were indeed in some danger of being broken and swept away by the torrent of runaways, all pressing to get first to the pass of Duleek, and were forced to fire repeatedly on these despicable allies. The retreat was, however, effected with less loss than might have been expected. For even the admirers of William owned that he did not show in the pursuit the energy which even his detractors acknowledged that he had shown in the battle. Perhaps his physical infirmities, his hurt, and the fatigue which he had undergone, had made him incapable of bodily or mental exertion. Of the last forty hours he had passed thirty-five on horseback. Schomberg, who might have supplied his place, was no more. It was said in the camp that the King could not do everything, and that what was not done by him was not done at all."

The Battle of the Boyne.
The climax to the Glorious Revolution. Numbers on this Dutch print identify the prime contenders and the turning points in the action. **1** – King William. **2** – Duke of Schomberg, who was killed. **3** – fording the Boyne, William's army crossing at three points with water to their waist and then swimming. **4** – attack on Vyard's camp. **5** – its sequel, with James's men put to flight. Courtesy the BBC Hulton Picture Library.

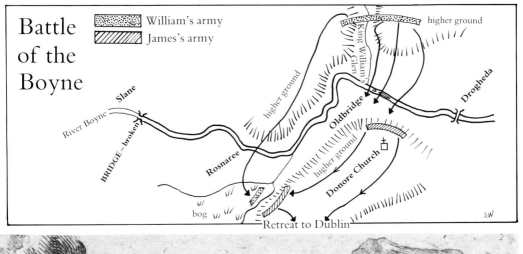

Battle
of the
Boyne

William's army
James's army

higher ground

King William's Glen

higher ground

Slane

River Boyne

BRIDGE — broken

Rosnaree

Oldbridge

Drogheda

higher ground

Donore Church

bog

Retreat to Dublin

SW

It is likely, on the other hand, that William, for his wife's sake, deliberately refrained from a close pursuit of James, and allowed him to escape to Dublin.

"The slaughter had been less than on any battle field of equal importance and celebrity. Of the Irish only about fifteen hundred had fallen: but they were almost all cavalry, the flower of the army, brave and well disciplined men, whose place could not easily be supplied. William gave strict orders that there should be no unnecessary bloodshed, and enforced those orders by an act of laudable severity. One of his soldiers, after the fight was over, butchered three defenceless Irishmen who asked for quarter. The King ordered the murderer to be hanged on the spot.

"The loss of the conquerors did not exceed five hundred men: but among them was the first captain in Europe. To his corpse every honour was paid. The only cemetery in which so illustrious a warrior, slain in arms for the liberties and religion of England, could properly be laid was that venerable Abbey, hallowed by the dust of many generations of princes, heroes, and poets. It was announced that the brave veteran would have a public funeral at Westminster."

[Schomberg was, in fact, buried in Dublin. Dean Swift and the Chapter of St. Patrick's Cathedral had a memorial erected to him there.]

"Walker was treated less respectfully. William thought him a busybody who had been properly punished for running into danger without any call of duty, and expressed that feeling, with characteristic bluntness, on the field of battle. 'Sir,' said an attendant, 'the Bishop of Derry has been killed by a shot at the ford.' 'What took him there?' growled the King.

"The victorious army advanced that day to Duleek, and passed the warm summer night there under the open sky. The tents and the baggage waggons were still on the north of the river. William's coach had been brought over; and he slept in it surrounded by his soldiers. On the following day, Drogheda surrendered without a blow, and the garrison, thirteen hundred strong, marched out unarmed.

"Meanwhile Dublin had been in violent commotion. On the thirtieth of June it was known that the armies were face to face with the Boyne between them, and that a battle was almost inevitable. The news that William had been wounded came that evening. The first report was that the wound was mortal. It was believed, and confidently repeated, that the usurper was no more; and, before the truth was known, couriers started bearing the glad tidings of his death to the French ships which lay in the ports of Munster. From daybreak on the first of July the streets of Dublin were filled with persons eagerly asking and telling news. A thousand wild rumours wandered to and fro among the crowd. A fleet of men-of-war under the white flag had been seen from the hill of Howth. An army commanded by a Marshal of France had landed in Kent. There had been hard fighting at the Boyne: but the Irish had won the day: the English right wing had been routed: the Prince of Orange was a prisoner. While the Roman Catholics heard and repeated these stories in all the places of public resort, the few Protestants who were still out of prison, afraid of being torn to pieces, shut themselves up in their inner chambers. But, towards five in the afternoon, a few runaways on tired horses came straggling in with evil tidings. By six it was known that all was lost. Soon after sunset, James, escorted by two hundred cavalry, rode into the Castle. At the threshold he was met by the wife of Tyrconnel, once the gay and beautiful Fanny Jennings, the loveliest coquette in the brilliant Whitehall of the Restoration. To her the vanquished King had to announce the ruin of her fortunes and of his own. And now the tide of fugitives came in fast. Till midnight all the northern avenues of the capital were choked by trains of cars and by bands of dragoons, spent with running and riding, and begrimed with dust. Some had lost their firearms, and some their swords. Some were disfigured by recent wounds. At two in the morning Dublin was still: but, before the early dawn of midsummer, the sleepers were roused by the peal of trumpets; and the horse, who had, on the preceding day, so well supported the honour of their country, came pouring through the streets, with ranks fearfully thinned, yet preserving, even in that extremity, some show of military order. Two hours later Lauzun's drums were heard; and the French regiments, in unbroken array, marched into the city. Many thought that, with such a force, a stand might still be made. But, before six o'clock, the Lord Mayor and some of the principal Roman Catholic citizens were summoned in haste to the Castle. James took leave of them with a speech which did him little honour. He had often, he said, been warned that Irishmen, however well they might look, would never acquit themselves well on a field of battle; and he had now found that the warning was but too true. He had been so unfortunate as to see himself in less than two years abandoned by two armies. His English troops had not wanted courage: but they had wanted loyalty. His Irish troops were, no doubt, attached to his cause, which was their own. But as soon as they were brought front to front with an enemy, they ran away. The loss indeed had been little. More shame for those who had fled with so little loss. 'I will never command an Irish army again. I must shift for myself; and so must you.' After thus reviling his soldiers for being the rabble which his own mismanagement had made them, and for following the example of cowardice which he had himself set them, he uttered a few words more worthy of a King."

Dr. Burnet describes his departure from Dublin: "Next morning he left Dublin: he said, too much blood had been already shed; it seemed God was with their enemies; the prince of Orange was a merciful man; so he ordered those he left behind him to set the prisoners at liberty, and to submit to the prince: he rode that day from Dublin to Duncannon Fort; but, though the place was considerably strong, he would not trust to that, but lay aboard a French ship that anchored there, and had been provided, by his own special directions to sir Patrick Trant. His courage sunk with his affairs to a degree that amazed those who had known the former parts of his life. The Irish army was forsaken by their officers for two days; if there had been a hot pursuit, it would have put an end to the war of Ireland; but the king thought his first care ought to be to secure Dublin; and king James's officers, as they abandoned it, went back to the army, only in hopes of a good capitulation. Dublin was thus forsaken, and no harm done, which was much apprehended; but the fear the Irish were in was such, that they durst not venture on any thing which must have drawn severe revenges after it. So the protestants there, being now the masters, they declared for the king. Drogheda did also capitulate.

"But, to balance this great success, the king had, the very day after the battle at the Boyne, the news of a battle fought in Flanders, between prince Waldeck and the marshal Luxembourg, in which the former was defeated."

Tyrconnel and Lauzun with their forces marched out of the City of Dublin towards the plateau of Kildare. When the people of Dublin saw how the situation had changed, the Protestants emerged from hiding. Some demanded arms from their oppressors, and the prisoners were freed. The Bishops of Meath and Limerick, now turned moderate Whigs, formed a provisional government and sent a messenger to William's camp welcoming him to Dublin.

Macaulay continues: "At eight that evening a troop of English dragoons arrived. They were met by the whole Protestant population on College Green, where the statue of the Deliverer now stands. Hundreds embraced the soldiers, hung fondly about the necks of the horses, and ran wildly about, shaking hands with each other.

"On the morrow a large body of cavalry arrived; and soon from every side came news of the effects which the victory of the Boyne had produced. James had quitted the island. Wexford had declared for King William. Within twenty-five miles of the capital there was not a Papist in arms. Almost all the baggage and stores of the defeated army had been seized by the conquerors. The Enniskilleners had taken not less than three hundred cars, and had found among the booty ten thousand pounds in money, much plate, many valuable trinkets, and all the rich camp equipage of Tyrconnel and Lauzun.

"William fixed his headquarters at Finglass, about two miles from Dublin. Thence, on the morning of Sunday, the sixth of July, he rode in great state to the cathedral, and there, with the crown on his head, returned public thanks to God in the choir which is now hung with the banners of the Knights of Saint Patrick. There the remains of Schomberg were deposited, as it was then thought, only for a time; and there they still remain. Doctor King preached, with all the fervour of a neophyte, on the great deliverance which God had wrought for the Church. The Protestant magistrates of the city appeared again, after a long interval, in the pomp of office. William could not be persuaded to repose himself at the Castle, but in the evening returned to his camp, and slept there in his wooden cabin."

This was the last time that a monarch conducted a battle and led his troops to war in the British Isles. The Orange Men of Northern Ireland keep 12 July to this day as the Anniversary of the Battle of the Boyne.

"The fame of these great events flew fast," continues Macaulay, "and excited strong emotions all over Europe. The news of William's wound everywhere preceded by a few hours the news of his victory. Paris was roused at dead of night by the arrival of a courier who brought the joyful intelligence that the heretic, the parricide, the mortal enemy of the greatness of France, had been struck dead by a cannon ball in the sight of the two armies. The commissaries of police ran about the city, knocked at the doors, and called the people up to illuminate. In an hour, streets, quays, and bridges were in a blaze: drums were beating and trumpets sounding: the bells of Notre Dame were ringing: peals of cannon were resounding from the batteries of the Bastille. Tables were set out in the streets; and wine was served to all who passed. A Prince of Orange, made of straw, was trailed through the mud, and at last committed to the flames. He was attended by a hideous effigy of the devil, carrying a scroll, on which was written, 'I have been waiting for thee these two years.' The shops of several Huguenots, who had been dragooned into calling themselves Catholics, but who were suspected of being still heretics at heart, were sacked by the rabble. It was hardly safe to question the truth of the report which had been so eagerly welcomed by the multitude. Soon, however, some cool-headed people ventured to remark that the fact of the tyrant's death was not quite so certain as might be wished. Then arose a vehement controversy about the effects of such wounds: for the vulgar notion was that no person struck by a cannon ball on the shoulder could recover.

"The disputants appealed to medical authority; and the doors of the great surgeons and physicians were thronged, it was jocosely said, as if there had been a pestilence in Paris. The question was soon settled by a letter from James, which announced his defeat and his arrival at Brest.

"At Rome the news from Ireland produced a sensation of a very different kind. There too the report of William's death was, during a short time, credited. At the French embassy all was joy and triumph: but the Ambassadors of the house of Austria were in despair; and the aspect of the Pontifical Court by no means indicated exultation. [The Pope was at that time opposed to the policies of Louis XIV, and was very satisfied with the outcome of the Battle of Boyne.]

"Melfort, in a transport of joy, sat down to write a letter of congratulation to Mary of Modena. That letter is still extant, and would alone suffice to explain why he was the favourite of James. Herod—so William was designated—was gone. There must be a restoration; and that restoration ought to be followed by a terrible revenge and by the establishment of despotism. The power of the purse must be taken away from the Commons. Political offenders must be tried, not by juries, but by judges on whom the Crown could depend. The Habeas Corpus Act must be rescinded. The authors of the Revolution must be punished with merciless severity. 'If,' the cruel apostate wrote, 'if the King is forced to pardon, let it be as few rogues as he can.' After the lapse of some anxious hours, a messenger bearing later and more authentic intelligence alighted at the palace occupied by the representative of the Catholic King. In a moment all was changed. The enemies of France—and all the population, except Frenchmen and British Jacobites, were her enemies—eagerly felicitated one another. All the clerks of the Spanish legation were too few to make transcripts of the despatches for the Cardinals and Bishops who were impatient to know the details of the victory. The first copy was sent to the Pope, and was doubtless welcome to him.

The good news from Ireland reached London at a moment when good news was needed. The English flag had been disgraced in the English seas. A foreign enemy threatened the coast. Traitors were at work within the realm. Mary had exerted herself beyond her strength. Her gentle nature was unequal to the cruel anxieties of her position; and she complained that she could scarcely snatch a moment from business to calm herself by prayer. Her distress rose to the highest point when she learned that the camps of her father and her husband were pitched near to each other, and that tidings of a battle might be hourly expected. She stole time for a visit to Kensington, and had three hours of quiet in the garden, then a rural solitude. But the recollection of days passed there with him whom she might never see again overpowered her. 'The place,' she wrote to him, 'made me think how happy I was there when I had your dear company. But now I will say no more; for I shall hurt my own eyes, which I want now more than ever. Adieu. Think of me, and love me as much as I shall you, whom I love more than my life.'

"Early on the morning after these tender lines had been despatched, Whitehall was roused by the arrival of a post from Ireland. Nottingham was called out of bed. The Queen, who was just going to the chapel where she daily attended divine service, was informed that William had been wounded. She had wept much: but till that moment she had wept alone, and had constrained herself to show a cheerful countenance to her Court and Council. But when Nottingham put her husband's letter into her hands, she burst into tears. She was still trembling with the violence of her emotions, and had scarcely finished a letter to William in which she poured out her love, her fears and her thankfulness, with the sweet natural eloquence of her sex, when another messenger arrived with the news that the English army had forced a passage across the Boyne, that the Irish were flying in confusion, and that the King was well. Yet she was visibly uneasy till Nottingham had assured her that James was safe. The grave Secretary, who seems to have really esteemed and loved her, afterwards described with much feeling that struggle of filial duty with conjugal affection. On the same day she wrote to adjure her husband to see that no harm befell her father. 'I know,' she said, 'I need not beg you to let him be taken care of: for I am confident you will for your own sake: yet add that to all your kindness; and for my sake, let people know you would have no hurt happen to his person.' This solicitude, though amiable, was superfluous. Her father was perfectly competent to take care of himself. He had never, during the battle, run the smallest risk of hurt; and, while his daughter was shuddering at the dangers to which she fancied that he was exposed in Ireland, he was half way on his voyage to France.

"It chanced that the glad tidings arrived at Whitehall on the day to which the Parliament stood prorogued. The Speaker and several members of the House of Commons who were in London met, according to form, at ten in the morning, and were summoned by Black Rod to the bar of the Peers. The Parliament was then again prorogued by commission. As soon as this ceremony had been performed, the Chancellor of the Exchequer put into the hands of the Clerk the despatch which had arrived from Ireland, and the Clerk read it with a loud voice to the lords and gentlemen present. The good news spread rapidly from Westminster Hall to all the coffeehouses, and was received with transports of joy. For those Englishmen who wished to see an English army beaten and an English colony extirpated by the French and Irish were a minority even of the Jacobite party.

"On the ninth day after the battle of the Boyne James landed at Brest, with an excellent appetite, in high spirits, and in a talkative humour. He told the history of his defeat to everybody who would listen to him. But French officers who understood war, and who compared his story with other accounts, pronounced that, though His Majesty had witnessed the battle, he knew nothing about it, except that his army had been routed. From Brest he proceeded to Saint Germains, where, a few hours after his arrival, he was visited by Lewis. The French King had too much delicacy and generosity to utter a word which could sound like reproach. Nothing he declared, that could conduce to the comfort of the royal family of England should be wanting, as far as his power extended. But he was by no means disposed to listen to the political and military projects of his unlucky guest. James recommended an immediate descent on England. That kingdom, he said, had been drained of troops by the demand of Ireland. The seven or eight thousand regular soldiers who were left would be unable to withstand a great French army. The people were ashamed of their error and impatient to repair it. As soon as their rightful King showed himself, they would rally round him in multitudes. Lewis was too polite and goodnatured to express what he must have felt. He contented himself with answering coldly that he could not decide upon any plan about the British islands till he had heard from his generals in Ireland. James was importunate, and seemed to think himself ill used, because, a fortnight after he had run away from one army, he was not entrusted with another. Lewis was not to be provoked into uttering an unkind or uncourteous word: but he was resolute; and, in order to avoid solicitation which gave him pain, he pretended to be unwell. During some time, whenever James came to Versailles, he was respectfully informed that His Most Christian Majesty was not equal to the transaction of business. The high-spirited and quick-witted nobles who daily crowded the ante-chambers could not help sneering while they bowed low to the royal visitor, whose poltroonery and stupidity had a second time made him an exile and a mendicant. They even whispered their sarcasms loud enough to call up the haughty blood of the Guelphs in the cheeks of Mary of Modena.

"But her husband stood among the scoffers serene and well pleased with himself. 'Contempt,' says the fine Indian proverb, 'pierces through the shell of the tortoise,' but the insensibility of James was proof even against contempt."

For William, victory at the Boyne established without question the final success of the Revolution which he had led with such distinction. James was gone, never to return. There now remained some tidying up to do. The King, now in possession of Dublin, went on in August to besiege Limerick, where Sarsfield, in command of the

Irish, put up a brave and stubborn resistance, so that William, having lost 2,300 or more men, and faced with the prospect of his artillery sinking in the mud of a very wet August, abandoned the seige and returned to England in September, where he appointed John Churchill, Earl of Marlborough, commander of a fresh expedition, and sent it off to Ireland. Once in Ireland, Marlborough was joined by the Duke of Würtemburg with the regiments which had remained in that country, and in a short and brilliant campaign in Southern Ireland, Cork and Kinsale were captured by the English forces.

The Irish war continued into the next year, when Ginckel, a Dutchman now in command of William's army, attacked at Athlone on 30 June and at Aghrim twelve days later. Both towns capitulated when the English, as Fortescue observes, "showed their usual desperate valour, succeeding when experienced commanders like St. Ruth confessed with admiration that they thought their success impossible". In August 1691 Limerick was besieged again, and again Sarsfield held out stubbornly, buoyed up by promises of support from France, but his hope gradually turned to despair as the weeks passed with no sign of the French forces arriving, and he finally surrendered the town on 3 October, 1691. The conditions demanded by the Irish commander were rigidly observed by William, who had agreed that the people of Limerick should be allowed to continue to worship in their own way, and that any Irish soldiers who so wished might leave for France. Eleven thousand Irishmen sailed, and joined the French army.

William's inclination to be merciful, and his statesmanlike magnanimity in victory, were much in advance of his times, when victorious rulers would often inflict cruel vengeance on those whom they had defeated, as did James II after the Monmouth rebellion, and as was the French practice. For this reason, in the aftermath of conflict, those who had supported him sometimes turned bitterly against him when he failed to deal with his former opponents as hardly as they considered he should. After the surrender of Limerick relations between the King and the English inhabitants of Ireland became increasingly strained. He desired to grant a general pardon to all classes of Irish people, including the aristocracy. The Anglo-Irish colony, however, refused to support this, because, as Burnet writes, "they thought the present opportunity was not to be let go of breaking the great Irish families, upon whom the inferior sort would always depend. And in compliance with them, the indemnity now offered was so limited that it had no effect."

In spite of problems with the inhabitants, William took steps to restore the country's stricken trade, and in particular the linen industry. Many of his retired foreign officers, including some noblemen, and other immigrants to Ireland were offered naturalisation and freedom to exercise their religion. They settled at Youghal, Waterford and Portarlington (formerly the village of Cootletoodra) among many places, and there were many who came to live in Dublin. Here, as in London, these hardworking immigrants soon established profitable industries, including the manufacture of fabrics such as "tabinet", later known as Irish Poplin. Later, in 1697, William invited Louis Crommelin, a Huguenot refugee temporarily settled in Holland, to Ireland to establish the cultivation of flax and the making of linen, an industry which was set up in Lisburn. Crommelin epitomised all the good qualities of the Huguenots, especially their inventiveness and their industry, and William realised their worth in helping to provide work for the poor of Ireland.

William, throughout his campaign, from before the time he left Holland, never lost sight of his overriding purpose, which was to thwart the threatening might of France by ensuring that the power of England would be joined to that of Holland against their age-old foe. From the point of view of Britain, however, the success of the campaign extended far beyond the mere countering of the ambitions of Louis XIV of France. As Macaulay observes; "... Yet this revolution, of all revolutions the least violent, has been of all revolutions the most beneficient . . . The highest eulogy which can be pronounced on the revolution is this, that it was our last revolution."

The supremacy of Parliament was firmly and finally established. William of Orange, who bore on his standard the motto "For the Protestant Religion and Liberty" as he landed at Brixham, was in the estimation of Prince Albert, Queen Victoria's Consort, "the finest monarch England ever had".

His Royal Highness the Prince of Wales, who is patron of the British Tercentenary Trust which, jointly with the Dutch, is celebrating the "Glorious Revolution of 1688" in the year 1988, described William and Mary, whose accession marked the birth of a new relationship between Crown and Parliament, as being "very modern in their outlook." "They did not use religion as a political weapon," he said, "but desired religious tolerance above all else."

Lyme Regis, Dorset.
The Duke of Monmouth had landed here in 1685 to lead the previous rebellion against James II.

Bibliography

Contemporary Sources:

Bill of Rights   Record Office, House of Lords, Westminster.

Burnet, Dr. G.   *History of His Own Time.* Reeve & Turner, 1888.

Declaration of James II, 1688
Declaration of the Nobility, 1688 } Somerset Record Office, Taunton.
Prince of Orange's Circular, 1688

Fabric Accounts, 1688-9.   Salisbury Cathedral Archives.

Schwoerer, L. G.   *A Jornall of the Convention at Westminster Begun the 22nd January 1688/89*
Bulletin of the Institute of Historical Research, Vo. XL 1976.

Walker, Revd. G.   *A true account of the siege of Londonderry, London 1689.*

Whiffle, J., Chaplain of the Fleet.   *An Extract from a Diary (1688).* Published and Printed by A. G. Stevens, Brixham 1888.

Whittle, Revd. John.   *An Exact Diary of the late Expedition of his Illustrious Highness the Prince of Orange 1689.*

Later Authorities:

Baxter, SD.   *William III.* Longmans Green & Co. Ltd., 1966.

Beckett, J. C.   *The Making of Modern Ireland, 1603-1923.* Faber, 1981.

Boulger, D. C.   *The Battle of the Boyne.* London 1911.

Chacksfield, K. Merle.   *The Dorset and Somerset Rebellion.* Dorset Pub. Co. 1985.

Colt Hoare, Richard.   *The History of Modern Wiltshire* (Vol. VI. Old & New Sarum) 1843.

Evelyn, John.   *Diary.* Ed. E. S. De Beer, Oxford, 1955.

Feiling, Keith.   *A History of England.* Book Club Association, 1950.

Firth, Charles.   *Commentary on Macaulay's History of England.* Macmillan, 1938.

Fletcher, J. M. J.   *Some Royal Visits to the City and Cathedral Church of the Blessed Virgin Mary at Salisbury.* 1935.

Fortescue, J. W.   *A History of the British Army.* Vols. I & II. Macmillan 1899.

Foxcroft, H. C.   *The Life of the First Marquis of Halifax (Sir George Savile) (1633-95).* 1898.

Green, E.   *William of Orange through Somerset.* 1892.

Hill, C.   *The Century of Revolution 1603-1714.* Thos. Nelson & Sons, Edinburgh. 1961.

Hutchins, John.   *The History and Antiquities of the County of Dorset.* Westminster, 1861.

Horsley, John E.   *A Short History of Brixham.* Brixham Museum. 1973.

Johnson, D. R.   *William of Orange's Expedition to England.* 1981.

Legg, Rodney.   *Wincanton's Directory.* Dorset Publishing Co. 1987.

Macaulay, Lord T. B.   *History of England* Vols. I & II. London 1889.

Miller, J.   *The Life and Times of William and Mary.* Weidenfeld & Nicolson, London. 1974.

Miller, J.   *The Glorious Revolution.* Longmans. 1983.

Norway, A. H.   *Highways and Byways in Devon and Cornwall.* Macmillan. 1900.

Packe, Joyce.   *The Prince it is that's come.* The Kemynyon, Newton Abbot.

Packer, Roy.   *Long ago in Ottery.* E.R.D. Publications, Ltd., Exmouth.

Pennington, D. A.   *17th Century Europe.* Longmans. 1972.

Seymour, D.   *Berry Pomeroy Castle.* 1982.

Simms, J. G.   *Jacobite Ireland 1635-1691.* Routledge. 1969.

Singer, S. W.   Ed. *Correspondence of Henry Hyde, Earl of Clarendon, to Laurence Hyde, Earl of Rochester. Diary of Lord Clarendon from 1687 to 1690.* Vols. I & II. London, 1828.

Smiles, S.	*The Huguenots.* London, 1881.
Sweetman, Geo.	*History of Wincanton.* 1903.
Trevelyan, G. M.	*The English Revolution.* Butterworth, 1938.
Williams, E. N.	*The Eighteenth Century Constitution.* O.U.P., 1960.
Wilson, Frank	*Uniforms of Marlborough's Wars.* Chas. Knight & Co., London, 1970.
Vlekke, B. H. H.	*Evolution of the Dutch Nation.* New York, 1945.
	The Dictionary of National Biography. Various editions.
	Encyclopaedia Britannica. 9th Edition.

Acknowledgements

The picture of Mary as Queen in her Royal Robes, by Wissing, is reproduced by gracious permission of Her Majesty the Queen.

Other illustration are published by kind permission of:

The Ashmolean Museum, Oxford.

The B.B.C. Hulton Picture Library.

Country Life, London.

The Mansell Collection, London.

The National Portrait Gallery, London.

The Tate Gallery, London.

The Record Office, House of Lords, London.

The Rijksmuseum, Amsterdam.

I am grateful to the following for their valuable help in the preparation of this book:

Air Vice-Marshal Sir Bernard A. Chacksfield, K.B.E., C.B., C.Eng., F.R.Ae.S., R.A.F.(ret.).

D. Chandler, Esq., M.A., Head of the Department of War Studies and International Affairs, Royal Military Academy, Sandhurst.

The Right Reverend J. A. Baker, The Bishop of Salisbury.

M. Blee, Esq., Headmaster, The Cathedral School, Salisbury.

P. Smith, Esq., The Cathedral School, Salisbury.

Canon Hoskins, Exeter Cathedral.

Reg Ward, Esq., Holwell, Dorset.

T. D. Weare, Esq., Headmaster, Bryanston School, Dorset.

H. W. Drax, Esq., Charborough Park, Dorset.

R. S. Noquet, Esq., Swanage, Dorset.

The Revd. A. Hughes, Rector of Wincanton, Somerset.

Dr. S. Mattar, Wincanton, Somerset.

P. Bowden, Esq. and Mrs. L. Reeves Barton, Wincanton, Somerset.

Mrs. M. Vooght, Little Bovey Farm, Devon.

Mr. Howell, Guide, Powderham Castle, Devon.

D. Langford, Esq., Salcombe, Devon.

R. Packer, Esq., Ottery St. Mary, Devon.

J. Guthrie, Esq., Publicity Officer, Salisbury.

Miss P. C. Williams, A.L.A. and the staff of the Swanage Branch of Dorset County Library.

Miss E. Black, Art Curator, Ulster Museum, Belfast.

Mrs. C. Coote, Librarian, Brixham Museum, Devon.

Mrs. M. Godley, Brixham.

Miss S. Eward, M.A., F.S.A., A.L.A., Librarian and Keeper of the Muniments, Salisbury Cathedral Library, Salisbury.

Miss D. Phillips, Principal Librarian (Local Studies), Library and Arts Department, Reading Central Library, Reading.

The Librarian, Salisbury Local Studies.

G. Langley, Esq., B.A., F.L.A., County Reference Librarian, Central Library, Bristol.

D. P. Hudson, Esq., Ll.B., The Town Clerk, Town Hall, Torquay Devon.

Miss P. M. Cobb, The Town Clerk's Office, Torquay, Devon.

D. Shorrocks, Esq., County Archivist, Somerset County Council.

My very special thanks to Robert Chacksfield, who took the photographs on the route which the Prince of Orange travelled and typed the manuscript; and also to Rodney Legg, my editor and publisher, for his constant support in the preparation of this book, and in particular for researching and writing the captions.

K. Merle Chacksfield

Swanage, Dorset.   January 1987.

Index

Act of Grace 16, 90, 162
Andover 79,80
Anne, Princess 16, 17, 80-82, 119
Antrim 166, 169, 175
Ardee 170
Argyll, Earl of 12, 146
Armagh 169
Athol 148
Athol, Marquess of 141, 148
Aughrim, Battle of (1691) 185
d'Avaux, Jean Antoine de Mesmes, Compte. 163, 165
Avignon 11
Axminster 80

Bath 16
Bath, Earl of 25, 30, 36, 60, 84, 85

Beachy Head, Battle of (1690) 173
Beaminster 85
Belfast 160, 161, 166, 169
Bentinck, Hans William, Earl of Portland 29, 101, 117, 119, 143, 171, 175
Barillon, French Ambassador 106, 118, 126
Berry Pomeroy 40, 46
Bill of Rights ratified (1689) 135
Blair Castle 148
Bovey Tracey 52
Boyne, Battle of (1690) 170, 171, 175-179
Brest 184
Bristol 76
Brixham 28-41
Bryanston School 60
Bunyan, John 10
Burnet, Bishop Gilbert 11, 14, 17, 18, 32, 53, 58, 62, 65, 101, 117, 166, 169

Carrickfergus 160, 166
Charborough Park 14
Charlemont 165
Charles I, King of England 7
Charles II, King of England 8, 10, 11
Chudleigh 53-55
Churchill, John, Duke of Marlborough
    64, 76, 79, 81, 83, 85, 139, 141, 143, 185
Churchill, Sarah, Duchess of
    Marlborough 80-82, 119, 136
Churston 41, 42
Clarges, Sir Thomas 125, 131
Clarendon, Henry Hyde, 2nd Earl of 60
    82, 90-94, 101, 110, 120, 125, 126, 153
Claverhouse, John Graham, Viscount
    Dundee 141, 142, 147-151
Compton, Bishop Henry 18, 122
Cornbury, Lord 59, 60
Cork 185
Coronation of William & Mary 142-145
Courteney, Sir William 36, 51
Covenanters 147, 148
Crewkerne 83, 85

Danby, Earl of 18, 63, 133, 143
Dartmouth, Lord 85, 129
Dartmouth Castle 37
Declaration of Breda 8
Declaration of Indulgence 10, 16
Declaration of Right 133
Declaration of William, Prince of Orange
    47, 57
Defoe Daniel 11
Delamere, Lord 63, 118
Devonshire, Earl of 18, 50, 51, 63, 64, 143
Dieren 35
Dorchester 10, 59
Dorset 12, 14, 59, 60, 141
Dorset, Earl of 82
Dover 25
Drogheda 170, 171, 175, 180
Dromore 153
Dublin 159, 162-163, 165, 166, 170, 177,
    180, 184
Dundalk 166, 169, 170
Dundee, Viscount Claverhouse
    see Claverhouse
Duncannon Fort 181
Dunkeld, Battle of (1689) 151-152
Dykvelt, Everard 17, 130

Edinburgh 140, 141, 142, 147, 148, 151
Elizabeth I, Queen of England 10, 16
Elizabeth II, Queen of England 16
Enniskillen, or Inniskilling 154, 158, 159,
    161, 175
Enniskilleners, The 177, 182
Erle, Thomas 14, 60, 141
Escot 59, 74
Evelyn, John 136
Exclusion Bill 10, 11
Exeter 36, 38, 52, 53, 55-64, 72

Faversham 117, 118
Feversham, Earl of 67, 79, 109, 111, 117
    118, 129
Finglass 182
Forde House 36, 50, 51
France 182
Furzeham Common 32, 35, 36

Galway 161
George, Prince of Denmark 80, 166
Germany 171
Ginckel, Godert Van 140, 171, 185
Glenmore 148
Gloucester 95
Godolphin, Sidney, 1st Earl of 93, 101,
    102, 103
Gordon, Duke of 141
Grafton, Duke of 76, 79, 83, 85
Greenwich 135

Hague, The 11, 16, 18, 163
Halifax, George Savile, 1st Marquis of 92
    93, 100, 101, 102, 103, 111, 112, 118,
    121, 123, 124, 133, 136, 143
Hamilton, Richard 141, 176
Hampstead Marshall 100
Hellevoot-Sluys (Hellevoet-Sluis) 19, 20
Henley 113
Herbert, Arthur, Lieut. Gen., Admiral 18
Het Loo Palace 35
Hicks 53
Holland, States of 18, 121
Honiton 59
House of Lords 126, 131, 132, 134, 137, 140
House of Commons 74, 126, 131, 134,
    140, 161

Huguenots 182, 185
Hungerford 100, 103, 106
Hutchins, John 14, 86

Inverlochy 152
Immortal Seven 18

James I, King of England 8
James II, King of England 7, 8, 10, 12, 14,
    16, 17, 25, 59, 65, 67, 74-82, 90-93,
    106-110, 114, 115, 117, 125, 129, 132,
    140, 154, 155, 162, 163, 165, 170, 173
    175, 177, 180, 181, 184, 185
James, Francis Edward Stuart, Prince of
    Wales 16, 107-108, 129, 131
Jeffreys, George, Judge 12, 74, 76, 119, 120
Jesuits 7

Kent 115, 117
Killiecrankie, Battle of, 1689 149-151
Kingsteignton 41
Kinsale 154, 185
Kirke, Percy, General 12, 57, 76, 85, 155

Lamplugh, Bishop of Exeter 53, 59
Lauzun, Antonine, Count of 107, 165,
    172, 175, 181
Limerick 184
Lisburn 160, 161
Littlecote 103, 104, 105
Lochaber 148, 149
Lochiel 149
Loughbrickland 169, 170
London 12
Londonderry, Siege of (1689) 153,
    154-158
Longcombe 44-46
Louis XIV, King of France 10, 11, 17,
    140, 165, 174, 184
Louvois, Francois-Michel Le Tellier,
    Marquis de 165
Lumley, Richard, Earl of Scarborough 18, 94
Lundy 154
Lyme Regis 186

Macarthy 158
Macclesfield, Earl of 96
Macdonald of Keppoch 147
Mackay, General 28, 142, 147, 148

Maclean of Duart 147, 150
Maidenhead Bridge 116
Margate 135
Marlborough, John Churchill, Duke of
    see Churchill
Mary Beatrice d'Este, Queen of
    England 7, 10, 16, 107-108, 129,
    165, 184
Mary, Queen of England, Princess of Orange
    7, 10, 17, 18, 131, 132, 135-137, 165,
    168, 183
Monmouth & Buccleuch, James Scott,
    Duke of 11, 12, 28, 40, 52, 60, 185
Mordant, Lord Charles (also Mordaunt)
    16, 53
Mulgrave, Lord 109, 112
Mutiny Act 140, 161

Netherlands see "Holland"
Newcastle-on-Tyne 64
Newry 160
Newton Abbot 41, 47-51
Newto(w)n Butler 158, 159, 172
Nijmegen, Treaty of, 1678 139
Northumberland, Earl of 109
Nottingham 75, 77, 102, 103
Nottingham, Daniel Finch, Earl of 93,
    101, 166

Oldbridge 171, 172, 175
Omagh 159
Orange, House of 11
Ormond, Duke of 80, 85, 143, 171, 172
Ottery St. Mary 59, 60, 72, 74
Oxford 95
Oxford, Edward Russell, Earl of 90,
    101, 171

Parnham 83
"Parliament", Devon 45-46
Parliament, Irish 159
Paignton 41
Pembroke, Earl of 166
Philip II, King of Spain 10
Plymouth 25, 30, 36, 60, 84, 85, 139
Portland, Hans William Bentinck, Earl of
    see Bentinck
Portarlington 185
Portman, Sir William 60, 61
Powderham Castle 50, 51

Ramsbury 100
Reading 72, 79, 105, 106
Rochester 117, 118, 119, 120, 126
Roope 36
Russell, Lord William 11, 25, 36, 63
Russell, Edward, Earl of Oxford 11, 16, 18, 60
Rye House Plot (1683) 11

St. Germains 184
St. James 117, 118, 120, 121
Salisbury 64–67, 76–79, 96–98
Salisbury Cathedral School 66, 67, 77, 78
Sancroft, William, Archbishop of Canterbury 16, 76, 111, 112, 122, 125
Sarsfield, Patrick 70, 159, 172, 175, 184, 185
Sarum 67
Scarborough, Richard Lumley, Earl of see Lumley
Scheveningen 19
Schomberg, Friedrich Hermann, Duke of 18, 30, 56, 79, 101, 110, 120, 139, 143, 155, 160, 162, 165, 166, 170, 172, 176, 177, 180
Scotland, insurrection in 147–152
Seven Bishops, Trial of 16
Seymour, Sir Edward 40, 46, 60, 62
Shaftesbury, Lord 10, 11
Shales, Henry 160, 161
Sheppey, Isle of 114
Sherborne 83, 85–87
Shovel, Sir Cloudesley 166
Shrewsbury, Earl of 18, 94, 101, 118, 133
Sidney, Henry, Earl of Romney 11, 18
Sion House 119
Sittingbourne 117
Skelton, Bevil 12
Solmes, Count of 28, 118, 171, 172, 175, 176
Speke, Sir Hugh 72, 87, 114
Stirling 142, 151
Stonehenge 99, 100
Swift, Jonathon 180

Teignmouth 173
Test Act 10
Tiverton 57

Topsham 38
Tor Bay 25, 173
Torquay 39
Torre Abbey 39
Totnes 9, 10
Tyrconnel, Talbot Richard, Earl of 117 123, 129, 140, 153, 164, 165, 170, 172, 176, 181

Ugbrooke 53, 54
Ulster 154, 161
United Provinces – States General 130, 139, 140, 171

Varwell, Peter 28, 32, 35
Versailles, Palace of 184
Villiers, Anne 17
Vooght 52

Waldeck, George Frederick, Count Von 60, 121, 129, 138, 141, 181
Walker, Revd. Dr. George 154, 172, 180
Waterford 170, 185
Westminster 82, 107, 120, 126, 139, 140 142, 143, 161, 175, 184
Whitehall 80, 117, 118, 119, 173, 183
Wincanton 68–72, 87, 88–90
William III, King of England, Prince of Orange 7, 8, 10, 11, 12, 14, 16, 18, 19, 20, 25, 28, 29, 30, 31 32, 44, 51, 53, 55, 58, 59, 62, 67, 72, 74, 83, 90, 95, 98, 100, 103, 105, 110, 113, 117, 120, 122–130, 132, 135–137, 140, 161, 162, 163, 165, 166, 169, 170, 172, 175, 176, 177, 179, 180, 182, 184, 185, 186
Wilton 96
Windsor 110, 115, 117, 120
Wolseley, Col. 158, 171
Worcestershire 94, 95
Wren, Sir Christopher 12, 169
Würtemberg-Neustadt, Charles Frederick Duke of 162, 171, 185

Yalberton 43, 44
Yeovil 72, 114
Yonge, Sir Walter 59, 74
Youlden 28, 30

Zuylestein (Zulestein) William Van Nassau 117, 118